Paradigm Shifts in Christian Witness

Marguerite (Meg) and Charles (Chuck) Kraft

Paradigm Shifts in Christian Witness

Insights from Anthropology, Communication, and Spiritual Power

Essays in Honor of Charles H. Kraft

Charles E. Van Engen
Darrell Whiteman
J. Dudley Woodberry
Editors

ORBIS BOOKS

Maryknoll, New York 10545

Founded in 1970, Orbis Books endeavors to publish works that enlighten the mind, nourish the spirit, and challenge the conscience. The publishing arm of the Maryknoll Fathers and Brothers, Orbis seeks to explore the global dimensions of the Christian faith and mission, to invite dialogue with diverse cultures and religious traditions, and to serve the cause of reconciliation and peace. The books published reflect the opinions of their authors and are not meant to represent the official position of the Maryknoll Society. To obtain more information about Maryknoll and Orbis Books, please visit our website at www.maryknoll.org.

Library of Congress Cataloging in Publication Data

Paradigm shifts in Christian witness : insights from anthropology, communication, and spiritual power : essays in honor of Charles H. Kraft / Charles E. Van Engen, Darrell Whiteman, J. Dudley Woodberry, editors.
    p. cm.
  Includes bibliographical references and index.
  ISBN 978-1-57075-771-6
  1. Witness bearing (Christianity) I. Kraft, Charles H. II. Engen, Charles Edward van. III. Whiteman, Darrell L. IV. Woodberry, John Dudley, 1934-
  BV4520.P27 2008
  266.009'09511—dc22

                                                              2007034150

Contents

NOTES ON CONTRIBUTORS   vii

PREFACE
Charles E. Van Engen   xiii

FOREWORD
C. Douglas McConnell   xix

SKETCHING THE LIFE OF CHARLES H. KRAFT
Paul E. Pierson   xxi

INTRODUCTION
R. Daniel Shaw   xxxi

Part I
CULTURAL ANTHROPOLOGY

1   ANTHROPOLOGY AND MISSION
An Uneasy Journey toward Mutual Understanding
Darrell Whiteman   3

2   ANTHROPOLOGY, MISSIONS, AND EPISTEMOLOGICAL SHIFTS
Paul G. Hiebert   13

3.   ANTHROPOLOGY AND MISSIOLOGY
Reflections on the Relationship
Robert J. Priest   23

4.   A NEW HEAVEN AND A NEW EARTH?
The Future of Missiological Anthropology
Michael A. Rynkiewich   33

Part II
COMMUNICATION

5.   REFLECTIONS ON CULTURES, LANGUAGE LEARNING, AND COMMUNICATION
Eugene A. Nida   47

6. **GO AND COMMUNICATE GOOD NEWS**
    Viggo Søgaard   57

7. **NEGOTIATING THE GOSPEL CROSS-CULTURALLY**
    The Contributions of Intercultural Communication to Missiology
    Roberta R. King   66

8. **COMMUNICATION THEORY IN MISSIOLOGY**
    Where to from Here?
    Knud Jørgensen   76

Part III
SPIRITUAL POWER

9. **MISSIOLOGY AND SPIRITUAL POWER**
    C. Peter Wagner   91

10. **POWER AND BLESSING**
    Keys for Relevance to a Religion as Lived
    J. Dudley Woodberry   98

11. **DEEP-LEVEL HEALING PRAYER IN CROSS-CULTURAL MINISTRY**
    Models, Examples, and Lessons
    John and Anna Travis   106

12. **SPIRITUAL CONFLICT**
    A Challenge for the Church in the West with a View to the Future
    Tormod Engelsviken   116

Part IV
SUMMING UP

13. **AN OVERVIEW OF THE WORK OF CHARLES H. KRAFT**
    Robert J. Schreiter   129

THE PUBLISHED WORKS OF CHARLES H. KRAFT
    Compiled by Dean Gilliland   137

BIBLIOGRAPHY OF WORKS CITED   147

INDEX   161

Notes on Contributors

Tormod Engelsviken is professor of missiology at MF Norwegian School of Theology in Oslo, Norway. His Ph.D. in systematic theology is from Aquinas Institute in Dubuque, Iowa (1981). He served as a missionary in Ethiopia (1971-1973), taught at Fjellhaug School of Mission in Oslo (1976-1978), and at MF since 1978. He has also been a visiting professor at the Central University for Nationalities in Beijing, China. He did postdoctoral studies at Fuller Theological Seminary in 1983 and 1987. Engelsviken's publications include *The Gift of the Spirit* (doctoral thesis, 1981); *Ånden i Ordet (The Spirit in the Word)* (1987); *Besettelse og åndsutdrivelse (Possession and Expulsion of Evil Spirits)* (1988); *Spiritual Conflict in Today's Mission* (2001); and *Missiologi i dag (Missiology Today)* (coeditor and contributor, 2nd edition, 2004).

Dean Gilliland received the B.D. from Evangelical Theological Seminary, the Th. M. from Princeton Theological Seminary, and the Ph.D. from Hartford Seminary Foundation. He served for twenty-two years as a missionary to Nigeria in church planting and education for ministry. Gilliland is senior professor of contextual theology and African studies at the School of Intercultural Studies, Fuller Theological Seminary. His publications include *Pauline Theology and Mission Practice* (1983); *The Word among Us: Contextualizing Theology for Mission Today* (1989); and *Announcing the Kingdom: The Story of God's Mission in the Bible* (with Arthur Glasser, Charles Van Engen, and Shawn Redford, 2003).

Paul G. Hiebert was born and raised in India where he also served as a cross-cultural missionary. He was the distinguished professor of mission and anthropology at Trinity Evangelical Divinity School, Deerfield, Illinois, since 1990, having formerly taught at the School of World Mission of Fuller Theological Seminary. Paul wrote his chapter for this book shortly before being called to the presence of the Lord in March 2007. His publications include *Anthropological Insights for Missionaries* (1985); *Anthropological Reflections on Missiological Issues* (1994); and *Missiological Implications of Epistemological Shifts: Affirming Truth in a Modern/Postmodern World* (1999).

Knud Jørgensen is a journalist. He received the M.Th. from the University of Copenhagen in 1970 and the Ph.D. in Missiology from Fuller Theological Seminary in 1985. Jørgensen has been program director at Radio Voice of the Gospel in Ethiopia, executive secretary for communication within the Lutheran World Federation in Geneva, director of the International Mass Media Institute in Kristiansand, principal of the Go Out Center in Hurdal, director of information within Norwegian Church Aid, dean of the leadership department at the Mekane Yesus Seminary in Addis Ababa, and since 1998 director for the mission foundation Areopagos. His publications include numerous articles in addition to *Proclaiming Christ to His World* (Hanne-Grete Brommeland and Knud Jørgensen, editors, 1984); *Medie-og kommunikasjonsstrategi* (redaksjon, with Hanne-Grete Brommeland, Knud Jørgensen, 1985); *The Role and Function of the Media in the Mission of the Church* (with particular reference to Africa, 1986); *Radioarbeid: programproduksjon og radiojournalistikk* (with Halvard Colbjørnsen and Kåre Melhus, 1987); *Local Churches and Missions: A Report from a Working Party on Local Churches and Missions* (Knud Jørgensen, editor, 1988); *Visjon og hverdag: lederskap i misjon og menighet* (1991); and *Missiologi i dag* (with Jan-Martin Berentsen and Tormod Engelsviken, 2004).

Roberta R. King is associate professor of communication and ethnomusicology at Fuller Theological Seminary. For twenty-two years, King served as a cross-cultural missionary in Africa. Based at Daystar University in Nairobi, Kenya, she worked in eleven countries in Africa with WorldVenture, applying principles from ethnomusicology to develop contextually appropriate cultural music for mission. Her publications include *Pathways in Christian Music Communication: The Case of the Senufo of Côte d'Ivoire* (1989, forthcoming reprint in the ASM Dissertation series); *A Time to Sing: A Manual for the African Church* (1999); "Toward a Discipline of Christian Ethnomusicology: A Missiological Paradigm" in *Missiology*, Vol. XXXII, No. 3, July, 2004, pp. 293-301; "Variations on a Theme of Appropriate Contextualization: Music Lessons from Africa" in *Appropriate Christianity* (Kraft, 2006); and *Music in the Life of the African Church* (forthcoming).

C. Douglas McConnell is dean of the School of Intercultural Studies and associate professor of leadership at Fuller Theological Seminary. McConnell served for fifteen years as a cross-cultural missionary in Australia and Papua New Guinea with Asia Pacific Christian Mission (APCM, now PIONEERS). From 1992 to 1998, he was an associate professor and chair of the Department of Missions/Intercultural Evangelism at Wheaton College Graduate School. Prior to coming to Fuller, McConnell served as the first international director of PIONEERS, from 1998 to 2003. His publications include *The Changing Face of World Missions* (coauthor, 2005); "Children of the Kingdom: Missiological Reflections on Children at Risk" (in *Changing Our Response: Mission in the Era of HIV/AIDS, The International Bulletin of Missionary Research* by OMSC Publications, 2005); and *Understanding God's Heart for Children* (coeditor, 2006).

Eugene A. Nida is a linguist, teacher, and Bible translation theorist. Nida was awarded the B.A. in Greek from UCLA (1936) and a master's degree from USC in Greek New Testament (1939). Each summer from 1937 to 1953 Nida taught at the Summer Institute of Linguistics (SIL) of Wycliffe Bible Translators, along with Kenneth L. Pike. In 1943, Nida received a Ph.D. in linguistics and anthropology from the University of Michigan and joined the American Bible Society

(ABS) as its translations secretary. In that position he traveled seven to eight months a year all over the world for 40 years. He has worked in over 85 countries and some 200 languages, studying the linguistic, cultural, and translation problems that translators face, giving them guidance, holding seminars, and lecturing. Nida's publications include *Morphology: The Descriptive Analysis of Words*; *Learning a Foreign Language*; *God's Word in Man's Language*; *Customs and Cultures*; *Message and Mission*; *Toward the Science of Translating*; and *The Theory and Practice of Translation* (with Charles R. Taber).

Paul E. Pierson is dean emeritus (1980-1992) and senior professor of history of mission and Latin American studies at Fuller Seminary's School of Intercultural Studies. Previously he served as a cross-cultural missionary sent by the Presbyterian Church U.S. to Brazil (1956-1970) and Portugal (1971-1973). His publications include *A Younger Church in Search of Maturity: Presbyterianism in Brazil from 1910 to 1959* (1974); *The Good News of the Kingdom* (edited with Charles Van Engen and Dean Gilliland, 1993); and *Transformation from the Periphery: Emerging Streams of Church and Mission* (2004).

Robert J. Priest is professor of mission and intercultural studies and director of the Ph.D. program in intercultural studies at Trinity Evangelical Divinity School. He holds the Ph.D. in anthropology from the University of California, Berkeley. With interests in short-term missions, anthropology of religion, and culture and moral discourse, his work has appeared in various journals, such as "Missionary Positions: Christian, Modernist, Postmodernist" in *Current Anthropology*, Vol. 42, 29-68, and in various edited books, such as his own coedited *This Side of Heaven: Race, Ethnicity and Christian Faith* (2007).

Michael A. Rynkiewich is director of postgraduate studies at Asbury Theological Seminary and professor of anthropology in the E. Stanley Jones School of World Mission and Evangelism. Rynkiewich trained as an anthropologist at Bethel College (now Bethel University in St. Paul) and earned his M.A. and Ph.D. in anthropology at the University of Minnesota. He taught at Macalester College from 1971 to 1981. He received the M.Div. degree from Asbury Seminary, is an ordained elder in the South Indiana Conference, and served as a missionary in Papua New Guinea for five years with the General Board of Global Ministries of the United Methodist Church. His publications include *The Nacirema* (1975); *Ethics and Anthropology* (1976); *Traders, Teachers and Soldiers: An Anthropological Survey of Colonial Era Sites on Majuro Atoll, Marshall Islands* (1981); *Politics in Papua New Guinea* (2000); and *Land and Churches in Melanesia* (2001). He also served as the editor of the journal *Catalyst: Social Pastoral Journal for Melanesia*.

Robert J. Schreiter, a member of the Congregation of the Precious Blood, is the Vatican Council II professor of theology at Catholic Theological Union in Chicago. Robert Schreiter is an internationally recognized expert in the areas of inculturation and the world mission of the church. He is interested in how the gospel is communicated in different cultures and in how a theology of reconciliation might shape missionary activity today. He holds the professorship of theology and culture sponsored by the Edward Schillebeeckx Foundation at the University of Nijmegen, The Netherlands. His publications include *Constructing Local Theologies* (1985); *Reconciliation: Mission and Ministry in a Changing Social Order* (1992); *The New Catholicity: Theology between the Global and the Local* (1997); *The Ministry of Reconciliation: Spirituality & Strategies* (1998); *Doing Local Theology: A Guide for Artisans of a New Humanity* (with Clemens Sedmak, 2002); and *In Water and in Blood: A Spirituality of Solidarity and Hope* (2007).

R. Daniel Shaw (Ph.D. in anthropology) conducted field work among the O'otham (Papago) of southwestern Arizona (1967-1968) and the Samo of Papua New Guinea (1969-1981) where he served as a Bible translator. He is currently professor of anthropology and translation at Fuller Seminary's School of Intercultural Studies. Dan serves on the Mission Aviation Fellowship board of directors. His publications include *Transculturation: The Cultural Factor in Translation and Other Communication* (1988); *Kandila: Samo Ceremonialism and Interpersonal Relationships* (1990); *From Longhouse to Village: Samo Social Change* (1996); *Understanding Folk Religion: A Christian Response to Popular Beliefs and Practices* (with Paul Hiebert and Tite Tiénou, 1999); and *Communicating God's Word in Today's World: God's Truth or Hocus-Pocus?* (with Charles E. Van Engen and Lamin Sanneh, 2003).

Viggo Søgaard is senior professor of communication in the School of Intercultural Studies at Fuller Theological Seminary. Based in his native Denmark, he travels around the world as communication and media consultant for the United Bible Societies and various other organizations, teaching and developing non-print-based translation procedures. Prior to Fuller, Søgaard served as a cross-cultural missionary in Thailand where he founded Voice of Peace, a media ministry of radio, cassettes, and television. He has served as senior associate for the communications track of the Lausanne Movement and also directs the Asian Institute of Christian Communication. His publications include *Audio Scriptures Handbook* (1991); *Everything You Need to Know for a Cassette Ministry* (1975); *Communicating Scriptures* (2002); *Media in Church and Mission: Communicating the Gospel* (1993, 1998); and *Research in Church and Mission* (1996).

John and Anna Travis have worked in cross-cultural ministry to unreached peoples for the past twenty years. Both have been trained under Chuck Kraft in the ministry of deep-level healing. Today their ministry of coaching and training others in healing and deliverance has taken them to Africa, the Middle East, and many parts of Asia. Anna is the author of a handbook on deep-level healing entitled *The Undivided Heart Prayer Model*. Both are pursuing graduate degrees in the area of spiritual dynamics and cross-cultural ministry. They presently reside in Asia.

Charles (Chuck) Van Engen is the Arthur F. Glasser Professor of Biblical Theology of Mission in the School of Intercultural Studies at Fuller Theological Seminary. Born and raised in Mexico of missionary parents, he founded a seminary and was involved in extension theological education, leadership formation, and training evangelists for the National Presbyterian Church of Mexico, from 1973 to 1985. Among his publications are *The Growth of the True Church* (1981); *God's Missionary People* (1991); *Mission on the Way* (1996); *God So Loves the City* (with Jude Teirsma, 1994); *Evangelical Dictionary of World Missions* (edited with A. Scott Moreau and Harold Netland, 2000); *Announcing the Kingdom: The Story of God's Mission in the Bible* (with Arthur Glasser, Dean Gilliland, and Shawn Redford, 2003); and *Evangelical, Ecumenical, and Anabaptist Missiologies in Conversation* (edited with James R. Krabill and Walter Sawatsky, 2006).

C. Peter Wagner, who taught in the School of World Mission at Fuller Theological Seminary for thirty years, now resides in Colorado Springs. He serves as president of Global Harvest Ministries, chancellor of Wagner Leadership Institute, presiding apostle of the International Coalition of Apostles, and is author of sixty-nine books. His publications include *Your Church Can Grow* (1976); *Your Church Can Be Healthy* (1979, revised 1996); *Your Spiritual Gifts Can Help Your Church Grow* (1979, 1994, 2005); *How to Have a Healing Ministry* (1988); *Prayer Warrior Series* (1992-1997); *Churchquake: How the New Apostolic Reformation Is Shaking Up the Church as We Know It* (1999); and *Changing Church* (Regal Books, 2004).

Darrell Whiteman is vice president for Mission Education and resident missiologist with the Mission Society in Norcross, Georgia. Previously he was professor of cultural anthropology and dean of the E. Stanley Jones School of World Mission and Evangelism at Asbury Theological Seminary. He is the past president of the International Association for Mission Studies, the American Society of Missiology, and the Association of Professors of Mission. He served as editor of *Missiology* from 1989 to 2002. His publications include *An Introduction to Melanesian Cultures: A Handbook for Church Workers: Book One of a Trilogy* (1984) and *Melanesians and Missionaries: An Ethnohistorical Study of Social and Religious Change in the Southwest Pacific* (2002).

J. Dudley Woodberry is dean emeritus and senior professor of Islamic studies in the School of Intercultural Studies at Fuller Theological Seminary. Dudley served with his family at the Christian Study Centre, Rawalpindi, Pakistan, and as the pastor in Kabul, Afghanistan, and Riyadh, Saudi Arabia. He has served as consultant on the Muslim world to President Carter, the State Department, U.S. AID, and other U.S. government agencies. His publications include *Muslims and Christians on the Emmaus Road* (edited, 1989); *Where Muslims and Christians Meet: Area Studies* (edited, 1989); *Missiological Education for the 21st Century: The Book, the Circle, and the Sandals* (edited with Charles Van Engen and Edgar J. Elliston, 1996); and *Muslim and Christian Reflections on Peace: Divine and Human Dimensions* (edited with Osman Zumrut and Mustafa Koylu, 2005).

Preface

CHARLES E. VAN ENGEN

It has been a delight to serve as general editor for this book. My long friendship and collegial partnership with Chuck Kraft have brought joy to this endeavor. And the topic of the book was something I had wanted to work on for a long time.

I grew up with missionary parents in Chiapas, the southern-most state of Mexico and home of the ancient Mayan civilizations. In the mid-1950s when I was eight or nine, I can remember heated debates among the missionaries about the role of anthropology in their mission strategy of Bible translation, evangelism, church planting, and leadership formation among the Mayan peoples of Chiapas. As I remember it, there were three viewpoints. Some of the early members of Wycliffe Bible Translators believed that the only thing the Mayans needed was the Bible in their language. The pioneer missionary of our Reformed mission, John Kempers, believed that the Mayans needed biblical preaching, theological teaching, and leadership formation. But some of the newer recruits like Albert De Voogd had begun to read Eugene Nida and a number of secular anthropologists and felt that what was needed was an in-depth understanding of Mayan worldview in order to learn indigenous Mayan thought forms and means of communication in Ch'ol, Tzeltal, Zoque, Lacandón, Tzotzil, and Tojolabal. But in those days, anthropologists were not friendly to missionaries, even in Chiapas, and conservative evangelical Reformed missionaries had deep misgivings about anthropology.

I remember that my father was a kind of mediator among the three positions. He was friend, traveling companion, and mission partner with some of those who would one day be well-known names in the field like Cameron Townsend, Ken Pike, Bill Wonderly, John Beekman, and Eugene Nida. Some of our younger missionaries were reading Eugene Nida's writings as soon as they would come off the press. But like the other older missionaries, my parents had been given no training, no tools, to understand the Mayan worldview of the peoples to whom they had been sent. Their basic approach to communication was just to love the people, listen carefully, learn the language, and "do as the Romans do, within limits," they used to say. As they became closer friends with new Mayan Christians, and as the Mayan churches grew amidst severe persecution, my parents and their missionary colleagues came face-to-face with the pervasive presence of the demonic—both territorial and personal. And they were not prepared to deal with those issues. They would have been greatly helped by what Chuck Kraft would later be teaching and writing.

In fact, years later, several of the next generation of American missionaries serving among the Mayan churches in Chiapas studied under Chuck Kraft and

xiii

were deeply impacted by what they learned. And now the Mayan Christians of Chiapas are preparing to send one of their own as a cross-cultural missionary to the Middle East, having studied Chuck Kraft's teachings in the three arenas of missiology that make up this volume.[1]

So you can see why I have so much enjoyed bringing this volume together. An added bonus was being able to work closely with Dudley Woodberry and Darrell Whiteman as colleagues and coeditors of this volume. I am deeply grateful for their involvement and assistance in designing the book, inviting the contributors, and bringing together the chapters in their respective sections. It has been an honor to work with them.

We hope this volume will serve as a textbook in the field. It has three parts that relate to Chuck Kraft's three major contributions to missiology: cultural anthropology, communication, and spiritual power. We wanted to create a textbook that could be used to introduce people to the way these disciplines interface with missiology.

Each section is organized loosely on a historical track. At the beginning of each section we seek to describe how that cognate discipline became part of missiology—and Kraft's role in making that happen. In the middle of each section we ask: What is at present the primary contribution of that discipline to missiology? How have missiological considerations impacted that discipline? In the third part of each section we ask, Where to from here? in terms of that discipline's place and contribution to missiology.

For many centuries, the Christian calendar has been composed of two parts: Before Christ (B.C.) and Anno Domini (A.D.), the "Year of Our Lord." Many of us have experienced life in a similar fashion: before and after marriage, before and after children, before and after a major job promotion, before and after a major change of living location, or before and after a major traumatic event in our lives. As I write, I am recuperating from a second knee-replacement surgery and it seems like I have just lived through one of those moments. My life is marked by BKR (before knee replacement) and AKR (after knee replacement) surgeries.

When I consider the developments in missiology during the past sixty years, I see something similar. As a multidisciplinary discipline, missiology has two parts: before the inclusion of the cognate disciplines highlighted in this volume (anthropology, communication, and spiritual power) and after such inclusion. And although he was, of course, not alone in this, one of the principal change agents who brought about such a paradigm shift in missiology is Charles H. Kraft. One might say that there is missiology before Kraft (BK) and missiology after Kraft (AK). The watershed volume that epitomizes this paradigm shift is Chuck Kraft's magnum opus, *Christianity in Culture* (1979a; Kraft with Kraft, 2005).

As editors of this volume, we have signaled this development in missiology

---

[1]During the past several years, Vern Sterk (Ph.D. in missiology, School of World Mission at Fuller, mentored by Chuck Kraft) and I have served as mentors to the Mayan church leaders as they have formed their own mission-sending society called the Asociación Misionera de Chiapas.

by using the phrase "paradigm shift." For the past fifty years or so, philosophers of science have talked about the existence of patterns of thought known as paradigms. A paradigm is a conceptual tool used to perceive reality and order that perception in an understandable, explainable, and somewhat predictable pattern. It is "an entire constellation of beliefs, values and techniques, and so on, shared by the members of a given community" (Hans Küng and David Tracy 1989, 441-442). A paradigm is a tool of observation, understanding, and explanation, an epistemological foundation that takes into account the sum total of definitions determining the way we perceive and explain our reality.[2]

In the history of human thought there have been moments of radical paradigm shift that have had enormous impact on the way humans have viewed their universe. In the history of science, for example, we could mention Copernicus, Galileo, Columbus, Newton, Einstein, and the space age—all of which have precipitated significant shifts in the way we understand reality.

We speak of paradigm shift because we now know that in its construction a new paradigm will always draw from prior knowledge as well as create new perspectives and understanding. The shift involves continuity with past knowledge while it also offers new insight that is discontinuous with what was known before. This is also the case with our understanding of God's mission and the construction of missiology as a discipline.

On the one hand, there is a sense in which "there is nothing new under the sun" (Eccl 1:9 NIV). In terms of our understanding of God's mission, there is nothing more to say once one has proclaimed to the world in word and deed that "God so loved the world that he gave his one and only Son . . ." (Jn 3:16 NIV).

Similarly, missiology has always known about cultures, communication, and issues of spiritual power.

Attempts to construct a contextual theology appropriate to both the Scriptures and a new receptor culture can be traced as far back as the work of Orthodox missionaries to the Slavic peoples, Cyril (826-869) and Methodius (815-885), and early Roman Catholic missionaries like the Jesuits Robert de Nobili (1577-1656) in India and Matteo Ricci (1552-1620) in China (see Moreau, Netland, and Van Engen 2000, 694, 834). Beginning with William Carey (1761-1834), whenever Protestant missionaries have encountered a new culture and a new language, like their Orthodox and Roman Catholic counterparts, they have been concerned with communicating the message of the Gospel to their receptors in languages and forms acceptable and understandable to the new receptors.

Since God spoke to Adam and Eve in the Garden of Eden we can appreciate God's adaptation to human cultures in communicating God's intended meaning, the forms God chose to communicate with humans, and the spiritual power struggles between God's desires for humanity and human sinfulness (cf. Dan Shaw and Charles Van Engen 2003). Since its birth the Christian Church has also encountered issues of spiritual power in its participation in God's mission, Philip's

---

[2]See, for example, Ian G. Barbour (1974), Thomas S. Kuhn (1962, 1977), Hans Küng and David Tracy (1989), and David Bosch (1991).

encounter in Samaria with Simon the Sorcerer (Acts 8:9-13) being a case in point.

On the other hand, missiology has undergone a momentous shift since the early 1950s, especially in relation to cultural anthropology, communication theory, and spiritual power. So much so that it is difficult to remember what the missiology of the early 1950s was like. In the post-World War II era, there was great perplexity regarding the church's mission. In 1981 I wrote the following about the mission thinking of the 1950s and early 1960s, using key terms much in vogue in those days:

> Some called it "more a venture than ever." Others felt that its foundations had been "shaken." Some called the discussion surrounding it a "great debate," while others felt that it belonged to an era long past and should suffer "euthanasia," or at least be placed under a "moratorium." Some felt the Church should carry it out, but others believed it was the Church itself. Some were convinced that it should lead to personal conversion, but others stressed that its meaning . . . should involve a life-and-death struggle against hunger, disease, poverty, racism, and unjust social structures. Still others would replace the whole idea with such notions as "inter-church aid" or "dialogue."

In the early 1950s Protestant mission practitioners were reading the missiological thought of people like Gustav Warneck (1892-1905), John R. Mott (1900, 1930), Robert Speer (1904), Arthur Brown (1907), Roland Allen (1913), Robert Glover (1946), Samuel Zwemer (1934), Edmund Davison Soper (1943), Max Warren (1944, 1951, 1955a, 1955b), Kenneth Scott Latourette (1946, 1953), Hendrik Kraemer (1947), Carl Henry (1947), Johan H. Bavinck (1948), Harold Lindsell (1949, 1955), Lesslie Newbigin (1952), Stephen Neill (1957), and John Nevius (1958).[3] Missiological reflection at the time was concerned primarily with theological, philosophical, historical, and some sociopolitical and economic issues. In the Roman Catholic world, the *aggiornamento* of the Second Vatican Council had not happened yet. Amidst suspicions about the need to draw insights from anthropology, communication, and spiritual power, missiology of the 1950s was dominated by historical studies, arguments over church and mission structures, theological discussions, and administrative matters regarding church-to-church partner relationships and the global sharing of resources. Important as those issues were, in the 1950s there was a growing awareness that cross-cultural missionaries needed to deal with the expanding cultural diversity of the church and the world on six continents.

Some folks were pointing to new ways of reflecting about and doing Christian mission. Missionaries the world over began to read the writings of creative thinkers like Eugene Nida, Alan Tippett, and a number of others whose names were prominent in *Practical Anthropology* and whom the reader will find referred to

---

[3]For a summary of the developments in evangelical theology of mission in North America from the 1940s through the 1980s, see C. Van Engen (1996, 127-144).

often in this volume. Charles Kraft drew from and built upon their thought. Over time, Kraft, along with a number of others, focused the contributions of linguistics, cultural anthropology, communication theory, and, more recently, spiritual power on rethinking and reengineering missiology itself. This led to the paradigm shift in Christian witness that this volume intends to describe. The depth and breadth of the paradigm shift is such that one can accurately affirm that the missiology of the twenty-first century is a far cry—it is a different world—from the missiology of the 1950s.[4] And a central figure in this paradigm shift in missiology has been Charles Kraft.

I want to express my deep appreciation to the following for their assistance in the creation of this volume.

Thank you to Meg Kraft for the information she provided for Paul Pierson's biographical chapter and for help in getting a photo of Chuck and Meg.

Thank you to Dr. Doug McConnell, dean of the School of Intercultural Studies, for his systemic and financial support of this project.

Thank you to Bill Burrows and Orbis for the advice, enthusiasm, and personal support in getting the manuscript ready for publication.

Thank you also to Catherine Holton for her work over months of coordinating this project, communicating with the various authors, typesetting, editing, and compiling this volume.

I am deeply indebted to all these and many others who helped bring this volume to completion. Any mistakes in this book are mine. And the delight and privilege of bringing this book to completion have also been mine. We praise God for the life and ministry of Charles Kraft.

---

[4]For a summary treatment of this shift, see, e.g., C. Van Engen (2005c).

Foreword

C. DOUGLAS MCCONNELL

L ike many contributors to this volume, it is hard to remember a time when the work of Charles H. (Chuck) Kraft was not a major influence in missiology. From my earliest years of study in cultural anthropology under his direction to the recent years of learning more about spiritual power as a colleague, the thought of Chuck Kraft has been a major contributor in my own development. For many of us, Chuck Kraft is an exemplary missionary scholar.

As an illustration of Kraft's scholarly contribution, one need only consider *Christianity in Culture* (1979a; Kraft with Kraft 2005) as arguably one of the truly influential volumes in twentieth-century missiological writing. It is fitting then that the vision for a festschrift for Chuck, conceived by his colleagues Drs. Charles Van Engen and Dudley Woodberry and his friend Darrell Whiteman, would come to fruition in this volume. The idea of a "celebration writing," the German concept embodied in the word *festschrift*, is seen throughout the work of each author in the pages that follow.

To conceive of Chuck as an exemplary scholar, one must appreciate that his intellect was matched by his love of experimentation. If the traditional wisdom indicated a given approach, Chuck was and is just as likely to approach it with a rival hypothesis. He has been willing to consider other perspectives that often have challenged and sometimes even riled other scholars and practitioners. In the process of exploring new understandings and practices, he has led the field in developing both theories and methods of mission that are now widely accepted.

In each of the three sections of this festschrift, the authors explore the three phases of Chuck's intellectual and missional development. In Part I, Whiteman draws together respected scholars to build on the intersection of anthropology and mission providing a strong basis for the nuanced engagement of the gospel and culture from what is now foundational to our missiological reflection. In Part II, the major contribution of communication theory to missiology is explored skillfully under the direction of Van Engen. From the musings of pioneer Eugene Nida, a friend of both Fuller School of World Mission and Chuck Kraft, to the insights of former students turned colleagues like Søgaard, King, and Jørgensen, the vital role of intercultural communication is well represented.

To demonstrate that Chuck is an exemplary *missionary* scholar we gathered input from those who serve as missionaries around the globe. The articles in Part III by Travis and Engelsviken provide this important input. On a recent trip to Lebanon, I encountered a missionary team deeply impacted by Chuck's work on spiritual power, using his writings as part of their regular teaching in churches. It is fitting that the final section is edited by Woodberry, who has been instrumental in helping missionaries understand the role of spiritual power in Christian encounter with Muslims globally.

It is our goal to truly honor Chuck Kraft through this festschrift. His life and work have been singularly committed to helping others come to know the Triune God and to become mature followers of Jesus Christ. The contributions to this volume serve to deepen our understanding of critical issues in missiological thought and missionary praxis and to broaden our appreciation of Chuck Kraft's unique contribution to them.

Sketching the Life of Charles H. Kraft

PAUL E. PIERSON

Charles Kraft (whom everyone knows as "Chuck") was born into a non-Christian family in Connecticut in 1932. When he was still a child his mother was dramatically converted through a letter from a cousin, a graduate of Wheaton College, who was a missionary in Sudan. So he grew up hearing about missions, Africa, and Wheaton. Soon after Chuck committed his life to Christ at age twelve, these interests led him to discover his own vocation. This small-town boy had never traveled any significant distance from his home before he went away to college. How different his future would be!

Wheaton, Ashland, and Hartford, 1959-1967

As he often said, he went to Wheaton to prepare for missionary service, find a wife, and prove to his father that he could succeed in athletics. He did all three. He played on the varsity football and baseball teams, studied anthropology and linguistics, and he and Marguerite (Meg) were married the day before their commencement in 1953. In their college studies the Krafts began to move beyond their traditional Western paradigm and learn to deal with other cultures anthropologically and biblically. This implied a much more positive attitude toward non-Western cultures than was common at that time. Their goal would be to bring people to Christ within their contexts rather than extracting them from their cultures as many Western missionaries had attempted to do in the past. At Wheaton Chuck also worked with Young Life, a ministry with high school students. Disdained by many in the traditional churches, Young Life was in reality a creative attempt to contextualize the gospel with unchurched youth, not a bad stepping-stone toward mission in Africa. After graduation Chuck began theological studies at Ashland Seminary while Meg taught school. In 1955-1956 they spent a year at the Kennedy School of Missions at Hartford, Connecticut, where Chuck continued to focus on anthropology, linguistics, and African studies, with additional work in ethnomusicology and Islamics. He was also accepted into the Ph.D. program. Returning to Ashland the following year, he completed his B.D. degree.

At Hartford Chuck was strongly influenced by Eugene Nida, Bill Reyburn, and Bill Smalley of the American Bible Society, primarily through their writings in *Practical Anthropology* and *Bible Society Confidential Papers*. These men were pioneers in advocating the presentation of the Christian faith in ways that affirmed the values and forms of receptor cultures. They were a great help to Chuck, who was already moving in that direction. As he brought his insights from anthropology and linguistics to his theological studies he began to develop what he later called ethnotheology. As a result, he took to Nigeria "Wheaton anthropology and linguistics and Ashland theology, honed into incarnational missiology at Hartford and in reading *PA* [*Practical Anthropology*]" (Kraft 2005a, 100).

Nigeria, 1957-1960

Chuck's pastor father-in-law was a member of the missionary board of the Brethren Church, which had begun to work in cooperation with the Church of the Brethren Mission in northeastern Nigeria. Recruited by that board, the Krafts were promised they would be able to apply their anthropological and linguistic insights in a newly opened field of the Mission. It appeared to be an ideal situation. So in 1955 Chuck was ordained into the Gospel ministry in the Brethren Church. In 1957, Chuck, Meg, and their nearly two-year-old twins sailed for Nigeria. They spent six months studying Hausa, the trade language, using a methodology that stressed conversation for specific situations. (It later became the basis of Chuck and Meg's book on how to learn Hausa [1973b].) Then they moved to a tribal area to work with the Kamwe people, where they lived in a village with no running water or electricity. Their assignment was to supervise a dispensary, two new primary schools, half a dozen small churches, and plant new congregations. In addition they were to learn the language and put it in written form. Soon after their arrival in Nigeria Chuck read Donald McGavran's *Bridges of God* (1955 and 1981), a work that presented essentially the same approach he had accepted but went further in some respects.

The Krafts went to the Kamwe with the basic orientation they had learned at Wheaton and Hartford, the desire to help people become followers of Christ within their own culture. Before their arrival two remarkable evangelists, one blind, the other a leper, were spreading the gospel message. It appeared that a genuinely indigenous movement could develop. Drawing on his studies in ethnomusicology, Chuck encouraged the use of African music instead of Western hymns. Drums, previously forbidden by the missionaries because of their use in spirit worship, were employed in worship. Hymns of praise were composed by the people and sung antiphonally, so hymnbooks were not needed. Most of the people were illiterate anyway. Chuck soon saw that his primary task was to train African evangelists, most of whom had only a fifth-grade education. These were mature men, heads of families, who had the respect of their communities.

If the style of music was an issue, a far more serious problem was the attitude toward polygamy in a culture where it was common. As the church grew, Chuck began to baptize more and more people, even though each one first had to go through six months of training. Some months he baptized as many as 150 people. But the traditional missionary view was that no polygamist could be baptized. What to do when men with two or more wives began to come to faith? There was no place for a divorced woman in the culture. She could not live alone, nor could she return to her family. And she had to abandon her children, leaving them to her husband. A terrible dilemma! Kraft attempted to walk a fine line, following the rules of the Mission but also acting biblically as he understood it. He welcomed polygamists into the church for worship but they could not be baptized or hold any church office. Soon the field committee of the Mission, composed only of missionaries (with no participation by Africans), asked Chuck to discuss the matter. He wrote an eight-page paper on the issue that he believed was well received, returned to his field, and continued to welcome polygamists into the church without baptizing them.

After two years Chuck was elected to the *Majalisa*, the local pastoral leaders' council, an entity run by Africans with few missionaries as members. Apparently this distressed the Mission leaders. Shortly before the end of their first term, Chuck was invited to teach a course in a Bible school operated by the Mission. There he stated quite incidentally that he understood Scripture to show that God accepted everyone in Christ, even polygamists. That raised a storm. The night before the Krafts left for furlough, the founder of the Mission talked again with Chuck about polygamy. Chuck once again gave assurances that he had not baptized polygamists. But most importantly, the church had grown rapidly, schools had been established, and leaders were being trained. Although there had been fewer than one hundred Kamwe believers when the Krafts had arrived, the number had grown to around one thousand, and today the church numbers over forty thousand. Fifteen years after the Krafts left, the *Majalisa* voted to baptize polygamists.

However, there is no question that Chuck was seen as a maverick by Mission leaders, not without some reason. He questioned the refusal to baptize polygamists, the prohibition of drums and dance in worship, the refusal to allow those who had not paid a certain tax to participate in Holy Communion, and other disciplinary rules established by the Mission. He believed he had strong biblical grounds for his positions. But of course he had left himself open to criticism as one who advocated breaking rules the Mission had established. It was not the last time his ideas would be controversial! Consequently, when they returned to Hartford where Chuck would continue his Ph.D. work, the Krafts were dismayed and surprised to receive a letter telling them they were not invited to return to Nigeria.

From Hartford to UCLA, 1963-1969

It is not unusual for Christian leaders to go through a desert experience in which they move forward without knowing their destination. Chuck completed his Ph.D. with a dissertation on Hausa syntax in 1963 and considered returning to Nigeria with Wycliffe Bible Translators. When that was not possible he accepted an invitation to join the African studies faculty at Michigan State University, teaching Hausa and African linguistics. A grant enabled him to do research in Chadic languages back in Nigeria in 1966-1967. The attitude of the Mission had changed somewhat and Chuck did his research. Meg was invited to teach Hausa to new missionaries. They were able to visit their former field. While at Michigan State from 1963 to 1968, Chuck encouraged various mission boards to send their candidates to study African languages and cultures. Between thirty and forty studied with him during those years.

Shortly after his return from Nigeria, the prestigious African studies department at UCLA invited Chuck to be a visiting professor. He planned to stay one year but soon was invited to continue for several years. The move to Southern California quickly opened a new and far greater door to ministry and mission.

The Fuller School of World Mission, 1969-

The School of World Mission (SWM) had been established in 1965 by Donald McGavran, who promptly invited Alan Tippett to join the faculty. Ralph Winter was soon added to the faculty. Its two major foci were the emphasis on the importance of the growth of the church, and a positive attitude toward non-Western cultures. Most of its students were mid-career missionaries with a sprinkling of international students. When the Krafts renewed their friendship with Ralph and Roberta Winter over a Sunday dinner early in 1969, they learned more about this new school. When Ralph asked Chuck if he would consider teaching there, Chuck replied, "Well, we've never felt that God has rescinded our call to be missionaries, so we'd consider it" (2005a, 102). The process moved along rapidly. McGavran called the next day. He had been favorably impressed with an article of Chuck's in *Practical Anthropology* entitled "Christian Conversion or Cultural Conversion" (1963). Soon Chuck met with the three faculty members, gave a lecture to students, passed Fuller's theology exam, and began to teach in the SWM. Because UCLA wanted him to stay, he took on a full-time teaching load at both institutions but received only a half-time salary from Fuller. That continued for four years, until in 1973 he left UCLA and devoted all of his time to Fuller. At that time Meg began to teach in the Missions Department at Biola University, where she in turn made an important contribution.

The appointment to Fuller's SWM brought significant convergence of Chuck's anthropological and linguistic studies, his Nigeria experience, and the continuing development of his thought. Added to his passion to see the gospel communicated in culturally relevant ways, this created a powerful mix. Even though SWM faculty members did not always understand each other, the environment was a congenial one that encouraged each faculty member to try out new ideas and push out the envelope of traditional missionary thinking. Chuck began to teach an introductory course in anthropology, one on culture change, another in African area studies, and a fourth with the intriguing title "Conversion with a Minimum of Social Dislocation." The title, formulated by McGavran, indicated the direction of the school and Kraft's own convictions. Alan Tippett's influence on Chuck was important in his continued development. If Eugene Nida was his first "guru," Tippett was his second. This brilliant Australian anthropologist, who did not always receive the recognition Chuck felt he deserved, was a great stimulus and encouragement to Kraft on his continuing intellectual journey. There was a door between their adjoining offices, and often they shared experiences and ideas at the end of the day. In some ways, Chuck was like a son as well as successor to Tippett.

Chuck introduced communication theory into church growth missiology in a course on intercultural communication. *Communication Theory for Christian Witness* was published in 1983 (1983b). But his magnum opus, destined to become a classic, was *Christianity in Culture*, first published in 1979 (1979a) and revised with his wife Marguerite in 2005. He began writing it in 1973, passing out drafts of chapters to students and others, receiving their suggestions, and honing the manuscript until its publication. To quote him,

> I attempt to develop what I have called "ethnotheology," a crosscultural approach to theological interpretation. In this book I presented an early evangelical approach to contextualization based on my own attempts to integrate what I had learned of theology and anthropology with what I had learned of how to deal with biblical data in a nonwestern context. In some ways it is an angry book, developed out of the frustration of working in a mission approach I call "extractionist" in contrast with Jesus' approach that I called "identificational" or "incarnational." (2005, 103)

At times, Chuck seemed to be unduly harsh in his criticisms of traditional missionaries. That was tempered, however, by the fact that he normally had his facts straight and was critical of himself as well as others. He brought authenticity to his lectures by using his own missionary experiences as case studies.

The book immediately provoked controversy in the evangelical circles with which Chuck identified. A student at Trinity Evangelical Divinity School wrote his dissertation with the title "Is Charles Kraft an Evangelical?" The answer was negative. Carl F. H. Henry, the highly respected evangelical theologian who had been a faculty member at Fuller, was also very critical. Committed to a philosophically based propositional theology, he could not agree with Kraft's approach. This writer will never forget sitting with Donald McGavran on a plane to Korea in 1980 when I was the newly appointed dean of the SWM. Dr. Henry, a passenger on the same plane, came to McGavran and began to denounce Kraft's book. Somewhat intimidated, I sat very silently throughout the conversation! Over the years I learned that Kraft could handle criticism without becoming vindictive or acrimonious. Convinced in his own mind that he was being faithful to the gospel and committed to its effective communication, he could bear criticism in the confidence that he would ultimately be vindicated, or perhaps corrected if necessary.

As a faculty member Chuck's wide-ranging interests soon began to manifest themselves. During the 1970s conciliar missiologists began to speak of contextualization, but often in a theological framework that evangelicals could not accept. Thus, the latter continued to use the term *indigenization*. But as the concept of churches appropriate to their contexts continued to emerge, Tippett, Kraft, and others began to prefer the term *contextualization*, believing it to be more accurate and carrying less historical baggage than other words. With the formation of the Lausanne movement in 1974, a number of consultations were held, among them one at Willowbank, Bermuda, in 1978. There, evangelical theologians including John Stott, James Packer, I. Howard Marshall, Rene Padilla, and Orlando Costas met with anthropologists including Tippett, Kraft, Jacob Loewen, and others to hammer out some of the issues related to the contextualization of the Christian faith in non-Western cultures. It was a significant step forward. The January 1978 issue of *Evangelical Missions Quarterly* further strengthened the case for contextualization in evangelical mission circles. Kraft and other younger anthropologists played an important role.

One of Kraft's qualities is the ability to see potential in others that they might not see in themselves, and encourage them to translate that insight into new programs. That led to great expansion in the curricula and ministry of the SWM. Chuck had been trained as a Bible translator, and his interest in that subject led him to approach Drs. Tom and Betty Sue Brewster about the possibility of initiating such a program at Fuller. The Brewsters were on their own financially. Tom, a quadriplegic, had income because of his disability. They had volunteered their services to various translation projects for groups such as Campus Crusade and Living Bibles, at little or no cost. The Brewsters did join the faculty in 1975, teaching half-time, but focused on language acquisition instead of Bible translation. Theirs was a unique and important contribution, especially as the SWM expanded and began to accept preservice people into its programs along with mid-career missionaries. They continued to travel across the world, teaching missionaries how to learn languages incarnationally and socially, by living with families in the new culture, and immediately using what they learned. Chuck's interest in Bible translation did not die, however, and thanks in part to Chuck's vision, Dan and Karen Shaw, Wycliffe Bible translators in Papua New Guinea (PNG), became associated with the SWM. With a Ph.D. in anthropology, Dan was invited to teach in the SWM as an adjunct faculty in 1980. At that time, Chuck challenged him to develop a curriculum for a Bible translation program at Fuller. Dan did so and then returned to PNG to continue his work with the Samo people, convinced he was to remain there. Only after a visit to PNG by the SWM dean and a clear word from God were the Shaws convinced that they were called to come to Fuller. Again, Chuck's vision resulted in a creative new program in which over one hundred Bible translators have done master's and doctor's degrees. They are in turn training other translators in Asia, Africa, and Latin America!

Chuck has been unselfish in his encouragement of his students and colleagues. He had known Dean and Lois Gilliland, as Methodist missionaries in Nigeria, and had encouraged Dean to do his Ph.D. studies at Hartford. When it became necessary for the Gillilands to leave Nigeria, Chuck took the initiative to bring Dean to Fuller as assistant professor of contextualized theology. In that position Gilliland was able to combine his biblical theology, African experience, studies in phenomenology, and interest in Islam in order to expand the offerings of the school in those areas. J. Robert (Bobby) Clinton had been Chuck's teaching assistant while Bobby did his D.Miss. in ethnotheology. Because Chuck and other faculty saw great promise in Clinton, he was called to the SWM's first faculty position in leadership in 1981. At the meeting of the Lausanne Committee in Pattaya, Thailand, in 1980, Chuck encouraged Viggo Søgaard, a former missionary to Thailand and specialist in communication, to do his Ph.D. at Fuller. Viggo then joined the SWM faculty half-time and served very effectively for many years. The Krafts had met Roberta King, a musician teaching at Daystar University in Kenya, and noted her deep interest in African music. Roberta later did her Ph.D. in ethnomusicology under Chuck, and subsequently joined the SWM faculty where at present she focuses on global worship, encouraging indigenous music in non-Western cultures. So Chuck, along with the various deans, played a major role in building up the faculty and increasing the programs of the SWM.

A Major Paradigm Shift: The Issue of Power

In Nigeria, Chuck was often asked by church leaders what to do about evil spirits. But he had no answer for them. He had never been taught anything about that subject in college or seminary. The question simply was not discussed in educational institutions, evangelical or otherwise, as far as he knew. Nor had he ever been in a church that dealt with demons or faith healing. Yet they were of great importance in Africa. As Chuck would later recognize, for many, if not most, people in Africa and elsewhere, the first question to be asked of the Christian faith was not about truth, it was about power. Was the God of the missionaries more powerful than the spirits? So when in 1982 the SWM invited John Wimber, founder of the Vineyard movement, to assist Peter Wagner in teaching a course on signs, wonders, and church growth, the Krafts attended. Chuck wrote,

> Seeing the Holy Spirit make His presence manifest in our classroom by healing people was breathtaking for me. Often there were 8-10 people healed each evening. However I found the "words of knowledge" even more impressive . . . It was clear . . . that God was doing something new . . . The experience was nothing less than transforming. We watched. We went through a paradigm shift in our thinking. (2005a, 168-169)

After the course was cancelled because of the controversy it caused in the seminary, Chuck was allowed to offer a course on physical healing, and in 1990 gave a course on power encounter. Since then, at times with the participation of Peter Wagner, he has taught courses on healing and spiritual warfare, each with a focus on doing such ministry, not simply thinking about healing, deliverance, and spiritual warfare. He has been determined to see that his students would not go to their fields as ignorant as he had been concerning how to work in the power of God. But he has always made it clear that power encounter was not to be an end in itself. His simple but profoundly biblical statement is that the purpose of power encounter is to lead one to truth encounter, which in turn is to lead the person to allegiance to Christ as Lord. Consistent with his approach throughout, he decided that "an incarnational approach to contextualization demands that we do as Jesus did—healing, delivering people from demons, and conducting missions as spiritual warfare—as well as teaching what Jesus taught" (ibid., 103-104). At times, Chuck spoke of this transforming event as a second conversion. His personality changed significantly. He had always been a people person, concerned about people even above his academic pursuit. But with his incisive mind at times he seemed cynical and had a tendency to shock and disturb students. After his "paradigm shift" in relation to spiritual power, he became a more gentle, humbler, more caring person. To quote a colleague, "His shift from Spirit-talk to Spirit-power and Spirit-love was radical, and in light of the years since, the real thing" (Gilliland 2006).

The focus on inner healing came as an outgrowth of his ministry of praying for physical healing. After Wimber convinced him that anyone could exercise the gift of healing, Chuck began to pray for people to be healed physically. But not much happened. Then a man came, seeking prayer for a bad ankle. As Chuck attempted to analyze the problem, he asked when the ankle had been injured. He discovered that the man had turned his back on God and the problem had begun at that time. That led Chuck to see the need for inner healing before dealing with the physical problem. The man was healed physically after they had dealt with the spiritual issues. So Chuck saw that often the physical problem was the result of a spiritual problem. This new emphasis led him to a whole new calling, a ministry of deep-level inner healing that eventually went worldwide. Often there have been lines outside Chuck's office, with students and others waiting to see him and ask him to pray for them. He has led seminars on inner healing in various countries of the world and helped many, his own students and others, to engage in this ministry. To quote a colleague, "Chuck rejoices when persons who are in need receive help, often miraculous help, through his ministry. His availability for helping-healing is a gift he shares liberally . . . He is very open about this and always gives the glory to God" (ibid.). Yet he has continued his scholarly work. His revision of *Christianity in Culture* (1979a) was published in 2005 (Kraft with Kraft), and he edited *Appropriate Christianity*, to which he contributed eleven chapters, also in 2005 (2005b). This was in addition to other works published on issues of spiritual power.

How to describe such a life in a few words? His friends and students will speak of his keen mind, his openness to the new things God is doing in the world, but also his boyish playfulness, the cartoons on his office window that depict jokes on him along with the rest of us. Sometimes when he is telling his own jokes, he snickers so much he can scarcely finish them. He often uses humor effectively to make his point. I remember the first time I met him at a mission conference in Menlo Park, California, in the 1970s. He was speaking on the importance of using the unexpected in communication and cited a Charlie Brown cartoon. In it, Lucy told Charlie he was too fat. The reply was "I'm not fat; I just have a husky stomach." I had no idea at the time we would ever become colleagues at Fuller, but I will never forget the impression he made on me. As another colleague put it, "Even though he is analytical and original in his thinking he has an unsophisticated and straightforward style that makes him approachable and willing to listen on the spot" (ibid.). In other words, in Chuck, what you see is what you get!

As his friend and former dean, I suggest that the consistent thread in Chuck's life has been the passionate desire to help men and women come to know and follow Jesus Christ in ways that are authentic in their own contexts and consistent with Scriptures, and to see them experience the fullness of the gospel of forgiveness, reconciliation, and power in their lives. That has been Chuck's purpose in both his academic work and his ministry. By constantly aiming toward that goal, Chuck Kraft has made an immeasurable contribution to the world mission of Jesus Christ.

Introduction

R. DANIEL SHAW

Anthropology: What people do
Communication: What people talk about
Spiritual Power: What people understand about spiritual dynamics

Anthropology, communication, and spiritual power—interesting bed fellows that extend back to the beginning of the church and provide key themes for the book of Acts as well as the Apostle Paul's ministry. The New Testament is a record of human interaction in particular contexts about which people communicate and in which they recognize a plan that is bigger than themselves. 1 Corinthians 9:19-23 demonstrates how Paul put it all together enabling him, through the power of the Holy Spirit, to connect with people in any context, interact in ways appropriate to that context, and present the Gospel so as to be relevant and meaningful. He went beyond forms and meanings to present God's intent within each context so that his audience would be persuaded of the presence of God in their midst. And through it all, Paul says that he was the primary benefactor; he learned from every circumstance and was able to apply each to the next (see Woodberry in this volume). So it is with the one we honor in this collection of articles reflecting his lifetime commitment to these three subdisciplines. He has learned from many others around the world and has generously, through word and deed, passed it on to us, enabling us to benefit for the sake of God's Kingdom.

While the juxtaposition of these three subdisciplines may seem a bit incongruous, especially within the purview of one individual, they all combine, and in fact define the career of Charles H. Kraft. Given "Chuck's" interest in mission from an early age, and his intentional preparation for missionary service through his studies at Wheaton, Ashland, and Hartford, the anthropology focus is not surprising. In his mission work in Nigeria, he became involved in linguistics and its application to Bible translation, so the communication focus is also no big surprise. Through his teaching and writing, anthropology and communication have been critical tools he has developed for "Christian witness," words that often feature in the titles of his books. But spiritual power? Kraft, himself, admits this was a surprise, a "second conversion," a "paradigm shift," in his words. The appropriation of spiritual power in mission raised many new questions regarding the nature of the Holy Spirit's role in the realm of human beings. This, in turn, affected how Kraft interpreted worldviews, and engaged in mission endeavors. With his new view of the human condition, he sought to coordinate issues from below with his developing awareness of God's power from above. I seek, here, to record the key role these disparate subdisciplines have had in our ongoing understanding of the nature of missiology as an overarching discipline that Kraft has helped to develop at a transitional moment in mission history. As we actualize a major paradigm shift from past realities to new views of the world as it is, we draw from Kraft's experience to understand new constructions of reality that move us from particularity to wholism, from the said to the unsaid, from the weak to the powerful, from the seen to the unseen.

Kraft's Missiological Impact

I first met Kraft in 1977 when on furlough from my role as a Bible translator in Papua New Guinea (PNG). The next time I saw him was in PNG as he lectured from his then new book, *Christianity in Culture* (1979a). I was impressed with his forward thinking and the impact of the issues he presented on how, as translators, we thought about our theological and communicational task of clearly presenting God's Word. The cultural implications were immense, and Kraft drew attention to them in a creative and dynamic way. We chatted on many levels. Subsequently, I was invited to a meeting with the technical studies director and Kraft to discuss the possibility of my teaching a course at Fuller during my upcoming furlough. The purpose was to familiarize myself with the School of World Mission curriculum in order to consider the possibility of teaching Fuller courses for credit in PNG, thereby reducing the time translators needed to spend in study programs away from the field. This made sense, and I enjoyed my time at Fuller teaching, interacting with the faculty, and reflecting on my work on the Samo translation program.

During that term at Fuller, Kraft challenged me one day: "What would a translation degree program look like?" I said I didn't know and that he should contact the Wycliffe leadership in Dallas. But Kraft wouldn't take "I don't know" for an answer and handed me two large folders full of material he had collected on translation programs. As I perused these folders I saw Kraft's dream, and that dream was realized two years later as I came kicking and screaming from the jungles of New Guinea to the asphalt jungle of Southern California.

I recite this story to focus on Kraft's desire to meet the needs of field missionaries. He has had a wide-ranging effect on training those who were directly involved in mission. He has been particularly interested in equipping those who would work with nationals who, in turn, could carry on missional roles within their own cultures. From 1975 to 1990, Kraft was directly involved in bringing six professors to Fuller and thereby developing academic programs that affected the future of missiology (see Pierson in this volume). This has resulted in hundreds of graduates (over one hundred in translation alone) who are now spread around the globe in key positions and who have transformed the face of mission in our changing world. Clearly many others have been involved as well, but at Fuller, Kraft has often been the catalyst for initiating new programs and redirecting careers to have a strategic effect on mission worldwide.

Bridging the Gap

Kraft's career has seen the transition from doing foreign mission to incorporating mission into cross-cultural interaction—from doing to being. He has witnessed and often encouraged the transition from the old colonial model, where the focus was on telling others what enlightened outsiders thought "locals" should know, as noted by Whiteman, Rynkiewich, and Søgaard (in this volume), to taking mission out there and enabling others to see Jesus in their context, as suggested by King, Woodberry, and the Travises (in this volume). This shift transitioned messengers from doing mission to being "God's missionary people" (Van Engen, 1991). Kraft epitomizes this missiological transition and has done much to promote and precipitate it. He encouraged the transition from older models of doing mission that often denigrated culture—that too often preached ideas strange to the new culture—and were usually powerless to apply appropriate cultural understanding and local communication styles to the spiritual connections people knew to be real. As missiologists, we need to recognize the impact of understanding what people do (Whitman and Part I), the role of communication in its many forms (Van Engen and Part II), and the effect of applying biblical guidelines for spiritual power to effective ministry (Woodberry and Part III).

In his development of the connections between these three subfields of missiology, Kraft has demonstrated that effective field missionaries must operate in the power of the Holy Spirit in order to match people's cultural expectations with their understanding of God's communication to human beings. Too often it has been the case that everyone but the missionary understood the role of power in spiritual transformation. Shamen and others like them have understood the value of spiritual power and have utilized it in their activities. Thus when missionaries emphasized knowledge over power (because for them knowledge was power) they came across as powerless to the people they sought to reach. And a powerless gospel was of no use to anyone. In his academic and intellectual perception, Kraft realized the necessity for power ministries to go hand-in-hand with knowledge and a relationship to God which in turn affected their relationship to other human beings. This was the essence of his crucial article on the three encounters—truth, allegiance, and power—in Christian witness (Kraft 1992a) that offered us a new view of mission.

Kraft's Intellectual Background

As any scholar, Kraft was influenced by others. His formative anthropology began with the reading of Eugene Nida's book *Customs and Cultures* (Nida 1954). Later, when he attended the Summer Institute of Linguistics, he met Nida and they became close friends—a relationship that continued to grow at Hartford. Nida's propensity for applying theory to the practical contexts in which theory had to work itself out influenced Kraft, and he often found himself in the midst of arguments where conventional mission wisdom and anthropological theory clashed in the reality of connecting a relationship to God to the reality of people's lives. This involved issues of baptism, communion, types and use of music, and the all important and often divisive matter of polygamy. Kraft often found himself arguing against mission leaders on behalf of the people he so wanted to reach with the incarnational message of the gospel. His focus on "receptor-oriented communication," mentioned so often in these pages, was formed during these in-field arguments that sometimes left the true audience (those for whom Christ died and to whom the missionaries were preaching) out of the loop. Kraft's anthropological insight often put him at odds with field administrators who, in the end, determined that they would do better without this troublesome scholar meddling with their field policies. It was at this juncture that Kraft completed his Ph.D. at Hartford and launched his academic career building on those often painful field experiences, continually encouraged by Eugene Nida's thoughts and writings (see Pierson in this volume).

When Kraft arrived at Fuller, he met Alan Tippett and they became colleagues as well as friends. In typical Australian style, office chats and table conversations as well as a shared interest in cultural anthropology and stamp collecting cemented their friendship. Common interests in applying anthropological theory to effective mission drove them both. The friendship flourished long after Tippett returned to Australia to display his stamps, do research, and write from his library in Canberra where Kraft often visited him.

The intellectual influence along with field experience and ongoing interaction with field missionaries (as when Kraft went to PNG in 1979) had an effect on Kraft's teaching and provided wonderful material for the countless stories that he would tell to illustrate his lectures and enliven his writing. He took the students beyond their experiences and challenged their assumptions as he encouraged them to apply the literature they were reading to their field contexts. He also gave international students a new appreciation for their own cultures. He encouraged them to be themselves as they applied course materials to the reality of their own cultural experience. On one occasion a student thanked Kraft for enabling her to finally be herself and apply her self-awareness to her relationship with Jesus. Kraft was touched and maintained that enabling posture, with reflection, throughout his career.

The third influence on Kraft's intellect came from a surprising source, a pastor of a charismatic church in Anaheim, California: John Wimber. Introduced to him by Peter Wagner, Kraft sat in on the first "signs and wonders" course out of curiosity and got hooked (see Wagner this volume). Wimber's influence was more in terms of ministry orientation than in an intellectual focus. But it changed Kraft's life and career. Wimber's focus on allowing God's Spirit to work without a lot of flash or excess noise resonated with Kraft, who was anything but charismatic. Yet, he recognized the importance of allowing the power of the Spirit to make a difference in people's lives as well as in the culture around them. Kraft brought his anthropological and communicational insights to an understanding of the work of the Holy Spirit in any context. Every culture is different and will manifest the working of the Spirit in ways that are often in keeping with specific, local cultural values and patterns. This was an important message that impacted Kraft's understanding for, and teaching of, inner healing. Kraft always used theory as a tool for effective practice, an approach inspired by Nida and Tippett and reinforced through an application to power ministry. For Kraft, missional practice always wins out over theory but is always informed by theory in order to be meaningful and appropriate. How do we take what he has given us and enable effective mission practice and reflection among future generations of missionaries? Rynkiewich, Jørgensen, and Engelsviken take us there and suggest we follow Kraft's example, remain humble, and let God do the work.

Moving beyond Chuck Kraft

In his role of transitioning missiology from the old missionary school approach, epitomized by his experience at the Kennedy School of Missions, to connecting with a postmodern, global village approach to the world, Kraft sought to build on lessons learned while connecting to new attitudes and issues. His adage that "we will always make mistakes—just make new ones" characterizes his approach. He has always been on the cutting edge of things, often making people uneasy. Yet he has opened the eyes of many to what they would not have otherwise seen. And what they see is a world in need of understanding of God's intent both for the world at large and for the particularities of a people living in their context (Shaw and Van Engen 2003).

Kraft has helped many of us to see the importance of doing ministry in context armed with anthropology, communication, and power tools designed to help us reach out to real people who seek a relationship with God. He investigated new vistas of culture in relation to biblical understanding and developed ethnotheology (see the chapter by Rynkiewich in this volume). He anticipated the interests of those who received the gospel and encouraged a multiplicity of media modes that would let people appreciate God's relevance in their midst (see the chapter by Søgaard in this volume). Furthermore, he recognized the value of using music and word in dynamic, interactive ways that would allow people to express themselves to God as they would to others (see the chapter by King in this volume). Through his study and practice of spiritual power Kraft helped people connect to God's power by way of their own spiritual understanding and apply it in their daily living.

Kraft understood Ajith Fernando's plea for missionaries to change their job description (Fernando 1988). In an age of increased non-Western, long-term mission involvement, missionary roles relate increasingly to equipping and enabling local people to reach God's chosen potential for them in their own context. The development of so-called Independent/Indigenous/Initiated Churches (particularly in Africa) was largely a reaction to powerless mission from missionaries with a colonialist attitude. Kraft demonstrated that God could move in the midst of people in ways that went beyond missionary expectations and that such was all right. God created people in God's own image and knew and valued them far more than the well-meaning but often uninformed and culturally insensitive missionary.

As we seek to enter into new and "appropriate" approaches to mission (as characterized in the title of Kraft's edited work in honor of his good friend and colleague Dean Gilliland [Kraft 2005b]), we need to follow in the spirit of Kraft's applicational appropriation of theory to practice. We need to recognize that the stakes are high in our increasingly dangerous and globalized world. Pierson, Whiteman, and Wagner encourage us to learn from the past and apply lessons learned to ongoing ministry in a globalizing, urbanizing, and changing church environment. We must come to understand the cultural context as Priest, Nida, and King make clear. We must appreciate the changing patterns of meaning as Hiebert, Rynkiewich, and the Travises note. We must value the source (extending all the way back to God's intention in communicating his Word) as well as the impact on receptors as Søgaard, Jørgensen, and Woodberry assert. Engelsviken and Wagner admonish us to appreciate the many manifestations of God's Spirit as well as the counterpoint of the power of the enemy at work in the world.

Kraft has demonstrated an attitude of "we can do anything" in God's power and "anything can and will happen." He has instilled in colleagues, students, and thousands of others who have listened to his lectures that God's Spirit is alive and well in the world and is engaged in battle with the forces of darkness that continually seek to cloud human minds (Kraft 1992b). This battle, however, has clear cultural parameters which permute from one context to another—we can never predict it; therefore, we must study the context and bring cultural understanding to enabling people in that context to experience God's grace for themselves. They in turn will respond by communicating to others, being missional, and doing so in ways that are relevant and meaningful. Their theologies will differ from those espoused by the ones who originally brought them the gospel, and they will express their Christianity in ways that are particular and meaningful for themselves (Shaw and Van Engen 2003, 67). Assumptions about worldviews will always produce geographic clashes as West meets non-West, communicational challenges as modern modes of thinking and communicating clash with the postmodern, and spiritual wars as those grounded in biblical theology interact with those who connect their life issues to thinking about God. In short, we must re-engineer our thinking about what God does, what God says, how God works, and what that means for people everywhere—an appreciation for worldview and the epistemological shifts required to appreciate both the text and the context as we compare them to how "we have always done it."

As we reflect upon Kraft's focus on the relationship between power, truth, and allegiance, we are forced to value the impact of incarnation as a biblical theme that flows through the whole of the canon but is epitomized in the life of Jesus. He learned to live in the context of second temple Judaism, spoke Aramaic and Greek, and allowed the Spirit to work through him to do the Father's will. Kraft's fascination with the incarnation and "communicating God's way," based on Jesus' life and ministry (Kraft 1983a), led him, in part, to a new understanding of power ministry (Kraft 1989). In Kraft's view, Jesus always operated as a human being, allowing the Spirit to work through him. This means that Jesus met people's expectations by performing miracles through the same power that he sent to indwell the disciples on the day of Pentecost. And it is that same power that dwells in God's people today.

An incarnational approach, then, has implications for how we go about doing mission. If we follow Jesus' example, we will apply methods that reflect on human interaction within a context (anthropology), connect God's truth to that context in ways that draw people into God's presence (communication), and enable the Spirit to work through them (spiritual power). All this will bring a new allegiance to Christ as Lord. But these are not merely missiologically theoretical principles. Rather, they represent missional pathways that pertain to the church's life and presence in the world, to the way contemporary people move beyond culture to effective communication, and to the use of spiritual power to meet human need. People who connect God to their world are the best representatives of Jesus in the midst of their people. They seek to apply Scripture to their context and become church planters, leaders, and Christians in the midst of the people, following Jesus' example. Missiological principles are increasingly relevant to the success of wholistic ministry in any context. Recognizing the pluralism extant in our world demands the application of approaches long associated with cross-cultural mission to being missional at home (Guder 1998).

Kraft spanned the gap from old-style mission to the new. He has been betwixt and between, neither one nor the other, and he often felt caught between the two perspectives. He has been a liminal figure who has bridged the colonial and postcolonial eras, yet not been comfortable in either. Intellectually he took us from one era to the other. And in practice he has sought to connect a powerless West to the power of those who experienced the reality of a spiritual presence but who, without Christ, accepted the devil's twisted lie for the reality of God's powerful presence. In understanding this, both the West and the non-West gain new insight and are able to redirect their beliefs and practices in line with God's expectations. Kraft has brought a greater awareness of God's power in particular contexts that then influences more effective communication of what God intends human beings (wherever they are) to understand about God.

We need to utilize Kraft's approach and attitude in ever-new contexts where issues created by the AIDS pandemic, children at risk, terrorism, wars and rumors of wars, and new religious responses to age-old questions rule. What impact do Kraft's principles have in a pluralist world which is interactively multicultural, multilingual, and trans-spiritual? Throughout his career Kraft challenged us to build on these subdisciplines for the express purpose of gaining new insights about new ways to offer a new (yet always the same ancient) message of God's love. In McCluhan's terms, "the medium is the message" (McLuhan 1967). Kraft escaped that near cliché, packaging his message in terms of relevance to various contexts, adapting to receptor-oriented communication styles necessary to ensure understanding, and presenting it, as best he could, to demonstrate God's power in the midst of the people.

In the pages that follow, the authors (all influenced by Kraft in one way or another) connect this triumvirate of subdisciplines with being missional in the reality of a changing world. Today's world represents much the same environment as that in which Paul addressed the Ephesians, as Woodberry points out in this volume. The world in which we live today faces the same concerns about local contexts and transformational challenges as the one faced by the early apostles who allowed the Spirit to walk in their midst and work through them. In so doing they communicated with each other and sought the will of God. Like them, we today join in the sentiment of the Jerusalem council and send a resounding note to all who read these pages: "it seems good to the Holy Spirit and to us not to place any extra burden on you" (Acts 15:28). In his conclusion to this volume, Schreiter connects missiology with advancing "God's Reign." In Kraft's terms, our focus is always on God's big "R" reality. Yet, we must recognize that in our humanity, every society is bound by its own small "r" perceptions which, together, bring new appreciation for the totality of God's creativity. In our human collectivity we come to new understanding as we learn to value others, who, in turn, reflect God's intentionality in creation. In the words of Jesus, "I will send you the Spirit who comes from the Father and shows what is true. The Spirit will help you and will tell you about me. Then you will also tell others about me" (Jn 15:26, 27 CEV). May these words ring true as you read and apply these paradigm shifts to your Christian witness.

Part I

CULTURAL ANTHROPOLOGY

Introduction by Darrell Whiteman

"Good missionaries have always been good 'anthropologists,' " Eugene Nida argued in the opening line of his landmark book *Customs and Cultures: Anthropology for Christian Missions* (1954). Charles Kraft, through his mission experience, his teaching, and his writing is a living example of how important anthropological insights can be for effective cross-cultural witness. Anthropological insights helped Kraft to make a significant paradigm shift as he went to Nigeria in the twilight of the colonial era. Despite the fact that much of early anthropology rode on the back of colonialism and modernity, Nida's important book and Kraft's subsequent mission experience and later scholarship helped pave the way for a post-colonial approach to mission: a way that recognized the importance of indigenous forms of ministry that may look and feel quite different from those introduced by the foreign missionary.

Since Nida wrote his book in 1954 and Kraft first went to Nigeria in 1957, anthropology and missiology have undergone significant changes, dramatic paradigm shifts, if you will. In fact, the entire context of God's mission in the world, influenced and shaped by urbanization, migration, and globalization, has changed. So, the question remains, what role is there for anthropology in the training of cross-cultural witnesses, in conceptualizing the mission task as we join in the *missio Dei*, and in influencing our understanding and practice of mission as we develop relationships with others across cultural boundaries? Anthropological insights can help us discover where God has already been at work, long before cross-cultural witnesses arrive on the scene. It will help us develop epistemological humility and become more vulnerable as we move into more of a learning mode so that the quest for understanding will become more important than the need for certainty.

In the opening chapter to this section on cultural anthropology, I chronicle the long and ambivalent journey that has led to the field of anthropology informing the practice of mission. Anthropology first had to get over its hesitancy to become an applied science. Once there was progress on that front, it was easier to see how anthropological insights could inform mission practice.

The late Paul Hiebert makes an important contribution to this book by helping us understand the epistemological assumptions of Modernity, Postmodern Deconstruction, and Critical Realism as they have informed anthropology, theol-

1

ogy, and mission understanding and practice. Unless we raise to a conscious level the epistemological assumptions that guide our practice and understanding of mission, we will more than likely, without realizing it, be embedded in worldviews and assumptions that are at variance with the Kingdom of God and biblical values. In research begun over 20 years ago, Hiebert demonstrated the influence of various epistemologies on anthropology and mission, and now in one of his last publications in a long life of prodigious scholarship, he has helped us better understand how anthropology can contribute to mission.

Robert Priest in his chapter on the relationship between anthropology and missiology notes that the integration of anthropology into the field of missiology is a dominant characteristic of North American missiology, in contrast to European missiology which focuses more on history and theology of mission and deals far less with the relationship of the social sciences to mission studies. He chronicles the key individuals and institutions that have helped to develop the field of missiological anthropology. Despite the potential for broader and deeper contributions of anthropological insights to missiology and despite the fact that anthropology is a significant player in North American missiology, Priest notes that it is still marginalized in theological conversations. Perhaps one reason for anthropology being sidelined in Christian colleges and seminary curriculums is because there are so few professional anthropologists who have used their training and scholarship in the service of mission and the church. Priest concludes with some helpful suggestions on how the field of missiological anthropology can be strengthened in the future.

This leads us to the final chapter in this section on cultural anthropology in which Michael Rynkiewich points to the future of missiological anthropology. In a rather sobering statement, he affirms that missiology is still stuck in the 1960s and has not yet taken advantage of insights from a more postmodern anthropology. Standard concepts and "household terms" in missiology such as "culture" and "ethnicity" are given a postmodern update, and newer concepts such as "agency" are brought into the dialogue with missiology. Despite his somewhat harsh critique of the past and present contributions of anthropology to missiology, Rynkiewich is hopeful and positive about the future of missiological anthropology.

Charles Kraft has been a creative and insightful contributor of anthropological ideas to the practice and understanding of mission. Picking up where Nida left off, Kraft introduced a whole generation of mission practitioners to the value of anthropological insights for cross-cultural witness. Building on his creative insights and applications, we can anticipate that future generations of missiological anthropologists will dig deeper and research whole areas of mission and anthropology that have yet to be explored and understood.

1

Anthropology and Mission

An Uneasy Journey toward Mutual Understanding

DARRELL WHITEMAN

The relationship between the academic field of anthropology and the practice of mission is an essential connection. Elsewhere I (Whiteman 2003a) have shown the significant missionary contributions to anthropological research and argued that missionaries need the insights from anthropology to enable them to identify incarnationally with the people among whom they serve. In this chapter I will discuss how the field of anthropology slowly emerged to become an applied science, an important stepping-stone to the development of the field of missiological anthropology.

The Ambivalent Relationship between Anthropology and Mission

The relationship between anthropology and mission has been an ambivalent one for over a hundred years (see Hiebert 1978; Stipe 1980; Luzbetak 1985; Sutlive 1985; Salamone 1986; Van Der Geest 1990; Burridge 1991; Priest 2001). Committed to the doctrine of cultural relativism, most anthropologists have viewed religion only as an epiphenomenon of culture, as a mere reflection of society (Durkheim 1915). They have thus concluded that Christianity is no different than other religions. It is simply a cultural by-product; it is human-made, they argue, not God given. Because there are so few anthropologists with personal Christian faith, it is not surprising that a fair amount of antagonism toward missionaries has come from anthropologists. For example, in his presidential address to the American Anthropological Association in 1976, Walter Goldschmidt (1977, 296) declared, "Missionaries are in many ways our opposites; they believe in original sin, the moral depravity of uncivilized man, and the evil of native customs. Because they wish to change the people we wish to study, we view them as spoilers."[1] This lack of appre-

---

[1] In this statement Goldschmidt ignores the fact that anthropologists also "spoil" when they enter a culture to study it, and that anthropologists also have a mission. For example, Bruce Knauft (1996, 5, 38*ff.*), a postmodern anthropologist with evangelistic zeal, calls for the need for passion and clear mission in anthropology.

ciation for, or understanding of, missionaries by anthropologists has been well documented and discussed by Robert Priest (2001; see also his chapter in this volume) in a recent provocative article in *Current Anthropology* entitled "Missionary Positions: Christian, Modernist, Postmodernist" (see also Stipe 1980; Sutlive 1985; Salamone 1985, 1986; Bonsen, Marks, and Miedema 1990; Van Der Geest 1990). Anthropologists have frequently stereotyped missionaries as narrow-minded destroyers of culture. And, unfortunately, some missionaries must confess, "guilty as charged." But the preponderance of evidence demonstrates that missionaries have often contributed to the preservation of languages and cultures more than to their destruction (Whiteman 2002). Lamin Sanneh (1989) has argued persuasively that through Bible translation into vernacular languages, missionaries have done much to preserve rather than destroy indigenous cultures.

If anthropologists have been suspicious of missionaries, missionaries in turn have been slow to show appreciation for the insights that anthropology has to offer them. Paul Hiebert (1978) several years ago described the relationship between missions and anthropology as a love-hate relationship. Twenty years ago Louis Luzbetak (1985) called for a better understanding and a closer cooperation between the two antagonistic groups of anthropologists and missionaries, and offered some practical suggestions as to how this could come about. Kenelm Burridge (1991), who is more sympathetic and understanding of missionaries than are most anthropologists, documents this long history of ambivalence between anthropologists and missionaries, and notes the significant ethnographic contributions many missionaries have made.

A Turning of the Tide in Anthropology and Mission

At the beginning of the twentieth century, anthropology as a discipline was becoming established and recovering from its obsession with evolutionary thought. Other theories were advanced to explain the diversity of human beings and their cultures. In reaction to the nineteenth-century evolutionary schemes, several different theories of cultural diffusion were pressed into explaining cultural diversity. The devastation left by World War I and the expansion of colonialism called for the application of anthropology to human problems. For example, in 1921 proposals were made for the establishment of a school of applied anthropology in Great Britain, suggesting that "the anthropological point of view should permeate the whole body of the people" and that the lack of this "was the cause of our present troubles" (Peake 1921, 174).

In 1929 Bronislaw Malinowski published an article in the journal *Africa* entitled "Practical Anthropology." He noted at the time the huge gap between the theoretical concerns of anthropology and the practical interests of colonial administrators and missionaries. Writing from the African context, Malinowski notes,

> Now I think the gap is artificial and of great prejudice to either side. The practical man should be asked to state his needs as regards knowledge on savage law, economics, customs, and institutions; he would then stimulate

the scientific anthropologist to a most fruitful line of research and thus receive information without which he often gropes in the dark. The anthropologist, on the other hand, must move towards a direct study of indigenous institutions as they now exist and work. He must also become more concerned in the anthropology of the changing African, and in the anthropology of contact of white and coloured, of European culture and primitive tribal life. (1929, 23-24; 1970, 13)

Despite the colonial tone of his words, Malinowski was calling for anthropologists to study people as they were undergoing change from the impact of colonialism and to stop pursuing a speculative anthropology that sought to reconstruct the lives and cultures of people from a bygone era. In contrast to this salvage anthropology, Malinowski was calling for the creation of a new kind of anthropology, one that would later come to be called applied anthropology. Malinowski, perhaps more than any other anthropologist in Britain, helped to popularize anthropology and get it into the hands of nonprofessional laypeople. From the London School of Economics, Malinowski trained a generation of anthropologists who slowly took up his challenge and conducted research that was helpful in the context of changing cultures under colonial influence. Later postmodern critiques of anthropology would be critical of anthropology's cozy relationship with colonialism (see Knauft 1996).

Applied anthropology emerged in the 1930s, in both Britain and the United States. American anthropologists such as Robert Redfield, Ralph Linton, Melville Herskovits, and Margaret Mead sought to merge practical anthropology and academic anthropology while at the same time distancing themselves from missionaries and their concerns. Postmodern anthropology would later attempt to "expose" both anthropology and mission for having an agenda (see Rynkiewich 2002, 301-321).

Malinowski began calling for the practical use of anthropology as early as 1929, and in 1938 argued that the time had come to make anthropology practical:

... the anthropologist with all his highly vaunted technique of field work, his scientific acumen, and his humanistic outlook, has so far kept aloof from the fierce battle of opinions about the future and the welfare of native races. In the heated arguments between those who want to "keep the native in his place" and those who want to "secure him a place in the sun," the anthropologist has so far taken no active part. Does this mean that knowledge serves merely to blind us to the reality of human interests and vital issues? The science which claims to understand culture and to have the clue to racial problems must not remain silent on the drama of culture conflict and of racial clash.

Anthropology must become an applied science. Every student of scientific history knows that science is born of its applications. (Malinowski 1938, x)

Bronislaw Malinowski did much to take anthropology beyond the academy and into the real world. His theory of functionalism, much maligned today, was a helpful schema for understanding how change introduced into one part of a culture would impact all other aspects of the society. As a theory, Malinowski's functionalism was not particularly fruitful, but as a guide for research and for interpreting the impact of one culture on another it is still helpful. This perspective became important for colonial administrators and, of course, for missionaries.

After the turn of the century, missionaries also started to get in touch with the value of anthropology for their work. Ecumenical mission conferences were held in New York in 1854, Liverpool in 1860, and in 1888 the Centenary Conference on Protestant Missions was held at Exeter Hall in London, with sixteen hundred representatives from fifty-three mission societies. Over this thirty-year period the missionary movement had grown statistically in a remarkable way; mission agencies also became more paternalistic, with more vested interests. There is little evidence of an awareness of the need for anthropological insight coming out of these conferences.

But Edinburgh 1910 was a different story. The report of the commission is a large series of nine volumes, with one devoted completely to the preparation of missionaries (vol. 5). The importance of understanding the cultures and customs of the people to whom missionaries go was stressed from this time onwards. Edinburgh is important because it shows that missionaries were struggling with all the points of criticism that anthropologists would eventually make. One of the features of this conference was the recognition of the fact of sociocultural change, as well as the need to move beyond ethnocentric evaluations of cultural differences. The call for anthropological training of missionaries was clearly sounded at Edinburgh. The report says,

> It is, therefore, clear that the missionary needs to know far more than the mere manners and customs of the race to which he is sent; he ought to be versed in the genius of the people, that which has made them the people they are; and to sympathise so truly with the good which they have evolved, that he may be able to aid the national leaders reverently to build up a Christian civilisation after their own kind, not after the European kind. (World Missionary Conference 1910, p. 170)

Edinburgh differed from other missionary conferences because it was the first time that such an emphasis was heard. Both the speakers at the conference and the reports offered from all over the world articulated what many missionaries were feeling very strongly, namely, a need for better understanding and deeper appreciation of the religion and the values of the people among whom they were working. They were beginning to realize that sympathy was not enough, that empathy and understanding were required, and that their evangelism would be far more effective if it took place within a worldview other than their own.

The leading advocate for applying anthropological insights to mission was Edwin W. Smith (1876-1957). Smith, born of missionary parents of the Primitive Methodist Mission in South Africa, served as a missionary in Zambia among the Baila-Batonga people from 1902 to 1915. Although he often thought of himself as an amateur anthropologist, he nevertheless was held in high esteem by contemporary anthropologists of his day. He was a member of the Royal Anthropological Institute of Great Britain from 1909 until his death in 1957, and served as its president from 1933 to 1935, the first and only missionary to do so. He contributed substantially to anthropology (Smith 1907; Smith and Dale 1968) and wrote frequently in the *International Review of Missions*. In 1924, in an article entitled "Social Anthropology and Missionary Work" Smith (1924, 519) argues that "the science of social anthropology [should be] recognized as an essential discipline in the training of missionaries." He goes on to note that we need to understand people from their point of view, not just our own, if mission work is to be effective. He notes in language characteristic of his time that, "a study of social anthropology will lead the young missionary to look at things always from the native's point of view, and this will save him from making serious blunders. Tact is not enough; nor is love . . . Tact needs to be based on knowledge; love there can hardly be without understanding" (Smith 1924, 522-523).

Ten years later in his 1934 presidential address to the Royal Anthropological Institute entitled "Anthropology and the Practical Man," Smith connected his Christian faith and missionary work with his anthropological perspective. He notes,

> I think that too often missionaries have regarded themselves as agents of European civilization and have thought it part of their duty to spread the use of English language, English clothing, English music—the whole gamut of our culture. They have confounded Christianity with western Civilization. In my view this is a mistaken view of the Christian mission. I am convinced that essential elements in Christian belief and practice are of universal value—that in other words, there are fundamental needs of the human soul that Christ alone can satisfy. But in the Christianity which we know there are unessential elements, accretions which it has taken on from its European environment and which it is not part of the Christian missionary's duty to propagate. (Smith 1934, xxvi-xxvii)

Smith goes on to note, in language that is similar to contemporary discussions of contextualization, that Christianity must take on appropriate cultural forms in each culture it encounters. And then with a spirit of optimism he claims,

> Here and there in the field academically trained anthropologists are to be found on the [mission] staffs. Some of us will not be content until such qualified persons are at work in every mission area and every missionary has had some anthropological training. In short, there are signs that the modern missionary is becoming anthropologically minded, without being any the less zealous in his religious duties. (Smith 1934, xxix)

I believe Edwin Smith's optimism was premature, for today many, if not most, missionaries are not anthropologically minded, even though we see there was a call for this as far back as Edinburgh 1910.

Another early advocate for connecting anthropology and mission was Henri Philippe Junod, missionary in South Africa and son of the missionary ethnographer Henri A. Junod (1962). Writing in 1935, Henri Philippe says, "I wish anthropologists would realize what they owe to missionary work. Many scientists do acknowledge this debt, but others forget the contribution of missionaries to science itself. It is not accidental if missionaries have sometimes proved to be the best anthropologists." He then bemoans the fact that "mission policy, however, has had too little to do with anthropology" (quoted in Junod 1935, 217). He goes on to say,

> I believe that anthropology can help us greatly. It can widen our views, it can open our eyes, it can teach us to understand, it can improve our educational policy and point out to us the dangers of the way. But we are not here to preserve native custom as a curio for some African museum. We are dealing with the realities of the present. (Junod 1935, 228)

Missionary anthropologists like Edwin W. Smith and Henri Junod had more impact on European missionaries from mainline denominations than on American evangelical missionaries. The first post-World War II era book on anthropology in the United States was written in 1945 by Gordon Hedderly Smith entitled *The Missionary and Anthropology: An Introduction to the Study of Primitive Man for Missionaries*. This is a very inadequate book, drawing too much on E. B. Tylor and John Lubbock, nineteenth-century evolutionary anthropologists. Smith argues for the importance of anthropological training as part and parcel of missionary preparation, but given the shortcomings of this book, it is not surprising that it had limited influence.

During the 1940s and continuing well beyond the end of WWII, Wheaton College in Wheaton, Illinois, became a center for preparing missionaries. The distinguished and popular Russian-born Dr. Alexander Grigolia developed a strong anthropology major and course program, and he was succeeded at Wheaton by a series of young anthropology instructors committed to both providing balanced undergraduate anthropological training and teaching the conceptual and practical tools required for effective communication across cultural boundaries. Perhaps the most famous anthropology major from Wheaton was the renowned evangelist Billy Graham, who graduated from Wheaton in 1943 and who had chosen anthropology as a major partly because of an interest in becoming a missionary (Graham 1997, 64-65). Graham drew on anthropological concepts for his evangelistic ministry. Students such as Charles Kraft, Henry Bradley, and William Merrifield (class of 1953) would all go on to make important contributions to missiological anthropology. By 1953 Wheaton had graduated over two hundred majors in anthropology, many of whom were serving or were destined to work as missionaries.[2]

---

[2]As Wheaton College's anthropology program waned in the early 1960s, Bethel College, St. Paul, Minneapolis, began to establish a program in anthropology for training Christian missionaries, practitioners in development and other applied fields, and academics. Building on an already strong Sociology Department under the guidance of David

The Kennedy School of Missions of Hartford Seminary[3] was the equivalent graduate program where anthropology was taught and used in the advanced training of Protestant missionaries. Edwin W. Smith, upon his retirement in 1939, was a visiting lecturer of African anthropology and history at Hartford until 1943, and Paul Leser served as professor of anthropology. Charles Taber and Charles Kraft, two well-known anthropologically trained missiologists, received their Ph.D. degrees from Hartford before it closed the mission program in the mid-1960s, reflecting the decline in missionaries being sent by mainline Protestant mission boards. As the Kennedy School of Missions at Hartford was folding, schools of world mission with an emphasis on applying anthropological insights in missiology and employing trained professional anthropologists on their faculty were begun at Fuller Theological Seminary in 1965, Trinity Evangelical Divinity School in 1969, and Asbury Theological Seminary in 1983.

A high-water mark in the history of anthropology and mission came in 1954 with the publication of Eugene Nida's *Customs and Cultures: Anthropology for Christian Missions* (1954). Although Nida's Ph.D. was in linguistics rather than in anthropology, as a translation consultant for the American Bible Society, Nida traveled widely, working in some two hundred languages in seventy-five countries (Stine 2004). From this vast experience Nida saw firsthand the problems and challenges faced by missionaries and translators. His anthropological perspective enabled him to make keen observations and write copious notes from which *Customs and Cultures* was written in a brief six-week period while Nida was in Brazil between translation workshops. *Customs and Cultures* is conceptually rich and anthropologically well grounded. It is still used today in colleges and seminaries, although many of Nida's illustrations are dated, especially those from pre-Vatican II Latin America. Nevertheless, I have had students tell me they wished they had read Nida's book before they had sallied forth into cross-cultural ministry (Stine 2004; Shaw 2007).

Moberg, Claude Stipe established the anthropology program that became part of a blended department of sociology and anthropology. Soon linguistics was added and the department became known as the Department of Anthropology, Sociology, and Linguistics. Some of the key professors during this time period were Thomas Correll, Don Larson, William Smalley, Ken Gowdy, and Paul Wiebe. This team added James Hurd in the early 1980s. The department attracted a relatively small number of majors, but the graduates of this program in this era created careers of distinction. The anthropology graduates included Thomas Headland, Michael Rynkiewich, Stephen Ybarrola, Richard Swanson, and Douglas Magnuson. Between 1986 and 1988 all but Ken Gowdy and James Hurd took early retirement or left for other opportunities. Today the Department of Anthropology and Sociology has a major in sociocultural studies with four "tracks" that allow a student to specialized in anthropology, sociology, cross-cultural missions, or urban studies. The program attracts almost 70 majors a year (around sixty percent in the anthropology and cross-cultural mission tracks, twenty percent sociology, and twenty percent urban studies). The faculty consists of three anthropologists, Harley Schreck, James Hurd, and Jenell Paris Williams, and two sociologists, Samuel Zalanga and Curtis DeYoung.

[3]The Kennedy School of Missions was a direct response to Edinburgh 1910, and especially the Report of Commission V, *The Preparation of Missionaries*, which was

The Journal *Practical Anthropology*

One index that an academic field is reaching maturity is when a journal is published in that field. This was the case with missionary anthropology and the publication of *Practical Anthropology.*

Malinowski's article entitled "Practical Anthropology" published in 1929 was a call for anthropology to move beyond the sterile confines of academia and enter the world where cultures were clashing with one another and where colonialism was impacting indigenous cultures. Malinowski was not a man of faith, so it is perhaps ironic that his call for a practical anthropology was a harbinger of the practical application of anthropology to Christian mission.

Following World War II with the proliferation of Protestant evangelical missionaries and the beginning decline of colonialism, a new journal called *Practical Anthropology* was launched in 1953. Its humble beginnings occurred when Robert B. Taylor, anthropology instructor at Wheaton College, prepared and distributed two initial issues to test the level of interest in a journal on applications of anthropology in Christian thought and practice. The response was favorable, mainly among those interested in cross-cultural communication of the Christian message.

At Wheaton, Taylor typed the mimeograph masters and had them reproduced by the college copy center. Both at Wheaton in 1953-1954 and in Eugene, Oregon, in 1954-1956, he continued to develop the journal, keeping the subscription cost at $1.00 per year by doing all the work with the help of his wife, Floris, except for the mimeographing and, later, multilithing. Within a few years there were 250 subscribers. During these years of development, the project was helped along, perhaps indispensably, by the advice and writings of such pioneers as William Smalley, William Reyburn, Marie Fetzer Reyburn, Eugene Nida, and James O. Buswell III. When Taylor left the University of Oregon campus for doctoral field research, William Smalley became editor. Under Smalley's leadership *Practical Anthropology* developed into a journal primarily for missionaries and Bible translators needing the insights from anthropology and wanting a forum where they could share their ideas and their anthropologically informed experiences of mission in the field. This conformed to a vision Smalley had held for some time for just such a publication, and with the help of others, he built effectively on the journal Taylor had turned over to him.

Practical Anthropology ran for nineteen years, continuing as an outlet for anthropologically minded missiologists like Nida, Smalley, Loewen, the Reyburns,

chaired by W. Douglas Mackenzie, president of Hartford Theological Seminary. Attending the Edinburgh conference in the summer of 1910 was Mrs. John Stewart Kennedy, who, when approached by Hartford Seminary, agreed to give $500,000 toward the new School of Missions. The school was named in memory of her late husband, John Stewart Kennedy of New York (Geer 1934, 202-218).

and Charles Taber, all of whom were committed to cross-cultural mission and Bible translation. *Practical Anthropology* served as a venue for one of Charles Kraft's early publications, "Christian Conversion or Cultural Conversion" (1963), which caught the eye of Donald McGavran and contributed to McGavran inviting Kraft to join the School of World Mission at Fuller Theological Seminary in 1969. The pages of the early editions of this journal are full of stories and examples of how anthropology can illuminate the cross-cultural complexities of effective mission work. It is interesting to read letters to the editor wishing that the readers had possessed this kind of anthropological insight before they had begun their missionary careers. For example, Herbert Greig writing from Batouri, Cameroun, lamented, "If only I had this before I went to Africa, what a difference it would have made. With regret I look back upon the embarrassments and the lost opportunities, and would like to save others from like mistakes" (1957, 204).

After nineteen consecutive years of publishing six issues a year, *Practical Anthropology* ceased publication and merged into *Missiology*, the journal of the American Society of Missiology, in 1973. At this time there were over three thousand subscribers to *Practical Anthropology* (Shenk and Hunsberger 1998, 17) indicating the tremendous growth this journal underwent in a relatively short time. The need for insights from anthropology applied to the problems of cross-cultural mission was significant, and *Practical Anthropology* (*PA*) responded with timely, helpful articles. The last editor of *Practical Anthropology*, Charles Taber, noted that,

> From the beginning, *PA* took for its scope the entire field of cross-cultural communication, viewed from an anthropological perspective. Its potential audience included anyone interested in such communication, especially of the Christian gospel. Such concepts as ethnocentrism, cultural relativity, accommodation, identification, and so forth were introduced and discussed, and their implications for Christian mission explored. We believe that *PA* has served an important function and has been helpful to many by making *practical* applications of *anthropology* to their work in all parts of the world. (Taber 1973, 7)

The first editor of *Missiology* was anthropologist Alan Tippett from Fuller Theological Seminary's School of World Mission. He promised to continue the emphases in *Practical Anthropology* in the new journal *Missiology* (Tippett 1973a). And I, as an anthropologist and the fourth editor of *Missiology*, from 1989 to 2003, also kept the *Practical Anthropology* legacy alive. Kraft published his important article "Dynamic Equivalence Churches" (1973a, 39-57) in the very first issue of *Missiology*. William Smalley captured the best of *Practical Anthropology* in two books entitled *Readings in Missionary Anthropology* (1967) and *Readings in Missionary Anthropology II* (1978).

At the time that *Practical Anthropology* was launched in 1953 the common understanding among most Bible translators and missionaries was that if we could just get the Scriptures into indigenous peoples' languages, then they would come to think like us in the West. And so anthropology was pressed into the service of Bible translation and other aspects of mission. It would not be until the 1970s that we would come to appreciate the importance of contextualization and to realize that people in different cultures should not only not come to think like us once they have the Bible in their own language, but also have the mind of Christ within their own culture. This new insight would usher in the field of ethnotheology (Kraft 1973c) and contextualization (Whiteman 1997).

2

Anthropology, Missions, and Epistemological Shifts

PAUL G. HIEBERT

A nthropologists and missiologists are embedded in human contexts. It should not surprise us, therefore, that they are deeply shaped by the cultures and worldviews in which they live. This is particularly true because both anthropology and Western Protestant mission movements are, to a considerable extent, the children of the Enlightenment and modernity. To understand the history of anthropological and missiological theories, it is helpful to examine not only the interaction between them, but also the fundamental epistemological shifts that have been taking place with the emergence of postmodernity, and now post-postmodernity (Hiebert 1999).

Modernity

With the coming of modernity, science became the dominant form of creating human knowledge. The epistemological foundation was positivism. The focus of this was to discover truth that was universal and timeless by means of empirical observation and the use of Greek abstract algorithmic logic and digital sets. The British anthropologist Radcliffe-Brown wrote,

> The postulate of the inductive method is that all phenomena are subject to natural law, and that consequently it is possible, by the application of certain logical methods, to discover and prove certain general laws, i.e. certain general statements or formulae, of greater or lesser degree of generality, each of which applies to a certain range of facts or events . . . For social anthropology the task is to formulate and validate statements about the conditions of existence of social systems (laws of social statics) and the regularities that are observable in social change (laws of social dynamics). (1958, 7, 128)

Positivism holds that our scientific knowledge is an accurate, true photograph of the world, and corresponds one-to-one with reality. Its theories are not models, but facts. Scientists seek objective truth, and to achieve this they must eliminate feelings and morals from the rational/empirical processes because these introduce subjectivity. Scientific knowledge is seen as universal and timeless. It is true for everyone everywhere.

Positivism dominated anthropological theories until the 1930s. Anthropologists such as E. B. Tylor, James Frazer, and A. R. Radcliffe-Brown saw anthropology as a science and modeled their research after the natural sciences. They believed their theories of social organization were timeless and universal—they applied to all peoples down through history. The beliefs of the people they studied were primitive and need not be taken into account. The people needed to be educated in the truth, namely, modern sciences.

Positivism deeply shaped Western theology. Theological positivism holds that our central concern is truth, and that our theology corresponds one-to-one to Scripture. Other theologies and religions are false and must be attacked. We are concerned with truth and define it in rational terms. We divorce it from feelings and values, because these undermine the objectivity of the truth. Our concern is that people believe the gospel truth, because that determines whether or not they are saved. We define the truth in propositional terms and seek to transmit it unchanged. We see ourselves as God's lawyers and put our trust in experts who have studied Scripture deeply. We see the gospel as acultural and ahistorical. It is unchanging and universal, can be codified in abstract rational terms, and communicated in all languages without loss of meaning. Neither the sociocultural contexts of the listeners nor the messengers need be taken into account.

Underlying this theological search for truth was a belief that human rationality is based on universal laws of thought. True logic, it was thought, is transcultural and ahistorical. Its model is mathematics with precise presuppositions and abstract, algorithmic deductions. In such a logical system the exact nature of the facts and reason are necessary to construct a true theory. A single error in either calls the whole system into question. Knowledge must be accurate in every detail for the whole to be true.

The goal of positivist systematic theologians was to present a single, unified picture of truth that was self-contained, potentially exhaustive, and logically consistent. Biblical history was the data on which they built their theology, but they sought more than a theology that looked for truth in the context of history. They were looking for the unchanging verities that underlie reality.

Positivism deeply shaped the modern mission movement. As positivists we equate the gospel with our Christianity. We had the timeless eternal truth, and it was to be communicated without distortion to other peoples. Moreover, our Christianity gave rise to modern civilization. Charles Taber notes, "The superiority of Western civilization is the culmination of human development, the attribution of that superiority to the prolonged dominance of Christianity, the duty of Christians to share civilization and the gospel with the 'benighted heathen'—these were the chief intellectual currency of their lives" (1991, 71).

It was important, therefore, that new converts learn from us and our ways because we were Christians and this was the way we practice it. They should become Christians and civilized humans. There was little need for contextualization other than to translate the Bible as literally as possible into other languages. Missionaries built schools and hospitals alongside churches, and taught science as an essential part of the curriculum along with the gospel. In many parts of the world Christianity became equated with Western civilization and commerce, and the reshaping of the entire world in the image of "modernity" was a foregone conclusion (see Miller 1973, 99-107).

An example of this view is the Methodist Church in Sri Lanka. In 1841, Spencer Hardy, a Methodist missionary, wrote:

> The national religion of Ceylon is Buddhism, accompanied by the worship of demons and the propitiation of malignant infernal spirits . . . I rest my argument for the necessity of its destruction upon the simple fact that it is opposed to the truth—denies the existence of God—is ignorant of the only way of salvation, by faith in our Lord Jesus Christ—and is utterly impotent as a teacher of morals, or as a messenger of peace to the awakened consciences of its deluded votaries. (1841, 9)

Assessing the results of this view, W. T. J. Small wrote,

> . . . there was no attempt to adapt the form of worship to a national or truly Sinhala form . . . Sinhala renderings of the great Methodist hymns were produced and sung to Western tunes, to the accompaniment of an organ or harmonium; the few lyrics included in the hymn book were hardly used in the services inside the church, and were reserved for open air services. No one dared to play an eastern musical instrument or a drum in a Methodist Church in Ceylon. In short, a visitor from the West entering one of our churches during this period would find nothing to suggest to him in the ritual, music, or appointments that he/she was in an Eastern church. (Small 1971, 367)

K. M. De Silva writes,

> The Christian missions had come to Sri Lanka as the apostles of a new faith and as critics of indigenous society, and in preaching their new ideas the missionaries had been fortified usually by an unquestioning faith not merely in their own rightness but also in the intrinsic depravity of many traditional customs and beliefs. This latter had given the Christian missionary movement its characteristic feature of cultural intolerance . . . Christianity was interpreted on western lines and in non-indigenous concepts. The missionaries imposed on their adherents in Sri Lanka the conventional forms of western Christianity almost in their entirety. (1977, 395)

This view was not restricted to Methodists or to missionaries in Sri Lanka. It was characteristic of most Protestant missions around the world.

Postmodern Deconstruction

The privileged position scientists claimed for their knowledge was challenged by philosophers of science such as Karl Popper, Thomas Kuhn, and Paul Feyerabend. They studied scientists at work and found that they were deeply shaped by their cultures, and that they were part of the pictures they were studying. Scientists were not objective outsiders, but passionate, moralizing insiders for whom knowledge was not only about truth but also about power.

Anthropologists and missionaries were among the first to challenge positivism. As they studied other peoples and their cultures deeply, they began to see the world through the people's eyes, not their own. This shift led to the distinction between etic points of view, those the scientist brings with her, and emic points of view, the way the people see realities. Anthropologists continued to formulate broad general etic theories, but increasingly their focus was on in-depth, emic ethnographies that tried to help us see the world as other people see it.

The tension between etic and emic points of view raised difficult questions. Whose questions, categories, and theories were we to use for comparisons between them? Which of these was "true," and why was it truer than another? Now we were no longer comparing "facts" in different cultures, we were comparing different ways of looking at the facts. It was arrogant to claim that etic theories were superior to the emic understandings of the people. But without comparison between different emic views, there was no way to formulate general theories about humans. All we had left was many different cultural worlds, none of which could judge another. The result was cultural relativism, which came to dominate anthropological theories after the 1930s.

Cultural relativism raised a profound question: Can people from different cultures ever truly understand one another? Modernity assumed that all people lived in the same world. They simply attached different labels to the same realities. Postmodernity argued that people live in totally different conceptual worlds. How then could they communicate or understand one another? One answer was that the bridge between cultures consists in the fact that all humans have the same minds and think in the same ways. This assumes universal rationality common to all people that provides the bridgehead into other cultures. Further research, however, showed not only that people create different categories and do so in different ways, but that they have different logics, none of which is privileged and correct. The positivist assumptions of science itself were challenged, and it, too, lost its privileged position. It became one set of belief systems over against other belief systems such as religions and animism.

To see anthropologists and missionaries as humans deeply involved in the scenes they study, bringing with them the unexamined assumptions and worldviews of their own cultures, led to a new epistemology, namely, instrumentalism. This holds that all people see their worlds through their own cultural eyes, and that they cannot judge other cultures, claiming that their own is truer or better. The only judgments that can be made are based on pragmatics. This culture can produce more food than others, that culture develops stronger families than others. The result is cultural relativism.

The critique of modern positivist anthropology began in the 1930s, but the implications of postmodernity continue to be worked out even today. Some, like Clifford Geertz, argue that anthropology is not a science, but belongs to the humanities. It is dealing not with lifeless objects subject to impersonal laws. It looks at humans who are living beings beyond the range of mechanistic analysis. To understand them we need hermeneutics, not simply observation and testing.

Other anthropologists argue for a radical cultural relativism. Each culture is autonomous and whole, and there are no criteria for judging between them. We can only seek to mutually understand one another across cultural boundaries. They argue that we cannot develop general theories from detached points of view, that we can never really begin to understand another culture, and that, in research, anthropologists can only talk about what happened to them when they lived in other cultures.

Instrumentalism has influenced theology. Postmodern theologians are persuaded that all human knowledge is shaped by cultural and historical contexts. If this is true, then theology, too, is influenced by the culture and historical experiences of the theologians. There can be no totally objective theology. It is our human search for God, it is our God-talk, not God's revelation to us. This means we must speak of theologies, not Theology, for there are as many theologies as there are human points of view. There are African, Indian, and Chinese theologies, feminine and masculine theologies, and theologies of the oppressed, the powerful, and the middle class.

An instrumentalist epistemology changes our view of Christian mission. It has raised the difficult questions of contextualization—the need to embody the gospel in the local cultural forms in ways that the people understand. Can Christianity be done differently from the ways we do it? If so, how differently can Christians in other cultures do it? Is our Christianity normative for all? To what extent have our ways of doing Christianity been shaped by the gospel and to what extent by our culture? How can we avoid having the gospel seen by the people as foreign, and marginal to their lives?

The stress on contextualization calls for communication and Bible translation to be receptor oriented, measured not by what the speaker says, but by what the receptor hears and understands. It calls for radical contextualization in which conversion calls for a minimum of cultural dislocation.

In instrumentalism all religions are seen as autonomous, incommensurable paradigms. Therefore, we have no privileged position from which we can claim Truth; we must affirm differing paradigms as subjectively true. Instrumentalism argues that Christianity is arrogant in its claims to be the only way to God, and some believe that there is saving truth in other religions. The task of mission, therefore, is not to evangelize and seek to win people from other religions to follow Jesus Christ. All religions must be respected as different people's ways of seeking God. Dialogue is the basis of mission. Mission is also ministry to people according to their felt needs. We must begin where people are and let them define the agenda and the solution. Salvation is defined largely as justice and liberation from oppressive systems. Our task is to join in solidarity with those suffering dehumanization by identifying with them in their pain.

Post-Postmodern Anthropology

In recent years, there have been a growing number of critiques of postmodern anthropology. It has served as a corrective to the arrogance and imperialism of early positivist anthropology, which saw reason and empiricism as sufficient to determine truth. But postmodernity offers no answers to the questions humans face in living together in a culturally pluralist world full of oppression, violence, and poverty. Postmodern anthropology is ego centered. The anthropologist cannot tell us anything about the people she studies, only what happened to her while she lived among them. All meta-narratives are imperialistic and oppressive. All we can truly speak of is the many narratives of individuals as seen from their own perspectives. In the end, postmodernity is in danger of becoming voyeurism, a study of the exotic, with little to offer modern humans today other than entertainment.

Modernity fails because it is rooted in the worldview assumption that translation is possible, and propositions are true across languages and cultures. Mark Hobart writes,

> This 'myth of perfect communication' presumes that understanding cannot be partial, even in our own culture ... Behind the myth are several pernicious and related dichotomies. Either one understands people or one doesn't. Either statements are true or they are not. Either native beliefs accord with the universality of logic, perception, classification or what not, or they are culturally specific. Either native utterances are factual [propositional or rational] or they are symbolic. (Hobart and Taylor 1986, 38)

Postmodern anthropology fails because it holds that we can never understand other people at all. We are each locked up in our own subjective world, and there are no objective ways to test whether we see things the same way or not.

Post-postmodern anthropology challenges both modernity and postmodernity by seeking to discern both the nature of human knowledge and its relationship to "reality." It agrees that human knowledge is socially constructed by communities of people, but it argues that these constructs must, to a great extent, correspond to external realities for the people to live. In the hunt, the hunter does not simply imagine a deer. If he does, he will bring home no game. He must discern between his own illusions and reality in order to bring home food for the table. Similarly, a man driving down a city street must know in his mind what is going on if he is to reach home safely. This does not mean that his knowledge is complete—it is always partial. Nor does it mean that his knowledge is not culturally shaped—he may drive by the law, as Americans expect, or by relationships, negotiating his way past trucks, cars, motorcycles, ox carts, and pedestrians of many types: humans, cows, water buffalo, sheep, dogs, and chickens. But it does mean that he must seek to avoid hitting other traffic on the road, and to do so his knowledge in some significant ways must correspond to what is "out there."

Critical Realism

The foundation for the epistemology underlying this view of knowledge is critical realism. This is a much humbler view of human knowledge. It holds that there is a real world outside, and that people from different cultures experience it. They construct mental models or maps of this reality which can be quite different from one another, but each must correspond to outside realities in essential ways if they are to be of any use to humans. Critical realism holds that reason and empiricism are not sufficient to discern the truth, but they are useful guides we can draw upon. It rejects cultural relativism in which ethnographies are seen as elegant fiction, or ingenious and informative mental sketches. It recognizes that as humans we see through a glass darkly, but that we do see.

Critical realism allows us to study and compare cultures without the arrogance and domination of positivist science or the nihilism of instrumentalism. It sees all humans as seeking to make sense of the world around them. They do so by constructing knowledge systems that are attempts to understand a real world outside. The world outside does not fall into neat categories, such as "trees," "bushes," "grass," and so on. Each tree is different from the next, and each category we create overlaps with the others we use to make sense of our world. Critical realism acknowledges the fact that different cultures can construct different mental images of reality, but that these all need, in some way, to correspond to reality or life becomes impossible.

Knowledge, in a critical realist view, is like maps. Maps are selective. There are many kinds of maps: road, railroad, sewer, and electrical power maps. Moreover, maps are simplified schemes that claim to be true on certain things, but not on others. For example, a road map must show the relationship between various streets to be true, but it need not show each curve and bridge for it to be true. In fact, if a map contains too much information, it is useless. Knowledge in critical realism is always focused, partial, and approximate. Human minds cannot grasp the fullness of this universe, let alone the fullness of God.

The fact that maps differ does not mean they are contradictory. Rather, each one describes a certain aspect of reality. Similarly, different cultures (and different academic disciplines) focus on different parts of reality, and ignore what may be seen as central in other cultures. In anthropology it is important, then, to learn to see the world through different eyes, and realize that all have some validity and certain limitations. The development of an etic grid emerging from many emic perspectives can help us not only to translate between cultures, but also to see a much bigger picture of reality.

To use another metaphor, critical realist knowledge is like a montage. We see thousands of faces of people who have been patients of a certain doctor, but they are put together so that we see behind these pictures the face of the doctor who healed them. Or we see the faces of many Christians, and taken together we see the face of Christ.

Critical realism takes a humble view of human knowledge and does not grant a privileged position to science or any other belief system. This is not to say that all systems are equally effective in answering specific questions. None can claim sole authority to judge the others. Each can bear witness to what it claims to have found, and judgment between them is ultimately a matter of faith, not proof. Rather, it recognizes "the fact that even the truest description comes nowhere near faithfully reproducing the way the world is . . . [no true description] tells us the way the world is, but each of them tells a way the world is" (Goodman 1972, 29, 31). Critical realism also brings thoughts, feelings, and morals together. All three are present in all belief systems. Bracketing out feelings and morals does not lead to objective knowledge.

Critical realism is based on community hermeneutics. No one specialist sees and knows the whole picture. It is through dialogue that we see reality from different perspectives. Burke writes, "It is by the approach through a variety of perspectives that we establish a character's reality . . . [W]e could say that characters possess degrees of being in proportion to the variety of perspectives from which they can with justice be perceived" (Burke 1969, 504).

Cross-cultural understandings begin with recognizing that there are different ways of representing reality, and that a dialectical process is needed for each party to understand the other, and to compare the two. We begin by using all kinds of information to try to grasp what our informants tell us about what we see. Our first impressions are often wrong, but as we interact with the people, our previous assumptions are modified, and our knowledge and understanding comes closer to theirs. This dialectic between our informants and our own representations goes both ways. As we study them, they are studying us, and as we increasingly learn to think as they do, they begin to understand us. We need to keep in mind that in all communication, even within a culture, there will be widespread miscommunication, but there is also a possibility of basic communication. Our mutual understandings are never complete or perfect, but they do enable us to communicate, to learn from one another, and to understand one another more fully.

We must also remember that in an increasingly globalized world, people from many cultures interact with one another, and that knowledge from one to another is spread, reinterpreted, misunderstood, and corrected. No culture is an island unto itself. It has links to the world that are bridgeheads for the development of mutual understandings.

How does theology look in a critical realist mode? Evangelical critical realists would differentiate between theology and Scripture, and ascribe final and full authority to the latter as the inspired, divinely superintended record of God acting and entering in human history. The Bible is divine revelation, the source and criterion against which we measure theological truth. Theology, on the other hand, is our best human understandings of Scripture. It is our personal and corporate confession of what we believe. To say that it is a confession is not to reflect doubt, but to affirm our strong conviction not only to understand but also to live by these truths.

As Evangelical critical realists we would recognize that our theologies, though rooted in Scripture, are also influenced by our human contexts, both cultural and historical. We may "see through a glass darkly" because of the limits of our human knowledge, but we do see. We are not simply looking in a mirror. To recognize that our understanding of Scripture is always shaped by our contexts, we need to study both Scripture and our context to see how our contexts shape our interpretation of divine revelation.

The contextual nature of theology raises a difficult question. Committed Christians in different historical and cultural contexts develop theologies that differ in the categories they construct, the questions they ask, the assumptions they make, and the logics they use. We must therefore speak first of theologies, for each theology is a human understanding of divine revelation in a particular historical and cultural context. This does not deny theological truth as God knows it. Rather, it recognizes that all human theologies are partial and culturally biased, and that the truth in the Scripture is greater than our understanding of it. There is room, therefore, for spiritual maturation and growth in our theologies, but this means we must constantly test our theologies against Scripture and the theologies of our brothers and sisters in Christ acting as a hermeneutical community. Divine revelation and historical realities do not change, but our understanding of them does.

Implications

What are the implications for mission of a critical realist perspective? The first set of implications has to do with our understanding of evangelism and discipleship. Positivists claim to know objective truth, and see evangelism as proclaiming theological verities. They often attack other religions to discredit them with the hope that their followers will turn to Christ. But this rarely works. Attacks and arguments often drive people away from the gospel as they seek to defend their beliefs. Non-Christians see this polemical stance as arrogant and accuse such missionaries of being more interested in proving correct doctrines than in listening to them as humans.

Critical realists hold to objective truth, but recognize that it is understood by humans in their contexts. There is, therefore, an element of faith and personal commitment in the knowledge of truth. This subjective appropriation of objective truth offers a second set of implications for Christian mission. First, critical realists have deep convictions about the truth and bear testimony to them. Mission to non-Christians begins with witness, in affirming "I believe . . ." E. Stanley Jones wrote,

> When I was called to the ministry, I had a vague notion that I was to be God's lawyer— I was to argue his case for him and put it up brilliantly . . . In my ministry [I learned] I was to be, not God's lawyer, but his witness. That

would mean that there would have to be living communication with Christ so that there would always be something to pass on. (1925, 141-142)

Second, conversion in this view is not simply mental acceptance of a set of theological truths. It is a change in a person's central allegiance and a personal commitment to follow Christ in life and in death. It is both a point and a process. Justification and sanctification are inseparable elements of the same transformation.

This view recognizes both felt and real needs, and seeks to minister to the whole person. We may start with felt needs, but we must move to the ultimate human needs of salvation, and reconciliation both here and in eternity.

Third, a critical realist stance has implications for how we view contextualization. The response of positivist missionaries has often been one of radical displacement. To become Christians people had to become modern. In reaction, anticolonial advocates, mostly instrumentalists, called for radical contextualization, assuming that all cultures are good and that all forms of Christianity are syncretistic to some degree. Critical realists see cultures not as morally neutral, but as mixtures of personal and corporate good and evil. They call for critical contextualization, an ongoing response of the church that sees that the gospel as divine revelation is outside culture and cannot be equated with any particular culture. It recognizes that for this revelation to be made known to humans it must be put into cultural forms that the people understand. It sees the gospel not as information to be believed, but as a transforming power that changes individuals, communities, and cultures to Christlikeness and in conformity with the Kingdom of God. This process requires a deep study of human cultures (phenomenology), a thorough study of Scripture (hermeneutics), a thoroughgoing interaction with God's creation (theology), an evaluation of human situations in the light of revelation and reality checks (ontology), and a process to transform persons and cultures in the light of ontological truth (missiology).

In our post-postmodern world, it is important as Christians and missionaries that we examine our own cultural assumptions in the light of biblical teachings. This is especially true of our epistemological and semiotic assumptions, for these are foundational to the way we think about Christianity and do missions. This new era also affords us tremendous possibilities in Christian missions. We no longer have to be God's lawyers, proving to people the truth of the gospel. We can be bold witnesses to what we have experienced and know. The gospel we bring is not abstract propositional truth; it is a living relationship with Jesus the Christ that involves our whole being: cognitive, affective, and moral. We no longer come with a sense of arrogance and superiority, as those who have found the whole truth. We invite people to follow Christ and the church and to let him transform their cultures.

3

Anthropology and Missiology

Reflections on the Relationship

ROBERT J. PRIEST

This chapter provides a brief historical overview of the relationship of anthropology and missiology, identifies current tensions and issues in that relationship, and suggests needed correctives to current weaknesses.[1]

Historical Overview

Missionaries were among the earliest Europeans to have long-term close relationships with non-Europeans. Well before anthropologists were doing fieldwork, there were missionaries writing rich ethnographic reports. Notable examples include Bernardino de Sahagun (1499-1590), Robert H. Codrington (1830-1922), and Henri A. Junod (1863-1934).

While there have been outstanding European Christian anthropologists, the links with missiology have been fewer than in North America. Father Wilhelm Schmidt (1868-1954) was an influential anthropologist in his day, founding, in 1906, the respected anthropology journal *Anthropos*. But while Schmidt was a member of a Catholic missionary order, the Society of the Divine Word (SVD), and indeed the journal is still owned by the SVD, Schmidt had no interest in using anthropology to develop missiology. He conceptualized his calling and that of the journal (including its many missionary contributors) as "scientific," rather than practical or applied. His anthropology did have a clear apologetic purpose, however. It was oriented toward the European secular setting, rather than to field contexts in which anthropological data were collected. In the European setting he was influential in using ethnography to critique evolutionary paradigms of religion that assumed that monotheistic ideas were only late evolutionary developments.

[1] I want to thank Dean Arnold, Alex Bolyanatz, Douglas Hayward, Tom Headland, Brian Howell, Jon Kirby, Rick Malloy, Douglas Pennoyer, Kersten Bayt Priest, Enoch Wan, and Edwin Zehner for valuable assistance and/or feedback provided in the preparation of this chapter.

On the Protestant side, one thinks of Maurice Leenhardt (1878-1954), a missionary in New Caledonia who was quite willing to use anthropology for missiological ends. But his own missionary society refused to let him teach in their missionary training school. So he replaced Marcel Mauss at the *Ecole Practique des Hautes Etudes*, eventually upon retirement relinquishing his anthropology chair to Claude Levi-Strauss (Clifford 1992). Leenhardt's major contributions were to secular anthropology, not missiology. That is, even where Christian anthropologists wished to work missiologically, European theological institutions and missionary training institutions appear to have had little place for them.

While one can think of individual European anthropologists who are missiological (such as Lothar Kaiser from Germany or David Burnett from England), mission studies in Europe have been incorporated into theological education under structures that allow space for history (one thinks of Stephen O'Neill and Andrew Walls as exemplars) or theology (along the lines of J. H. Bavinck and David Bosch, for example) but not for anthropology. While some European Christian anthropologists focus theologically and/or pastorally (Douglas Davies, Timothy Jenkins), there has not been the same presence of missiological anthropologists in European missiology that there has been in American missiology.

The Kennedy School of Missions. At the Edinburgh 1910 world missionary conference, the problem of missionary preparation was raised. With the help of a major donor, the Kennedy School of Missions at Hartford Seminary was founded. This school focused its work on comparative religion, linguistics, and anthropology. Notable linguists (William Welmers, William J. Samarin, Al Gleason), sociologists (Peter Berger), and anthropologists (Absolom Vilikazi, Paul Leser, Morris Steggerda, Edwin Smith) taught there. These were recognized and active scholars in their disciplines. Edwin Smith, for example, had served as president of the Royal Anthropological Institute of Great Britain and would later give leadership to the Rockefeller Foundation's initiatives in Africa. Dozens of missiologists received Ph.D.'s in missiology, linguistics, or anthropology from there, including such notables as George Peters, Dean Gilliland, Charles Taber, and Charles Kraft. This largely mainline Protestant school closed its doors in the 1960s with the marked retrenchment in commitment to missions by mainline Protestants.

The Summer Institute of Linguistics (SIL) (1934-). With Cameron Townsend's vision for the "Bibleless tribes," the Summer Institute of Linguistics was formed, a program that stressed the value of linguistic scholarship. Kenneth Pike (1912-2000) and Eugene Nida (1914-) were two of the first SIL members to pursue Ph.D.'s in linguistics. Led by outstanding scholars like Pike and Nida, SIL schools of linguistics were founded at various universities around the world. In the largest of these at Norman, Oklahoma, between 1941 and 1987 nearly ten thousand Christian students received training in linguistics and, to a lesser extent, anthropology. Many Christian anthropologists not with SIL also went through the SIL training: Louis Luzbetak, Myron Bromley, Robert Canfield, and Charles Kraft, to name a few. Hundreds of SIL members eventually earned Ph.D.'s in linguistics, and more than two dozen earned Ph.D.'s in anthropology or linguistic anthropology, for example, Elinor Abbot, Jon Arenson, David Beine, Alex Bolyanatz, Hank Bradley, David Coombs, Karl Franklin, Barbara Dix Grimes, Tom Headland, Marvin Mayers, Rob McKee, Carol McKinney, William Merrifield, Barbara Moore, Armin Peter, Daniel Shaw, and James Yost. Since SIL actively cultivated its image as a scientific and service organization rather than a missionary organization, SIL scholars have not tended to frame SIL commitments in missiological terms. SIL members were not encouraged to do advanced work in seminary settings, and those SIL members who became anthropologists were ambivalent about framing their own intellectual commitments as missiological. So the influence of SIL on missiological anthropology has been more indirect than direct. And with many notable SIL anthropologists now retired, and with the average age of active-status SIL anthropologists today at sixty-one, the future influence of SIL on Christian anthropology is uncertain.

Society of the Divine Word (SVD). Under the influence of Father Wilhelm Schmidt, SVD missionaries were encouraged to study anthropology, although not with missiological ends in view. This changed, in part, under the influence of Louis Luzbetak (1918-2005). With the Second World War, Schmidt felt that America was a more stable base for carrying on his work. So he recruited Luzbetak, an American studying theology in Rome, to study anthropology under him and be his successor. Luzbetak's own field studies led him to recognize that field missionaries were not applying anthropological understandings missiologically. After Schmidt died, Luzbetak shifted his work to an explicitly missiological direction, writing an influential text in missiological anthropology that was first published in 1963, reprinted in 1970, and completely revised in 1988. However, despite respect given to Luzbetak, the SVD has not provided a strong base for missiological anthropology. With the departure of a significant proportion of its younger anthropologists in the post-Vatican II fallout of the late 1960's (such as Johannes Fabian and Ernest Brandewie), the actual number of anthropologists in the SVD declined. And the historic emphasis of the Anthropos Institute on "scientific" rather than "applied" anthropology has remained influential. For the most part, then, remaining SVD anthropologists do not orient their work missiologically. One exception to this would be Jon Kirby, a field missionary in Ghana with a Ph.D. in anthropology from Cambridge who founded and directs the Tamale Institute of Cross Cultural Studies. In short, while there are many Catholic missiologists with anthropological training, there are relatively few Catholic missiologists with Ph.D.'s in anthropology. Notable exceptions would include Anthony Gittins (CSSp) and, as mentioned, Jon Kirby (SVD).

Christian colleges and universities. Wheaton College, a leading Evangelical college, began an anthropology major under the leadership of Dr. Alexander Grigolia, who arrived at Wheaton in 1936. The first three anthropology majors graduated in 1939. With a student body interested in missionary service, and anthropology presented as ideal for missionaries, Wheaton's anthropology major was popular. By 1953, the year Charles Kraft graduated, Wheaton had already graduated two hundred anthropology majors (Whiteman 2003b, 78-89), including Billy Graham. Many Wheaton graduates later went on to earn Ph.D.'s in anthropology, such as Miriam Adeney, Dean Arnold, Hank Bradley, James Buswell III, David Coombs, Terry Hoops, William Kornfield, Charles Kraft, Sherwood Lingenfelter, Marvin Mayers, Penny McGee, Barbara Moore, William Merrifield, Laura Montgomery, and Claude Stipe. In 1953, at Wheaton, Robert Taylor, an anthropology professor, founded the journal *Practical Anthropology*, to which Charles Kraft would later contribute. Over the years many anthropologists have taught at Wheaton, some who wanted anthropology to serve missiology, and others who have felt that the connection compromises the scientific and scholarly side of anthropology. Because missiology is taught in Wheaton Graduate School and anthropology is taught in the college, the links between the two have not been close. The master's degree in intercultural studies does not require or offer a single course in anthropology. For a while (1980-1998) the anthropology major was eliminated altogether from Wheaton College's curriculum. Currently the anthropology program has two faculty members (Brian Howell and Dean Arnold) and forty majors. Bethel University (St. Paul) is another school which has had many anthropology faculty of note (William Smalley, Donald Larsen, Claude Stipe, Thomas Correll, James Hurd, Harley Schreck, and Jenell Williams Paris), with many of their graduates going on to earn Ph.D.'s in anthropology—perhaps the most notable being Thomas Headland. In short, a significant proportion of all Evangelical Christian anthropologists got their start at either Wheaton or Bethel. Today four Evangelical colleges of the 102 CCCU member schools offer majors in anthropology: Wheaton College, Vanguard University (with three anthropology faculty Vince Gil, Craig Rusch, James Huff), Lee University (with three anthropology faculty Murl Dirksen, Richard Jones, Alan Wheeler) and Biola University. The strongest of these is now Biola University. In the mid-1980s Biola recruited top anthropology faculty (Marvin Mayers and Sherwood Lingenfelter), began an anthropology undergraduate major, and developed master's and doctoral degree programs in intercultural studies and missiology with a strong anthropology base. Biola currently (fall of 2007) has 6 anthropology faculty (Douglas Pennoyer, Douglas Hayward, Sue Russell, Katrina Greene, Paul Langenwalter, and Kevin Pittle), 63 undergraduate majors in anthropology, and 214 intercultural studies majors with a strong anthropology emphasis. With its opening of a master's degree in anthropology in fall 2007, Biola may well be central to the future of Evangelical presence in the discipline.

Eugene Nida and the Bible Societies. Shortly after finishing his Ph.D., Nida began working for the American Bible Society. Over the years he consulted with hundreds of translators around the world, and wrote extensively both about linguistics and anthropology. His 1954 book *Customs and Cultures* was enormously influential in introducing missionaries to the practical value of anthropology (1954). Nida helped build a team of linguist-anthropologists (William Wonderly, William Smalley, William Reyburn, Marie Fetzer Reyburn, Jacob Loewen, Charles Taber, and Charles Kraft) who communicated closely with each other, read each other's works, and formed an "invisible college" of missiological anthropologists. The journal *Practical Anthropology* (1953-1972) needed a home, and with funding from the American Bible Society, Nida and his colleagues supported it and filled its pages with practically oriented anthropological insights for field missionaries. This journal introduced and inspired many missionaries as to the value of anthropology. But in 1973 when the American Bible Society stopped supporting *Practical Anthropology*, despite a circulation of three thousand (Whiteman 2003b, 78-89), it was turned over to the American Society of Missiology, a society made up of historians, theologians, comparative religionists, and educators, as well as anthropologists. So the name was changed to *Missiology*, and the journal shifted its focus, with anthropology no longer playing the central role.

The Network of Christian Anthropologists. Christian anthropologists gathered at Wheaton in 1976 (August 23) and voted on a steering committee "to initiate the organization of a community of scholars for the purpose of studying data of common concern to anthropologists and missionaries." Although a mailing list of Christian anthropologists was begun and occasional gatherings were held, it was not until 1987 under the leadership of Darrell Whiteman that the Network of Christian Anthropologists was officially formed. This network meets annually at the American Anthropological Association (AAA) with typically thirty to fifty in attendance. It primarily serves to connect and encourage its members. Often members of the Network plan session proposals for the following year's AAA meetings. With a listserve hosted by Bethel University, Network members carry on conversations together. While many anthropologists in attendance each year are themselves missionaries or teach in missiology programs, the network has not formally focused on missiology. It has contributed to missiology rather indirectly by encouraging, strengthening, and networking Christian anthropologists.

Ph.D. programs in missiology/intercultural studies. Just as the Kennedy School of Missions was closing down, Donald McGavran founded the School of World Mission at Fuller Theological Seminary (1965). He immediately invited missionary anthropologist Alan Tippett (1911-1988) to join the faculty. Other anthropologists that joined the faculty over the years include Charles Kraft, Paul Hiebert, Daniel Shaw, and Sherwood Lingenfelter. For a time, Fuller replaced the Kennedy School of Missions as the single place for doctoral studies in missiology and missiological anthropology. But soon Trinity Evangelical Divinity School (TEDS) and Asbury Theological Seminary joined Fuller as schools offering Ph.D.'s in missiology and/or intercultural studies with anthropologists on their faculties (Paul Hiebert and Robert Priest at TEDS; Darrell Whiteman, Michael Rynkiewich, and Stephen Ybarrola at Asbury).

Denominational impulses. The Roman Catholic Church has produced a number of anthropologists, including Jesuits like Raymond Bucko, Luis Calero, Richard Malloy, and Michael Steltenkamp, or members of the SVD like Jon Kirby, Louis Luzbetak, or Sjaak Van Der Geest, and anthropologists from other traditions like Gerald Arbuckle (a Marist) and Anthony Gittins (a Spiritan). A number of other denominational traditions stand out as having produced anthropologists. From the Methodists came anthropologists like Edwin Smith, Alan Tippett, Vincent Sutlive, Darrell Whiteman, Phil Thornton, Michael Rynkiewich, and Harold Recinos. The Mennonites have generated their share of anthropologists: Robert Ramseyer, Jacob Loewen, Paul Hiebert, Don Jacobs, Elmer Miller, Eloise Meneses, and Ron Stutzman. And from the Christian and Missionary Alliance (C&MA) have emerged numerous anthropologists: Gordon Hedderly Smith, William A. Smalley, Linwood Barney, Myron Bromley, Norman Allison, Enoch Wan, Gordon Larsen, Wade Seaford, John Ellenberger, and Edwin Zehner. The Reformed tradition, with exceptions (Ralph Winter, David Scotchmer, and Vern Sterk), has not been strong in anthropology. Thus, when Reformed Theological Seminary in Jackson, Mississippi, wanted to find an anthropologist to help start a Ph.D. program in missiology, it went outside the Reformed tradition and invited Enoch Wan (of the C&MA) to lead its program. In spite of their enormous size the Southern Baptists have not produced missiological anthropologists, and even their doctoral programs in missiology lack anthropologists.

Summary Observations about American Missiological Anthropology

American missiology (unlike mission studies in Europe) has made anthropology central to missiology. The largest Ph.D. programs in Evangelical missiology (Asbury, Fuller, and Trinity) all have anthropologists among their faculty. And across America in Bible colleges, Christian liberal arts colleges, seminaries, and other mission training institutions, anthropology courses are usually key features of the missiology curriculum.

The actual number of professors with Ph.D.'s in anthropology who are teaching in missiology is relatively small. This means that the majority of anthropological and/or culture-related courses taught in these missiology programs are taught by missiologists who have had, at most, a few courses in anthropology but who are not themselves anthropologists.

In recent decades missiological anthropologists have contributed introductory orientations to intercultural relationships (Lingenfelter, Mayers), introductory texts in anthropology for missionaries (Luzbetak, Hiebert, Kraft), and important writings on missiological theory (one thinks here of anthropologists like Charles Kraft and Paul Hiebert).

But missiological anthropologists have been weaker in actually carrying out ethnographic research in mission settings and writing up the reports and analyses in a way that would pass muster within their discipline as a contribution to anthropological knowledge. The contrast with history is fruitful here. Historians in mission studies publish historical research about missions in ways that both inform missiology and contribute to their discipline. Their research is often published in the scholarly venues used by other members of their discipline. An example of this would be the work of Dana Robert in Boston. With exceptions, missiological anthropologists have not created a high-quality research-based literature about missionaries and mission churches. Secular anthropologists are now starting to do this (Joel Robbins, Robert Hefner, John Barker, Danilyn Rutherford, Simon Coleman, and Webb Keane), making the anthropology of Christian groups an emerging research specialty.

The discipline of anthropology has posed challenges for Christians wishing to join the guild. The very subject matter poses enormous challenges for individual Christians to work through, including issues like human origins, religious diversity, and moral variability/relativism. The discipline itself, with its reward structures and mechanisms of social control, has not been hospitable to Christian presence (Arnold 2006, 266-282; Priest 2001, 29-68), especially when such Christians exhibit any sympathetic interest in missionaries and the missionary agenda.

This has meant that Christians have been underrepresented in the discipline. While sociology has numerous leading sociologists of religion, self-identified Christians, who teach at major Ph.D.-granting programs in sociology (Christian Smith, James Davidson Hunter, Robert Wuthnow, Robert Bellah, Peter Berger, Nancy Ammerman, and Michael Emerson), nothing comparable exists in anthropology. I am aware of only one self-identified Christian (Robert Canfield) currently teaching full-time in any Ph.D. program in anthropology. He is seventy-five years old and no longer supervising dissertations. While there are scores of Christians with Ph.D.'s in anthropology, they are not structurally central to their discipline. While the research of Christian sociologists has been backed by major funding sources (often to the tune of millions of dollars), no comparable funding sources support the anthropological study of missions and Christianity around the globe. And while the sheer numbers of Christian psychologists has allowed for whole journals devoted to the Christian intellectual engagement with psychology, the small numbers of Christian anthropologists have hampered any comparable developments in their discipline. While missiological historians have a high-quality journal devoted to their historical work (*The International Bulletin of Missionary Research*), the one journal which missiological anthropologists did have (*Practical Anthropology*) shifted away from anthropology as the disciplinary center when it changed its title to *Missiology* and its institutional home to the American Society of Missiology.

Christians in anthropology have also often faced challenges from Christian communities and institutions of which they are a part. Even anthropologists in the Society of the Divine Word (SVD), a missionary order which owns and runs the journal *Anthropos*, have sometimes perceived deep ambivalence towards anthropology on the part of colleagues and/or superiors. After the "Battle for the Bible" of the 1970s, North American Evangelicals worried about the danger represented by the social sciences and especially anthropology. Thus when Charles Kraft's groundbreaking book *Christianity in Culture* (1979) came out, responses by leading Evangelicals like Carl F. H. Henry (1980, 153-164) and Robertson McQuilkin (1980, 113-124) stressed the dangers and called for boundaries (see also Gross 1985) rather than sustaining substantive conversation and engagement with the issues. In theological studies, it is once again conservatives like the radical Orthodox theologian John Milbank (1990) who pit theological understandings against knowledge that emerges through social science research. While

I agree that many of the questions raised by Henry, McQuilkin, and Milbank are good ones, they have framed them in overly oppositional terms. That is, they construct the very presence of Christian anthropologists in Christian institutions as a sort of danger. In Evangelical theological education, conservatives have honed linguistic and philosophical skills, but have avoided acquiring in-depth understandings of anthropology. That is, even those anthropologists teaching advanced Ph.D. missiology students are generally teaching individuals with prior theological education of a sort that is weak in social science, if not actively hostile to it. Most of our students do not come with adequate grounding in social theory, or with training in social science methodologies.

Within the Evangelical missions community Christian anthropologists have been more appreciated, perhaps simply because field missionaries intuitively recognize their need for help in understanding cultural realities. But even here, the pressure on anthropologists has been to produce narrowly instrumental writings in the service of missions, with impatience over any requirement of more sustained and in-depth anthropological research. Neat typologies or broad generalizations about such things as worldview are preferred to the kind of anthropological research and writing normally practiced and valued within the discipline. Anthropology is almost universally present as a key component of North American missiology and mission studies. But it is present without much depth. As noted, most of those who teach these courses are not themselves anthropologists. And even in top Ph.D. programs in missiology, the actual amount of anthropology any individual acquires is a fraction of what they would get in a master's degree program in anthropology. With mission trends away from career service and toward short-term missions there is a growing impatience with any expectation of in-depth anthropological insight.

Missiology itself has not provided strong institutional underpinnings for the kind of in-depth research needed. There are few funding sources specifically designed to support missiological research. Academic professional associations in other disciplines are designed to encourage optimum participation in scholarly presentations by the largest numbers possible, with brief papers (fifteen minutes), many parallel sessions, a mix of Ph.D. students, and senior scholars reporting on current research. Missiological associations, by contrast, feature long presentations often presented in a single room without parallel sessions to choose from, offered by a few senior missiologists who are there by invitation only. Presentations feature magisterial addresses rather than research-based reports from those on the cutting edge of missiological investigation. Professional missiological associations currently do a poor job of socializing the next generation of missiological researchers (i.e., they fail to model the centrality of research to missiology) and a poor job of providing access into the guild by means of formal opportunities to present one's research results to a scholarly audience.

In summary, missiological anthropology is central to American missiology, but marginal both to anthropological scholarship and to broader North American (and European) theological conversations. While appreciated within mission studies, anthropology is most appreciated when it is mostly instrumental and abbreviated. Institutional support structures in missiology for high-quality ethnographic missiologically oriented research are weak.

Recommendations for Strengthening Missiological Anthropology

1. Missiological anthropology would benefit if there were more Christians in anthropology involved in scholarship on all anthropological topics: Christians who are active and academically productive scholars in the discipline, are present at professional meetings, publish in top journals of the field, and play central roles in major doctoral-granting institutions of anthropology.

2. Missiological anthropology would benefit if there were a significant number of Christian anthropologists focusing their research and writing in the area of anthropology of religion, and the anthropology of Christianities. We need Christians who are recognized within the discipline as leading scholars in the anthropology of religion and of Christianity.

3. Those anthropologists who teach in missiology programs must be active scholars in their discipline, continuing their own active programs of ongoing anthropological research, publishing part of their work through peer-reviewed channels within their discipline.

4. Missiological anthropologists must also continue to cultivate knowledge that is oriented toward applied mission settings, and need to continue to write for nonanthropological audiences. For example, short-term missions is an enormous phenomenon. Anthropologists must move to the cutting edge of research scholarship on short-term missions, must publish on the topic in standard anthropology forums, but must also write in ways that are understandable and helpful to the tens of thousands of youth pastors whose current job descriptions require them to lead annual short-term mission trips.

5. Missiological anthropology will be strengthened if Christian colleges and universities have a stronger social science emphasis (both theory and method), and if theological institutions (especially theologically conservative ones) develop more sustained appreciation for the social sciences and the value of empirically based research related to human ministry settings. That is, when social science is more central to the curriculum of Christian education, and when theological leaders recognize not only the challenges of social science, but the positive possibilities, then the social contexts in which missiological anthropology is taught will prove to be more constructive settings in which high-quality work can be done. And when an undergraduate major in anthropology becomes the routine building block for later advanced work in missiology, missiology will be more solidly anthropological.

6. Missiological anthropologists need to engage topics, in both research and writing, that are central to North American theological conversations. One thinks of the "worship wars," of debates on gender in the church and in Bible translations, and of discussions on the "emerging church movement." Many of these topics are ones that missiological anthropologists, if they took the time to re-

search them, would be ideally positioned to engage constructively. We must cultivate the ability to speak to broad audiences of Christians, bringing missiological and anthropological insight to bear on core concerns of everyday life and ministry. If we do this well, we will move out of the intellectual ghettos in which many of us live, writing only for relatively small audiences of missiologists and career missionaries.

7. Finally, missiology must become a discipline in which those who receive Ph.D.'s in missiology become contributors to high-quality missiological anthropology. This means their foundations in social theory and in method must be improved. Ethnographic research of the length and caliber normally practiced by anthropologists must become normal for missiologists. Missiology needs to become a field that values research-based ethnographically rich writings and validates those who contribute to missiological knowledge through such research. Missiologists need to nurture the institutional support structures (curriculum, research funding, patterns of professional scholarly involvement, and publishing initiatives, to name a few) that are essential elements in strengthening anthropological research in service of mission.

4

A New Heaven and a New Earth?

The Future of Missiological Anthropology

MICHAEL A. RYNKIEWICH

Introduction[1]

A long time ago, in an article about dynamic equivalent churches, Charles Kraft made the claim that "integral to sound theology is sound anthropology" (1973a, 39-57). It follows, then, that sound missiology depends, among other things, on a sound anthropology. The truth of this assertion was demonstrated during the rise of practical anthropology in the 1950s (Nida and Pike), the development of missiology in the 1960s and 1970s (Kraft, Loewen, Taber, Wonderly, Tippett, Hiebert, and many others), and the establishment of schools of mission grounded in biblical studies and anthropology (Fuller, Asbury, Trinity, Biola, Columbia, and others). The trialogue between anthropology, theology, and missiology has been very productive indeed (Conn 1984).

David Bosch made the claim that "the entire missionary enterprise is, to a very real extent, a child of the enlightenment" (1991, 274; see also Taber 2000), though this is contested by Stanley (2001, 1-21) and others (Pachuau 2004, 19-38). A missiology based on an anthropology whose origins itself are in the Enlightenment (Conn 1984) and whose early growth was firmly set in a Western colonialist context (Said 1979) cannot help but be modern. But that is no compliment.

The genealogy of modernist anthropology seemed well established in the first half of the 1900s. However, Bruce Knauft argues that during the 1950s, in a quest for legitimacy in modernist terms, anthropology began to rewrite its genealogy to replace Tylor, Boas, and Frazier with Durkheim, Weber, and Marx.

At least indirectly, moreover, each figure could be seen in retrospect to have left a key intellectual legacy to early anthropologists: Marx to Morgan and White in the study of material life, Durkheim to Radcliffe-Brown and Levi-Strauss in the study of social and mental structure, and Weber to Geertz in the study of cultural and subjective orientations. This telescoping of theoretical ancestry was significant for a discipline that had been developing for

[1]I thank Steve Ybarrola for his critique of an earlier draft of this chapter.

the better part of a century and was simplifying and repositioning its stories for a new period of unprecedented academic and pedagogical growth. (Knauft 1996, 31-32)

Following Foucault, Knauft argues that this was a "superficial invention—the production of terms and ideas that were accepted (or discarded) not because they were in any meaningful sense true, but because they were consistent with the overarching structure of Western knowledge as a kind of epistemic power" (Knauft 1996, 32). So, the anthropology to which modern missiology has looked for insights is rooted in modernity, and thus believes that the thinking self can know the mechanistic universe, that knowledge can be certain, that data collecting can be objective, and that more knowledge is a good thing because it will lead to mastery of the universe and progress for humankind. This progress is inevitable as long as rationality overcomes tradition and superstition, including religion. Honest doubt (skepticism) that produces facts is valued, while seemingly blind faith that produces values is deconstructed and left for dead (Newbigin 1989, 20-21; see also Sampson, Samuel, and Sugden, 1994; particularly Storkey 1994, 136-150).

Lately, Wilbert Shenk has asked: "How can the missionary maintain independence of the sociopolitical ideology of the West?" (1996, 31-45). A part of the hegemony of the West is the embeddedness of social science beliefs and practices that go unquestioned within ancillary disciplines. That is, while anthropology has deconstructed and reconstructed itself in ways that lead to a new understanding of the world as it seems to be, missiology remains attached to the modernist version of anthropology (see Hiebert this volume). While some are beginning to question these assumptions (Hiebert 1999; see also Hesselgrave 2005), for most practitioners, missiology is still stuck in the 1960s.

Without defending the brief critique that I have offered concerning the lag in the relationship between missiology and anthropology, let us instead look at places where missiologists could learn from theoretical developments in anthropology.

Culture

Missiologists are so accustomed to quoting Tylor's definition of culture that I intentionally resist doing so. Instead of listing attributes, the concept of culture established by Franz Boas and his students described a shared way of looking at the world that enhanced survival through the production of practices and artifacts. Boas also made it his life's work to disconnect race, language, and culture; that is, to demonstrate that neither culture nor intelligence was integrally connected to physical characteristics (Boas 1940).

Alfred Kroeber established culture as a concept that represented a reality that had hitherto not been recognized, at least in its diversity and unseen power to shape people's lives (Kroeber 1917, 163-213). Edward Sapir, along with Benjamin Whorf, suggested that people who live in different cultures and speak different languages actually live in different worlds, not the same world with different names.[2]

Ruth Benedict (1934) and Margaret Mead (1928, 1935) explored the patterns of culture that give meaning to the parts, and asked how children learn the cultures of their parents. Bronislaw Malinowski (1922, 1944) and A. R. Radcliff-Brown (1965) insisted that the parts of culture, or institutions of a society, each played a role in the survival of the people. And the list goes on: Robert Lowie, Melville Herskovits, E. Adamson Hoebel, Ralph Linton, all worked to establish anthropology as a discipline with a distinctive emphasis on cross-cultural study, participant observation, cultural relativity, ethnography, and ethnology.

By the 1960s, American cultural anthropology had come together with British social anthropology (E. E. Evans-Pritchard, Edmund Leach, and Max Gluckman) and French structuralism (Claude Levi-Strauss) into a fairly coherent discipline. The segue into cognitive anthropology and symbolic anthropology, as well as a concern for applied anthropology and ethics, characterized the 1960s and 1970s.

This model of anthropology was largely a culturally determinist model where culture and/or worldview so shaped human perception that resulting behavior was inevitable. There were a few dissenting voices arguing for *culture against man* (Henry 1963), but, for the most part, modernist anthropology imagined people as *victims of progress* (Bodley 1975) or as people hopelessly stuck in a *culture of poverty* (Lewis 1966, 19-25).

The modernist model is that culture and/or worldview is given by tradition, passed on through enculturation, and reinforced by various sanctions and taboos. This model gave rise to an imagined missiological situation where one person, with one culture and one language, sat across the fire from another person who had one culture and one language, and where the missiological task was to communicate a message as one sends a letter from here to be opened there. A culture, then, is presented as a bounded, well-integrated, adaptive but slow-changing whole, that is, a self-generating and self-validating entity.

Neither culture nor the missiological situation is like this anymore, and it seems questionable that it ever was. That bedrock concept of "functionalist integration" has been called an "organicist fiction" (Strathern 1988, 6-7; see also Lingenfelter 1996, 225). The notion that culture exists somewhere (in people's heads? in the public arena?) and is self-replicating has been called "naive essentialism" (Foster 1995, 6). Postmodern anthropology will not accept the reification of the concept of culture.

Part of that reification has been the "black box" problem: What is the inner cause of outer behavior? For some, culture is what is in the black box. Others want to make culture only what is observable (e.g., for Geertz, culture is public symbols [1973, 6, 12]), while claiming not to know what is in the black box. Others posit worldview as the cause behind culture. This approach has gone far-

---

[2]"Language and our thought-grooves are inextricably interwoven, are, in a sense, one and the same" (Sapir 1921, 232). See also Whorf (1956, 135-136).

ther in missiology than it has in anthropology, and perhaps we have pushed it to the limits of its usefulness.[3] The problem is that the observer can construct worldview in ways that even the insider might not recognize. We need to admit that this is an infinite regress game. We can always posit a *homolucus*, a person inside the person we see, but we need to embrace epistemic humility about what we do not see.

Then, what is culture? Culture is knowledge, values, and feelings that are learned, shared, and employed to define reality, interpret experience, and generate appropriate strategies for living. That understanding is helpful, as is the notion that there are assumptions behind the conscious patterns of culture that the people themselves usually are not aware of. But culture is also contingent, constructed, and contested.

Culture is contingent on things at hand: stories, myths, histories, texts, concepts, metaphors, memories, proverbs, legends, scientific accounts, canoes, offices, relationships, planes, trains, and cars. None of these mean anything until someone brings them into the conversation. They are not a part of culture until they are present to the people.

Culture is constructed, but not out of thin air. When these things are present (displayed, imagined, or remembered), then they can be used to construct a particular view of reality, to shape relationships, and to produce, distribute, and consume goods. The project of constructing culture is a daily project, a group project, a community project. Like-minded people build up culture daily, and then do it again tomorrow. Continuity comes from many sources: the environment, the goods, the available stories, and the available relationships.

Finally, culture is contested. What one person or one subgroup chooses from among the available cultural items and the way in which these items are constructed on a particular occasion may differ markedly from the way another person or group constructs its selected items. Then the contest continues. Whose view of reality is true? Whose priorities rule? What relationships are important? What relationships can be ignored or restructured? This is the stuff of daily life whether in a remote village or in the midst of a world-class city, whether in a heated political arena or at a sedate funeral.

This is not the modernist concept of culture. In fact, dissent was rarely recognized in the early years, which is why J. O. Dorsey's footnote that "Two Crows denies this" stands out in stark contrast (Sapir 1951, 569-570). Conflict was seen as dysfunctional until Max Gluckman and the Manchester School were able to show the positive and negative functions of conflict in society (1955). As I have said elsewhere, "We need to understand how culture is contingent on regional and global flows, how culture is constructed from materials brought into the present over historic and geographic distances, and how culture is constantly being con-

---

[3] For example, Kraft, himself, defines culture as "the complex structuring of customs and the assumptions that underlie them in terms of which people govern their lives," but then locates worldview as "included in culture as the structuring of the deepest-level presuppositions on the basis of which people live their lives" (1996, 31, 52).

tested in daily life. If we do not have such an understanding, we fail to grasp the missionary situation and to communicate the gospel properly" (Rynkiewich 2002, 316).

In sum, neither culture nor worldview is as "primordial," to borrow Lewellen's term (2002, 106-110),[4] or as "monocausal" as anthropologists or missiologists have thought. Both are helpful, but in constellation with other concepts such as personality, society, and those described below.

Person

Basic to the assumptions that lie behind non-Eastern social science is the notion that a person is a bounded individual, a node in the structure of society and an isolate that exists with or without others. For example, Talcott Parsons and Edward A. Shils positioned the individual, as defined and analyzed by Western psychology and sociology, at the center of the social system (1951, 201). "First, the orientation of action of any *one* given actor and its attendant motivational processes becomes a differentiated and integrated system. This system will be called the personality, and we will define it as the organized system of the orientation and motivation of action on one individual actor" (Parsons and Shils 1951, 7).

The problem is that, like culture, persons are constructed in different ways in different cultures. For example, in some cultures, it is relationships that are assumed to be ontologically prior to persons. Thus, relationships exist, then a baby is born, then that baby develops over time as her relationships shape her, and finally, she becomes a person. In other cultures, one person may be subservient to another person, and only the dominant one is considered a full person. Or, a person may be conceived as being divisible, with the parts capable of being given away according to the various relationships that define the person, and thus the people construct partible persons. "Far from being regarded as unique entities, Melanesian persons are as multi-individually as they are individually conceived. They contain a generalized sociality within. Indeed, persons are frequently constructed as the plural and composite site of the relationships that produced them" (Strathern 1988, 13). These possibilities drive the missiologist back to the ethnographic drawing board. How are people constructed in this place? What does that mean for the location of decision making in this culture? What might it mean for group formation and the problem of shifting allegiances to Christ and the church?

Identity/Ethnicity

Anthropologists used to talk about identity as a fixed self, integral to the person, that might be hidden beneath layers of achieved, imputed, or imagined selves.

---

[4]Geertz uses the same concept in his chapter "The Integrative Revolution: Primordial Sentiments and Civil Politics in New States" (1973, 255-310).

Even so, the fixed self was thought to be linked to tradition and bonded to others like the self. It followed, then, that rediscovering the fixed self was a healthy or healing process, that dealing with too many alternative selves was tantamount to schizophrenia, and that the denial of self indicated a lack of integrity. The colonial situation involved an attack on the self such that people were victims who ended up with damaged selves, leading possibly to madness (see, for example, Williams 1923; Fanon 1967). "One way of understanding this phenomenon is to view identity as a collective true self buried beneath layers of superficial and artificial selves; this hidden essential self is the one that has historical continuity, shares common codes with others of similar descent, and, when discovered and consciously affirmed, reproduces one people" (Lewellen 2002, 90).

The problem is that identity is only one end of a relationship; that is, one should always ask: Identity with respect to what Other and in what context? In a Papua New Guinea Highlands village, a person identifies with reference to a clan (descent), a number of relatives (kinship), and a big man (local politics). The next day, in town, that person identifies with a language group vis-à-vis other speakers and places himself somewhere along a rural-urban continuum as well as an employed-unemployed continuum. Two days later, after a flight to the capital city, Port Moresby, the person is suddenly a Highlander on a Highlands-Nambis (mountains-seaboard) continuum. The next week, after a flight to Brisbane, the person identifies as Papua New Guinean (ethnicity) vis-à-vis Aussies and other Pacific Islanders.

And this is only as perceived from one side of the equation. All along the way, others are creating their own categories of identity for him, whether he hears it, whether he accepts it, or whether he likes it or not. For example, the Australian may identify the Papua New Guinean as a *wog* (racist category). He has moved from a village to a national to an international identity. He is in danger of being defined by a race-based identity. And he is in the process of creating identities not only for himself but for the Others that he encounters. Each set of categories, for example, Highlands-Nambis, carries its own attributes. Each constructed identity is open to negotiation, but only within the realm of imaginable identities and relationships (contingent, constructed, and then contested).

The missionary situation that will be the most common in this century is a complex urban context where people are capable of projecting two or more identities as they negotiate their way through a maze of microcultural settings. People are not confused, but are demonstrating that they are competent in several languages, in several ethnic groups, and thus in projecting several identities. They are also into the business of maintaining boundaries, and that is what makes for shifting selves. Missionaries will struggle with the nostalgia for a true self, and will have to ask how the multiple and shifting selves they see in front of them can be brought into the discipleship of Christ.

Agency

In modern anthropology, the agent for change was presumed to be outside the culture at hand. Stories about the Yir Yiront (Sharp 1952), the Siriono (Holmberg

1954), the people of Peri village (Mead 1956), or the peons of Vicos (Holmberg 1958, 12-16) abound, in which outsiders inadvertently, intentionally, or insidiously intervene to change another culture forever. In these stories, the people are portrayed as victims of forces beyond their control. They can do nothing.

John Bodley captured this view in his book *Victims of Progress*: "This work assumes that government policies and attitudes are the basic causal factors determining the fate of tribal cultures . . . Industrial civilization is now completing the destruction of technologically simple tribal cultures" (1975, v-vii).[5] While postmodern developments in anthropology have foregrounded the issue of power, especially differential power in relations that lead to abuses of power, at the same time anthropologists have come to recognize that people are agents in their own right and that they exercise strategies to resist and shape power for their own purposes. People are not simply victims, though victimization occurs, nor are they simply obstacles to progress, though they may block development plans. Instead, within the parameters of the neo-colonial situation, people are in a position to make what choices they can to resist change, to accept change, and, most commonly, to be selective about what will change and what will not change.

What this means for missiology is that neither paternalism nor demonization is an appropriate stance toward other people. Missionaries must discover where and in what ways people have agency (what can people decide about?), what strategies people have used in the past to manage change, and how people negotiate with outsiders about the diffusion of innovations (Rogers 2003).

Migration and Diaspora

The anthropology of the past imagined a world of bounded groups relatively settled inside a culture area (Kroeber 1939). In our globalized world, nation-states, a modernist invention to begin with, are in decline while significant communities are emerging that are neither bounded nor centered. Diverse examples of such country-less, boundary-less, and decentralized, but nevertheless powerful, networks include free market capitalism, Al-Qaeda, and the emerging church. How will we be in mission between the nations?

By the early part of this century, more people had moved to urban areas than there were left in rural areas. The greatest human migration in the history of the world continues, creating ironies like this: except for some small nations, the country known for the Amazon rainforest has become the most urbanized country (82%) in the world (UN 2001, 273).

The causes of migration, the methods of migration, and the results of migration contribute to a complex taxonomy of terms. *Refugees* are those who have been pushed into migration by some catastrophic event, such as war, ethnocide, tsunami, earthquake, famine, etc. Transnationals are a new category of people who "maintain multiple contacts—social, cultural, political, economic—with both

---

[5]Note that a critique of Bodley's work is found in Eder (1992).

the country of origin and the host country" (Lewellen 2002, 130). People living in diaspora continue to nurture selected memories of the homeland and maintain community in tension with their hosts within the various lands where they have settled. The more well-known diasporas are the Chinese diaspora that produced "Chinatowns" in nearly every major city in the world; the Indian diaspora that scattered communities throughout the former British Empire, a complex situation that has, among other things, recently (in 2006) produced the third coup in Fiji in the last fifteen years; and the Japanese diaspora that began in the nineteenth century and has produced such ironies as a Japanese president of Peru (Alberto Fujimori) and ethnic neighborhoods in São Paulo composed of nearly one million Japanese, not to mention the Italian district, the Jewish district, and growing neighborhoods of Filipinos and Koreans (Ember and Ember 2002, 143-153).

Migrants, refugees, transnationals, and diasporic communities provide two challenges for mission. First, the host country churches, such as the American church, have an opportunity to rediscover one of the most long-standing directives in Scripture: treat the alien or sojourner who lives among you with justice (e.g., Lev 19:33-34). Second, those in diaspora have an opportunity to follow an even more ancient directive: scatter and multiply and be a blessing wherever you go (from Gen 12:1-3 to Acts 1:7-8). For example, Filipinos who go into diaspora in order to find work consider their presence to be an opportunity for mission, as many narratives attest (Pantoja, Tira, and Wan 2004, 287-360). Dealing with migration and diaspora forces us to rethink missiology so that mission is less concerned with nation-states and tribes, or with boundaries and territories, and more concerned with journeying along with global flows of people, ideas, and goods; less concerned with discerning between evangelism and social justice, and more concerned with proclaiming and demonstrating the gospel among people who are in need wherever they are (Wan 2004, 103-121).

Summary

The interplay between anthropology and missiology must continue. As the world changes, so must we find out where people are and go to them, whether they are settled or in transit. Missiologists would do well to shift their gaze to concepts that will prove important for the next generation. Urbanization and globalization have been two of the most dominant forces shaping the world at the end of the twentieth and beginning of the twenty-first century, and many people are becoming aware that they will affect the deployment of missionaries from here on out (Van Engen and Tiersma 1994). Colonialism and neocolonialism are not forces that affected only the past, but rather forces that spill over into the present. As examples, neither the Rwanda genocide nor the Darfur genocide has its roots in ethnic conflict, but rather in the colonial history and neocolonial divisions that have been fostered in those places. Mission history is only beginning to understand the role of missionaries in decolonization (Stanley 2003), and the place of missionaries in the neocolonial order that supports globalization (Bonk

1991).[6] The revitalization of Islam, Hinduism, and Buddhism has brought a fundamentalist fervor to the resistance of Christian mission. The spread of HIV-AIDS and the devastation it causes dwarfs even ethnic violence as a force that works against Kingdom *shalom* in the world. Any mission organization not pursuing an integral mission strategy will be poorly positioned to demonstrate God's sufficiency to minister to the needy and marginalized.

Finally, in a postcolonial, post-cold war world that seems to be overwhelmed by globalization, local intersections are emerging as sites of resistance that are constructed by migrants, refugees, transnationals, and diasporas. There are channels, centers, peripheries, and reversals in global flows, and these produce complex social settings where people exhibit multiple, shifting, and hybrid identities. This decenters the "building blocks" of Western social sciences: personality, society, culture, and environment. Even history is contested from multiple perspectives, and theology is no longer sourced from within "the tradition," but rather from various standpoints. Social science and theology, the twin pillars of missiology, have been destabilized (the center is moving and the boundaries are falling), and we are poised to become all the richer for it.

The point is that we live in a new earth, though it is not yet the one we are looking for, yet we imagine a new salvation, more holistic and more faithful to the Source. Our task now is to find the tools with which we can apprehend and describe the world well, then employ multiple methods of analysis, apply several alternative interpretative schemes, and strive not for elusive objectivity, but for perspectives that will allow as many voices as possible to be heard (a new Pentecost). Then we can join with indigenous Christians in their contextualization of the gospel, their construction of local theologies, and their call to be in mission to the world as it is becoming (Jenkins 2006).

---

[6]Note also that Joel Robbins (*Becoming Sinners: Christianity and Moral Torment in a Papua New Guinea Society* [Berkeley: University of California Press, 2004]) is editing a new series called *The Anthropology of Christianity* for the University of California Press.

Part II

COMMUNICATION

Introduction by Charles E. Van Engen

"And God said, 'Let there be light,' and there was light" (Gen 1:3, NIV). "And the word of the Lord came to [Jeremiah], saying . . ." (Jer 1:4, NIV). "In the beginning was the Word, and the Word was with God, and the Word was God (Jn 1:1, NIV). Communication is at the heart of God's mission (*missio Dei*), God's desire to relate in love to human beings who are God's creation. From the beginning of time, God has sought to communicate to humans through other specially chosen human agents like the prophets—and ultimately through his Son, Jesus Christ. And now, during the church age, since Pentecost, God seeks to communicate God's intended meaning in love through the body of Christ, "the Church, in the power of the Holy Spirit" (Moltmann 1977).

The close relationship between communication and Christian mission is nothing new. Yet, the inclusion of communication theory as a central supporting discipline in missiology is new. It is difficult to find a work in missiology prior to the 1950s that specifically addresses the complex endeavor we know as communication. In 1960, Eugene Nida pointed toward a major paradigm shift in the role of communication theory in mission thought and practice when he published *Message and Mission: The Communication of the Christian Faith.* In the preface to that work, Nida wrote:

> One highly significant fact in the present world is the recent converging of interest and effort in several fields of study and research on problems of communication. Linguistics, which would seem obviously related to the problems of meaning and communication, remained preoccupied for many years with the formal structures of languages. Within the last few years, however, keen concern has been shown for the relation of language to culture and of formal structure to the problems of meaning. Linguists have rendered important service to the theory and techniques of communication . . .
>
> Anthropologists have recently become increasingly absorbed in the problem of symbols and their relation to human behavior . . . Now . . . the almost innumerable ways of communicating are being studied in terms of their dynamic effect on behavior and culture change, thus providing significant insights for the whole field of intercultural communication.

Psychologists have always been keenly aware of the problems of perception and have struggled with the seemingly ever elusive meaning of words. Of late . . . meaning has taken on an even greater significance, for it has been recognized that people do not merely perceive the "outside world," but that they select, organize, and interpret all that they perceive. These findings have been an additional source of clues as to how communication actually takes place.

Information theory (also known as the science of cybernetics) . . . has likewise contributed appreciably to our understanding of communication. Even though such concepts as encoding, decoding, feedback, redundancy, noise, and transitional probabilities may seem too remote from our everyday experience to be of practical relevance, they have nevertheless provided . . . some of the most important insights into the process of communication . . .

In our study of communication we shall be concerned primarily with the ways in which the message of the Bible has been communicated . . . The message of the Bible deals with every aspect of life, and thus the problems of communication are fully representative of all types of difficulties . . . The communication of the gospel by its nature requires acceptance or rejection on the basis of a people's most keenly felt values . . . The New Testament comes . . . as the communication of a new way of life. Thus the impact of its dissemination is highly significant in any thoughtful study of the principles and procedures of communication. (1960, xi-xiii)

In this section of the book we seek to give the reader an overview of the phenomenal impact that communication theory has had on missiological thought and in mission practice. Fittingly, the first chapter is from Eugene Nida. Nida was the pioneer and trailblazer for Chuck Kraft's generation of linguists and missionary anthropologists. Nida first coined the concept of "dynamic equivalence," which Chuck Kraft took and broadened, deepened, and strengthened by joining the concept with Kraft's idea of "receptor-oriented" communication. This chapter by Nida is a series of vignettes drawn from real-life situations that illustrate in poignant fashion the difficulties of communication and meaning that have plagued and fascinated missionaries the world over.

Viggo Søgaard from Denmark offers us the second chapter in this section. Like Nida, Søgaard has worked for many years with the Bible Societies. Drawing from Chuck Kraft's writing, Viggo reminds us of the ways in which the Bible itself is a model for effective communication of God's intention for humanity. Søgaard proceeds to describe ten myths about communication. Most of us can recognize ourselves in one or more of them. Finally, Viggo gives us a series of communication principles that every reader of this volume will find helpful.

The third chapter in this section is written by a unique person who combines music, linguistics, anthropology, and missiology in a very special way. Having studied under Charles Kraft, Roberta King describes in detail the ways in which intercultural communication contributes to twenty-first-century missiology. The reader will find helpful and informative Roberta's summary of various models of appropriate communication. Going beyond those models, King proposes that communication is actually a continuous process of negotiation between the communicator, the receptor, and the cultural contexts of both. Here we gain a new appreciation for the complexity of communication and a hint as to the valuable contribution that communication theory can make to missiology.

The final chapter in this section looks from the present to the future. Knud Jørgensen moves communication from being an individual matter to being a corporate process. He wants the reader to understand that the church itself is the corporate agent of communication of God's grace to the world. The church's essence is to be witnesses: the church itself is to be the embodiment of the message of the Gospel. In Jørgensen's words, this involves "communication through community." Knud is drawing from Kraft's concept of "dynamic equivalence churchness" that calls for churches themselves, in their essence, to be missional churches, the physical embodiment of the message of the gospel. Jørgensen's emphasis echoes Lesslie Newbigin's understanding of the Christian congregation as the hermeneutic of the Gospel that is called to be a "community of praise," a "community of truth," a community that "is deeply involved in the concerns of the neighborhood," a community that actively exercises a "priesthood for the world," a "community of mutual responsibility," and a "community of hope" (Newbigin 1989, 222-33; cf. C. Van Engen 1996, 223). Darrell Guder said it this way, "The reason the Christian church exists . . . is to be Christ's witnesses . . . All Christians are witnesses, whether they choose to be or not; the question is whether they are useful, responsible witnesses, a community through which the good news of God's love does flow and reach out to others (Guder 1992, foreword). May we all learn better how to be faithful witnesses, communicating God's love by every means at our disposal to a lost and hurting world so loved by God.

5

Reflections on Cultures, Language Learning, and Communication

EUGENE A. NIDA

Editors' Note

Like many hundreds of cross-cultural missionaries of the 1950s, Charles Kraft was strongly influenced by the thinking, teaching, and writing of Eugene Nida.[1] Thus, the editors considered it a fitting tribute to both Nida and Kraft to include some "musings" by Eugene Nida in this volume. In the fall of 2001, Eugene Nida offered a series of missiology lectures in the School of World Mission at Fuller Theological Seminary in Pasadena, California. The unpublished lecture series was entitled "Culture, Communication, and Christianity." Those of us who had the joy of hearing him remarked that "this is vintage Nida." Nida had a special way of teaching. He would weave anthropological, linguistic, communication, and missiological principles into a series of real-life stories. The stories brought the principles to life and enhanced one of Nida's concerns: that the theory be applied and made to work in specific cross-cultural situations. Based on the experience of such cross-cultural interaction, the theory itself would be modified. One might say that his was a praxeological approach to cross-cultural communication.

Nida described what being a translation consultant for the United Bible Societies is like in something of a self-portrait: (1) a keen intellect with a sense of structure and scientific imagination; (2) a capacity to communicate effectively with others; (3) a fundamental empathy with the cause of communicating the Good News, and a willingness to work closely with all kinds of Christian groups; and (4) a warm personal touch and sense of humor with which to relate to others, and not to take himself too seriously (North 1974, xx).

---

[1]In the original 1979 publication of *Christianity in Culture*, Kraft cites Nida on forty different pages, more than any other single author.

Steven Hoke once wrote: "One of Nida's greatest contributions to missions was the development and popularization of dynamic equivalence translation, which seeks to capture the meaning and spirit of the original without being bound to its linguistic structure. This approach to translation is highly influential in modern Bible translation work."

In 1988, Nida himself wrote, "I have found [my] work throughout the world to be not only intellectually stimulating, but spiritually inspiring. Translating is one of the most complex intellectual activities in which people can engage . . . But constantly dealing with the Scriptures has meant an ever increasing appreciation for the true values of life and the meaning of selfless service . . . Another discovery . . . has been the realization that it is not what we do for people, but what we do together with people, that really counts" (1988, 62, 64).[2]

Recently, Dan Shaw wrote the following tribute to Eugene Nida: "Good missionaries have always been good 'anthropologists' " (Nida 1954, xi). Missionaries like this opening line of Nida's book *Customs and Cultures*, which has served as a basal anthropology text for thousands of missionaries around the world for fifty years. Nida also knew that they were desperately in need of anthropological theory that could work itself out in the reality of their field experience. He went on to point out that he had

Become increasingly conscious of the tragic mistakes in cultural orientation . . . of missionary work, something they do not like to hear. He concluded that opening paragraph by stressing the need for missionaries to take both theory and practice seriously. Nida understood that scientific theory must be combined with practical application of field-oriented researchers to benefit sufficiently from the theoretical input. Shaw observed that Nida had a knack for enabling his recipients to recognize the benefit of anthropology and linguistics.

Involved in mission toward the end of the colonial era, Nida realized that good missionaries needed to be good anthropologists. He devoted his life to enabling those who sought missionary vocations to do so more effectively through the application of cultural and linguistic understanding. He encouraged Christian and largely Western non-anthropologists who were mono-culturally oriented to become aware of the people around them and to treat those people with dignity. Thus, Nida used anthropological theory to sensitize an entire generation of missionaries to apply principles of cross-cultural sen-

---

[2]Some of Nida's best-known publications include *Morphology: The Descriptive Analysis of Words* (1949); *Learning a Foreign Language* (1950); *God's Word in Man's Language* (1952); *Customs and Cultures* (1954); *Message and Mission* (1960); *Toward the Science of Translating* (1964); and *The Theory and Practice of Translation* (with Charles R. Taber, 1969). Eugene Nida is married to Dr. Elena Fernandez-Miranda-Nida, an executive in the translations program of the European Union. They make their home in Belgium.

sitivity to the practice of Christian mission. This new attitude, in turn, has contributed hundreds of cultural descriptions, orthographies, grammars, and translations that have provided unprecedented field data for anthropological analysis that would otherwise be unavailable.

Nida's lectures and writing were filled with stories and illustrations from "the field." But every example was grounded in a theoretical construct or issue that could be demonstrated in many different contexts. The response to a lecture or article could easily be, "he just told stories." But, when examined, there was a rationale for the stories that emanated from theoretical approaches out of anthropology, linguistics and translation theory. (Shaw 2007, 2)

Here, then, are some "musings" by one of the praxeological pioneers in whose debt we all stand.

On Cultural Relevance—Connecting with People

After a bumpy flight from Guatemala City to Chichicastenango in the heart of the M'am Indian region of Guatemala, I immediately ran to get a taxi. But when I asked to go to the residence of Paul Burgess, the taxi driver immediately replied, "Oh, you want to see Tio Peruchi; he's a great man and I read him every morning." For a moment I did not understand this use of an affectionate title *Tio*, literally "Uncle" in Spanish, neither did I understand the M'am adaptation of the English name *Burgess*. But it began to make sense to me as the taxi driver insisted that he always began each day reading Tio Peruchi's almanac that contained vital information for everyone about the phases of the moon, time for planting various crops, advice on controlling insects, and a very meaningful short passage from the Bible with Tio Peruchi's insightful comments.

I had met Dr. Paul Burgess (Ph.D. from Heidelberg, Germany, and distinguished Bible scholar) some years before, and I was anxious to have more time to talk with him because he was without doubt the best informed and most insightful missionary working among the ancient peoples of Latin America. Do you wonder why he would publish an almanac? Simply because almost everyone wanted to consult an almanac regularly, and in this way thousands of people also had a relevant message about life, as well as about the seasons.

Paul Burgess and his wife had finished the translation of the New Testament into the M'am Mayan language, and I needed to know more about the way in which the local people had understood some of the difficult passages of the Epistles. But I was even more interested in knowing how Tio Peruchi had earned the trust of everyone. The people of that area respected and trusted Burgess so much that at one point a band of outlaws had "captured him" so that their leader, who had just died, could have a man of God to conduct the funeral and burial.

As Paul and I talked at length about problems of cultural differences between the Spanish and the Mayan worlds, Burgess mentioned that he was leaving in a couple of days for an area about sixty miles north of Chichicastenango, and I commented about how nice it was that the new Pan American highway now passed so close to his destination. But he disagreed. He insisted that he would walk because the people he wanted to talk to were not accustomed to riding in cars. In fact, he said, "I have never met a person I could not talk to about Jesus, if we were walking down the same trail together."

Some months later I was asked to address a group of over three hundred students and faculty at a Baptist College in California, and I tried to share with them the really important aspects of Christian faith as experienced in various parts of the world. I discovered, however, that my audience was far more interested in the proper form of baptism, and during a question time people insisted on knowing what I believed about immersion, and especially, whether people should be immersed face-up or face-down. After I had explained the variety of views about baptism and the impossibility of being dogmatic about such a rite, my audience melted away. The next day only eight people came to listen to me. What a contrast to what I had seen Burgess doing in Guatemala!

On the Value of Language

Few people realize the enormous range of functions performed by language: (1) providing information in the seemingly endless verbal negotiations that constitute the core activity in so many enterprises, from family arguments to major international congresses, (2) altering the state of persons, for example, sentencing criminals, marrying and divorcing, adopting infants, accrediting specialists, baptizing, and stimulating changes in sexual state, (3) commanding and controlling the activities of persons, (4) educating and training, (5) aesthetic expression, for example, writing poetry and designing effective prose, (6) communicating with supernatural persons and powers by means of prayer and sacred texts, (7) verbal games, such as crossword puzzles and Scrabble, (8) expressing emotional states of anger or affection, and (9) thinking, because most mental activity depends on verbal and visual symbols. In fact, cognition is undoubtedly the most common use of language.

In order to use language for such a wide range of activities, states, entities, and characteristics, most people need and use a vocabulary of at least 20,000 to 50,000 words. But most people do not realize that the Hebrew Bible has a vocabulary of only about 8,000 words, ten percent of which occur only once. Similarly the vocabulary of the New Testament is about 5,000 words. Perhaps the only people who try to communicate truths with only a few hundred words are (cross-cultural) missionaries who think they can "get by" in the local languages.

On Language and Culture Learning

The quality of church life does not depend on the number of rules for behavior any more than the number of vowels in a language is a mark of linguistic superiority. For example, the Quechua languages of South America normally have only three vowels, Spanish has five, Portuguese has seven, and American English has eleven or twelve, depending on the dialect in question. But the number of vowels has nothing to do with communicative effectiveness.

Some persons, however, believe that tonal distinctions such as exist in different dialects of Chinese are signs of linguistic superiority. But if such were true, most of the languages in Africa south of the Sahara would have to be regarded as linguistically very superior, because most of these languages have highly complex tone systems. In fact, Bushman and Hottentot would win the linguistic prize for complexity and abundance of tone patterns. Many missionaries, however, flatly deny the existence of tonal differences. In one area of Congo a missionary with many years of experience in the field denied the existence of tone despite the fact that he mispronounced fully eighty percent of the words. Nevertheless, he assured me that in speaking to an audience he automatically got all the tones right because the people loved to hear him preach.

I was intrigued with the confidence of the preacher and so I talked with some of the workers at the mission station, who did go to hear the missionary whenever he spoke. In fact, after the missionary finished speaking, the congregation gathered in the African section of the mission station and for an hour or more howled in laughter at the many mistakes. They could all remember prize examples of what a person should not say in the local language.

If, as a new (cross-cultural) missionary, you are commended on the quality of your use of the local language, you can be sure that you are really not too good. But when people no longer comment about your use of the local language, you are highly competent—or hopelessly inadequate and therefore the people have simply given up hope of your ever learning.

Most missions allot three years for a new missionary to learn the local language, but this is nonsense. No one can learn any language adequately in three years, even if a person concentrates almost totally on language learning. A person is fortunate to learn how to engage in fast developing informal conversation in a period of ten years, but in order to speak relevantly in a language one must also have some grasp of the culture, which is more difficult to understand than even a language.

Not only do different languages have distinct ways of putting words together grammatically in phrases, sentences, and paragraphs, but different groups of people have very distinct ways of talking about human experience. For example, in English we speak of the future as being ahead of us, because we seem to be walking into the future. But in many languages the future is said to be behind because the future cannot be seen by the "eyes of the mind." In some languages people "leave a fever," rather than saying "the fever left." Similarly, in some languages a person does not "go to a town," but "pulls the town to himself."

Different languages also have different levels or registers: 1) ritual (the language employed in elaborate ceremonies, for example, marriage and burial, 2) formal (when speaking to persons one does not know), 3) informal (with friends and office colleagues), 4) recreational (at a picnic or during a soccer match), and

5) intimate (within the family or clan). Compare the following series of invitations to dine: "The guests may now proceed to their places in the banquet hall," "Please be seated," "Let's eat," "Come and get it," and "Dig in."

But we also need to know the meaningful gestures in the culture. For example, when a clerk says "How we love our boss!" and at the same time draws two fingers across her throat, you soon realize that she would like to kill him. In some cultures gestures are a continuous accompaniment of language. In fact, I have often seen Italians gesturing with two hands in a glass telephone booth as they shelter the telephone speaker between the shoulder and the head.

On the Vagaries of Language

When you want to say something to someone about the food being served in the dining room of the school, do you say to yourself, "Now let's see. First the article and then the noun, but just before the verb put in the adverb, and then the object of the verb?" You do not have to do that because in your mother tongue all those rules have become almost completely automatic. You talk without thinking about the grammar because you are concerned with the content. In fact, most grammar rules are automatically employed by the time a child is five years of age.

But there are also cultural rules that soon become automatic. Usually children of three years of age know perfectly well how to pit their mother against their father in order to get precisely what they want. And by five years of age most children are expert manipulators of their care-givers. But missionaries do not have such golden opportunities to learn a foreign culture.

Even on the simple level of initial language learning there are a number of "rules" that seem to make no sense. What, for example, is the difference in meaning between "He tied the package" and "He tied up the package"? Probably only a slight degree of intensity, but certainly nothing to do with elevation. And what about expressions such as "tie up traffic," "the boss is tied up till five o'clock," "the man turned up?" Although metaphorically there is some "upness" in the phrase "he upped the price" because such an increase seems to be something higher.

Or consider the phrase "ran into the house," which can be understood in a completely literal sense if someone is actually running and ends up inside of a house. But if a person in a car "runs into the house," the car is usually going to be hurt more than the house. In such a statement there is impact, but in the statement "during the convention he ran into his old friend" there is no running, but only unexpected meeting with someone.

On Believing Is Not Necessarily Seeing

The only way we can receive information or communicate our feelings is by means of our senses of hearing, sight, touch, smell, and taste. Without one or more of these senses, we are cut off from our world and especially from our interpersonal world, which is far more important for healthy survival than any other kind of experience.

When we choose to live in another language-culture, we cannot experience the culture as children do because we are already tuned to a different kind of world. Anthropologists have learned that it is extremely important to pay close attention to the behavior and explanations of children at different ages because they are often naively capable of explaining their ideas and behavior in unusually meaningful ways.

A society may, however, develop a false view of how the sense of sight functions. For example, the New Testament speaks about light by saying, "If the light in you is darkness, how intense is the darkness," because people in biblical times believed that the eyes were instruments that sent out light to identify objects, rather than being instruments for simply registering light as it impinges on the focal portion at the back of the eyes.

On Perceiving Biblical and Local Reality

Unfortunately, many people have so little background in cultural differences that they naively assume that local people will understand the Bible in essentially the same way as Americans or Europeans understand it. This applies especially to the contents of John 3:16 which is often regarded as "the gospel in a single sentence." But in the Buddhist world the statement, "God so loved the world" is entirely misleading because "love of the world" is regarded in Buddhism as the basis for all sin and deception. And the following declaration about God's only son is regarded as a defamation of God, because the greatest power in the universe would never be guilty of having a son with a virgin. But the most misunderstood part of this verse, "will never perish, but have ever lasting life" means to a Buddhist that he will never escape the endless series of births and deaths and so never attain the bliss of Nirvana.

Misunderstanding the text of the Bible is a constant hazard in the life of missionaries who genuinely desire to share their faith. On one occasion a Buddhist priest visited the Bible House in Bangkok in order to buy a New Testament, because he had heard that Jesus was a famous teacher and he wanted to learn more about him. Accordingly, he bought a New Testament and left, but a month later he returned and exclaimed, "This man Jesus was indeed a remarkable teacher, because he lived and died, lived and died, lived and died, and lived and died, and in only four reincarnations he attained Nirvana, when Gautama, the founder of Buddhism required a thousand births and deaths before entering that blessed state." For this Buddhist priest the four Gospel accounts were interpreted as four reincarnations on the path to Nirvana.

Words only have meanings in terms of the culture of which the language is only a part, though it is an indispensable means for the functioning and the perpetuation of the culture. A missionary can learn a language fairly well in ten years, but no one ever completely masters a new culture within a lifetime.

On Cultural Tolerance

I have always discouraged the idea that people who are unlikely to succeed in their own culture can succeed in another culture . . . An American bishop phoned me one day about a brilliant young man in one of the church's seminaries who was good in Hebrew and Greek, but whose personality would not be adequate as a minister in an American church. Therefore, the bishop wondered whether we in the United Bible Societies might use his help overseas. I immediately assured the bishop that someone who would not be successful in his own culture would certainly not succeed in giving leadership to a program in a different language and culture.

Some persons involved in judging the qualifications of people for overseas work have drawn up tests to diagnose potentiality for success as missionaries. Most of the tests focused on their ability to get along with other missionaries—often an important consideration. But what the analysts failed to realize is that in work overseas what is important is the capacity to identify with the out-group (the foreign people), and not the in-group (fellow missionaries). The profile questionnaire should have asked how many of the candidate's friends come from local out-groups. Do they identify with the underdog in conflicts? How many poor countries can they name? Describe the morals and beliefs of various immigrant groups in America. And what would you think of a local church in Haiti that has as its name, "Methodist, Pentecostal, National, Cathedral of Erzuli," with a note explaining that Erzuli is the fertility goddess of West Africa? The tendency for religious expression to borrow forms and beliefs from various sources is one of the fundamental characteristics of religious beliefs and practices.

On Cultural Re-entry

Problems of cultural adjustment are far more widespread than most people imagine. (And this impacts those who re-enter their own culture as well.) On one of my frequent trips to Africa, I was seated next to a young African who had just completed his university studies in accounting and business management in one of the leading universities in North America. I asked him about his experience in an American university and how he looked forward to getting back to the Congo.

He described enthusiastically his time in the United States and especially his love of classical music and the freedom of association with all kinds of students. But what worried him was facing a return to Congo. He was certain that his father had already chosen a wife for him from the village of his clan, and he realized that by working in the treasury of the Congo, he would be under great pressure to provide funds for all of his begging friends. A house full of self-seeking relatives was a frightening prospect. He faced more serious interpersonal problems than any missionary ever had.

On Attitudes toward Local People

In place of the motto "Helping others," the key to effective missionary service is "Helping others help themselves." This principle was remarkably demonstrated by a friend of mine who went to live in a heavily forested area of Central America where there was little space for gardens and cutting timber with hand saws was completely unrealistic. But some of the local leaders came to my friend and asked if he would help them build a sawmill that could be powered by a nearby stream. He told them that he would be happy to advise them about the construction and operation because he had worked for a while in the forests of North America. But he also made it clear that he did not have any money to invest in such an enterprise. Nevertheless, if they would raise the money, he would show the people how to build and operate such a mill.

Within a few months the mill was working fine, and the demand for the local lumber was excellent. People could buy better clothing, have more to eat, and even build a school. But the tropical rains that summer were torrential, and in one evening the entire mill was smashed and floated downstream. But the next morning the workers at the mill came to see my friend. They had collected enough money from the people in the village to buy all the necessary equipment. And they were already talking about how they could improve the location of the mill and the production of lumber.

If my friend had provided the money for the first mill from supporters in America, the local people would have simply waited for him to provide the cash again. But since it was their mill and he had worked with the local leaders and not for them, they felt a sense of pride and responsibility for the economic transformation of the region.

Similarly, some Mennonite missionaries in East Africa had some real problems about thirty years ago when local leaders in the churches were convinced by local politicians that the missionaries merely wanted to exploit and dominate the local people. Accordingly, the missionaries came to a meeting of the local churches and handed over all the keys to the cars, trucks, and houses. The next morning the local preachers, evangelists, and teachers went to the missionaries and said, "Regardless of what some of the politicians say, we need you, so here are your keys, because you are a part of us."

On Sanctification That Is More Than a Dream

It is a serious mistake to assume that only people from the so-called civilized world can find solutions that fit people's needs in diverse cultures. For example, Ephraim Alphonse from Jamaica became the minister of a church among the Valiente Indians of Panama. One morning his principal assistant came to tell his boss that he had "dreamed the dream" and therefore he would die within sixteen days, even as so many other people who had dreamed this dream had died in about two weeks.

Ephraim Alphonse knew that it would not do any good to deny the power of the dream, so he said to his assistant, "But you can't die. You owe me a month's salary that I gave you in advance. You cannot die till you have paid what you owe me." The young man agreed to work off the debt, and so Ephraim immediately went to talk with his two sons and explained to them that their father's assistant had dreamed the deadly dream that had caused the death of so many people. One or both sons must be with the assistant all the time. They must see that their father's helper ate plenty of food so that he could work hard. Finally, the sixteen days passed and everyone in the area was astonished to see that Ephraim's assistant was still alive and the power of the dream was destroyed.

Ephraim Alphonse was not a student of psychiatry, but a remarkable Caribbean who understood more about human nature than many professionals. He was also a good translator of the New Testament into the Valiente language. He realized that it would do no good to ask the local people for a Valiente word for "sanctification," because they would never know what he was talking about. But Ephraim noticed how the women washed their dirty clothes in a nearby stream, put the washed clothes on bushes to dry, and then placed the neatly folded clothing in baskets that only kept clean clothes, so he constructed an admirable equivalent for sanctification as "being washed by the Spirit of God and kept clean."

On What We Write Is Not What We Say

Our culture is increasingly a culture of writing, especially as we are drowning in email and the internet. Why do we so often say, "But put it in writing!" Do we no longer have confidence in oral language which is so much richer in meaning than any written text? When we receive a letter from a good friend, how often we wish that we could have heard the words from our friend's own lips.

On the other hand we so elaborate in our writing that we disguise our thoughts, and we think that the Good News that Jesus talked about is only understandable in the third volume on biblical hermeneutics. The parable of the Father and Two Sons has more theological insight than most volumes on theology.

Do you really want to be a successful missionary? I have three very simple words of advice:

1. Immerse yourself in the language and the culture of the people!
2. Live like you think Jesus would have lived if he were in your place!
3. Be yourself!

6

Go and Communicate Good News

VIGGO SØGAARD

Communication is not something accidental and supplementary for human beings. We communicate because, from our beginnings, we are communicators by nature. During the last few decades, the interest in communication has been increasing, and almost every discipline concerned with human society and human behavior is concerned with communication. A widening interest has also been evident in Christian mission as effective and relevant mission is inconceivable without paying careful attention to communication principles. Charles H. Kraft has made one of the most important contributions to communication theory as it relates to missiology with books like *Communication Theory for Christian Witness* (1983b, 1991a).

Communication and Missiology

The word *communication* is used here in a broad sense to include all the procedures by which one mind may affect another. This, of course, involves not only written and oral speech, but also music, the pictorial arts, the theater, and in fact all human behavior.

Communication is a complex subject where definition is difficult, and writings on communication theory show a great variety of perspectives. No one model is sufficient to explain and illustrate all aspects of the communication process (see Hiebert in this volume), but as we analyze available definitions, we find that each one has its own strengths and its own usefulness. So, due to the difficulties with definitions, it is more fruitful to describe communication rather than trying to arrive at a single definition (Søgaard 1993, 30).

Actually, the attempt to understand the process of communication and how to communicate more effectively started a very long time ago. Kegemni, the oldest son of Pharaoh Huni, is reported to have received an essay on effective speaking in c. 3000 B.C. (McCroskey 1968, 3). The documented history of rhetorical communication began in Syracuse, Sicily, in the fifth century B.C., where Corax developed an "art of rhetoric" for ordinary people to use, when proving their claims in court (Slate 1976, 17-18). In a review of the science of communication in the West our attention would also be drawn to people like Aristotle, Cicero, and Quintilian. These ancients thought of communication as an art, its theory being termed "rhetoric" and its practice being called "oratory." Aristotle defined rhetoric as the art of discovering in every case the "available means of persuasion." The persuader was successful to the degree to which he actually brought the audience to "right" belief and action (Schramm and Roberts 1971, 22). His *Rhetoric*, published in approximately 330 B.C., was one of the most influential works on communication ever conceived. Aristotle viewed communication in relationship to three points of reference: the speaker, the speech, and the audience. His model has been the basis for many models of communication theory ever since. But despite such ancient beginnings, it has only been during the last few decades that the field of communication has exploded with numerous publications.

The development of communication as a special discipline in missiology is interwoven with the development of Fuller Theological Seminary's School of World Mission (SWM) and the writings of Charles Kraft. The major writings about Christian communication started during the decade before the launch of SWM and flourished during the forty years of the SWM (now the School of Intercultural Studies).

Another significant center of development was Wheaton Graduate School, where communication thinking, research, and strategy came into clear focus under the leadership of James F. Engel. Its graduate degree in communication was established at approximately the same time as the launch of the SWM. While Engel and his colleagues focused more on secular theories of communication and strategy, adapting them to Christian mission, Kraft and his colleagues turned to a study of the biblical perspectives on communication. It was not just a question of using communication theory, but actually discovering a superior communication theory from the Scriptures themselves.

If we were to select a few writers on the topic of missiological communication, we would mention Eugene Nida, one of the early writers on the subject from a missionary perspective. From a perspective of anthropology and Bible translation he pointed to the central significance of communication theory (Nida 1960). Charles Kraft came from a similar background, including missionary experience in Africa. James Engel, who became the primary spokesperson for the communication department at Wheaton Graduate School, came from a background of marketing and consumer behavior (Engel 1979). Robert Weber provided theological insights to communication (Weber 1980). Working in an African context at Daystar Communication in Nairobi, Donald Smith provided several distinct propositions regarding communication (Smith 1992), and David Hesselgrave worked on mission applications (Hesselgrave 1978). Knud Jørgensen, in his doctoral dissertation (1986), highlighted the issue of incarnational communication and the use of media. William Fore has from a more ecumenical perspective challenged the whole use of media in the United States (Fore 1987). My own writings have focused on media, strategy, and research.

The development of communication as a specific discipline in mission was both helpful and important, but it was also problematic. We can note that Wheaton Graduate School no longer offers a master's degree in communication, and Fuller's School of Intercultural Studies (SIS) no longer emphasizes a concentration in communication. The problem is one of integration and application, as communication needs to be an integrated function in all aspects of missiology. We could take the example of development communication. Outstanding work was done in the Philippines and elsewhere, but as the topic became a theory by itself, it lost its cutting edge. Development communication functions within actual development programs, making them effective. Similarly, communication functions within all disciplines of missiology, and it is extremely important to have communication courses as part of leadership training, international development, pastoral care, psychology, media, public relations, promotion, fund-raising, or any other missiological discipline.

The Bible as a Textbook on Communication

Jesus spent much of his time with his small group of disciples, but a significant amount of time was also spent communicating with the multitudes or, we could say, with mass audiences and large crowds. It was very much a holistic "program," that included plenty of stories (parables), stories the listeners could understand and in which they saw themselves as actors in a drama. Jesus demonstrated his power to them by healing the sick and casting out demons. He fed the thousands who had nothing to eat and he confronted the power structures with prophetic announcements. But when Jesus was alone with his disciples, he taught them "theory." He explained the meaning of things and how the various items fit together in a conceptual framework. Likewise, we need to utilize the created ability to conceptualize and theorize, work with symbols and signs, and arrange concepts into theories that help us understand and visualize processes. For this we can also turn to the Bible.

Charles Kraft writes, "As one who specializes in communication and Bible translation I am increasingly fascinated by the communicational dimensions of the Word of God. I am, of course, convinced that God knew what he was doing communicationally. I am, however, surprised that it has taken us so long to look at the Bible from this point of view. For generations, we who seek to communicate God's Word have looked to the Bible for our message. I am afraid, though, that we have seldom looked to the Bible for our method. I have become personally convinced that the inspiration of the Bible extends both to message and to method" (1979b, 3).

So, based on his study of Scripture, Charles Kraft presents a list of observations concerning God and his communicative activity (1979b, 4-8).

1. God seeks to communicate, not simply to impress people. In God's communication it is the message that is at the center, but the message is combined with the method and the messenger. We have all had the experience of preachers or soloists who have been trying to impress the congregation with their performances, reaping prolonged applauses. When a vehicle of communication calls attention to itself, the message is lost. But in God's communication it is different, and his total communication of himself was in Jesus, who was the image of the invisible God (Jn 1:14; Heb 1:1-3a).

2. God wants to be understood, not simply admired. God is, of course, impressive and greatly to be admired, but if our interaction is simply to admire, the communication is thwarted. In order to be understood, God uses human language, and he took on a human shape. Jesus taught through parables that people understood, relating spiritual truths to their daily lives.

3. *God seeks a response from his hearers, not simply passive listening.* Communication is an interactive process that implies response, and God's interaction with human beings is characteristically in the form of dialogue, rather than monologue. Throughout Scripture we see God's concern for community and relationships. Christ wants us to commit to him and to his church as he has committed himself to us and to the community of believers.

4. *God has revealed in the Scriptures not only what to communicate, but how to communicate it.* We see that God takes the initiative to communicate with us, and enters our frame of reference. God's communication is personal, achieving great impact. It is an approach where the person is challenged and invited to personal discovery.

5. *God is receptor oriented.* In the communication process we have three basic elements: the communicator, the message, and the receptor. Receptor-oriented communicators are careful to bend every effort to meet their receptors where they are. They will choose topics that relate directly to the felt needs of the receptors. They will choose methods of presentation that are appealing to them. They will use language that is maximally intelligible to them.

6. *God's basic method of communication is incarnational.* The ultimate incarnation of God's communication was in Jesus Christ, but the use of human beings to reach other human beings is also an incarnational method. When we look at God's incarnation, we are looking at the center of communication and the essential essence of communication theory. By studying this incarnational communication of God we will not refute human communication, but rather will discover the key that can redeem and restore the human communication process (Jørgensen 1986, 27).

Misconceptions and Miscommunication

In spite of clear receptor-oriented communication theory, it seems quite obvious that much Christian communication practice is based on a one-way concept. This has left us with message-oriented theories of communication, where emphasis is placed on the design of the message rather than on the intended listener. Several books have highlighted the lack of good communication in mission and in the church. The Anglican vicar Gavin Reid gave a strong challenge in his book titled *The Gagging of God* (1969). Charles Kraft started his theoretical journey by observing mission practices in Nigeria in the late fifties, and his first article, "Christian Conversion or Cultural Conversion," appeared in *Practical Anthropology* in 1963. Kraft's earlier writings challenged the miscommunication approaches that were taking place due to what he described as colonial practices.

Most of Kraft's writings on communication are from his years at Fuller's School of World Mission, where he was teaching missionaries and other Christian workers. From his 1971 article "The New Wine of Independence" in *Culture, Communication and Christianity* (2001, 172-176) to the publication of *Communication Theory for Christian Witness* in 1983 (1983b), we see a theory developing. Later publications seem to be revisions of these writings. A significant input to communication is also evident in his major book, *Christianity in Culture* (1979a). Kraft often has a humorous way of pointing toward problems with mission and church, which is evident from his "Ten Myths Concerning Communication" (1983b, 3-37).

Myth 1: "Hearing the gospel with one's ears is equivalent to being reached with the gospel." Often we have a far too simplistic understanding of the words in Romans 10:17: "faith comes by hearing" (NIV). What is said is often not what is heard, and the actual meaning created in the minds of the receiver is often quite different from the intention of the speaker. The tone of voice, the body language of the speaker, the dress, the context, and the background of the listener all influence the interpretation of the words received.

Myth 2: "The words of the Bible are so powerful that all that people need to bring them to Christ is to be exposed to hearing or reading the Bible." There is no magic to the words themselves, and if they are not understood, then the Holy Spirit will not be able to illuminate the minds of the readers. A King James Version may be beautiful language, but if it does not communicate, then the person will hear nothing. This writer has observed that in most churches, very few people pay attention to Bible readings. It is a mere ceremony.

Myth 3: "Preaching is God's ordained means of communicating the gospel." Preaching is basically monologue, and if communication is to take place through monologues, then the finer points of communication theory must be adhered to. One way is to work with microphone distance, tone of voice, or a dialogue approach where a response may be elicited.

Myth 4: "The sermon is an effective vehicle for bringing about life change." The sermon will never stand alone, but will need to be integrated into a wider communication strategy, including life involvement, if life change is to take place.

Myth 5: "There is one best way to communicate the gospel." Communication tools or channels all have their distinct advantages and disadvantages. A canned approach based on one medium or specific approach will never succeed in the long run.

Myth 6: "The key to effective communication is the precise formulation of the message." The receptor has the final word regarding interpretation and application. The question is, Is the concern for precise formulation for the benefit of the speaker, for an academic, or for a nonliterate farmer?

Myth 7: "Words contain their meanings." There are numerous ways of saying yes and many more ways of saying no. The receptor will interpret according to his or her understanding of the word. In Thai, for example, the word used for God is the same word as used for the king. Since Buddhism does not have a concept of God, then the word will have a completely different interpretation in the mind of the receptor. The pronouncement of a word, or the emphasis given to a word, can also completely change the message.

Myth 8: "What people really need is more information." The problem is often one of relevance and motivation. Good news needs to be experienced as good news.

Myth 9: "The Holy Spirit will make up for all mistakes if we are sincere, spiritual, and prayerful enough." It is fully accepted that the final results will depend on the Holy Spirit, but God has made his communication go through human communicators who can enhance or actually block the message.

Myth 10: "As Christians we should severely restrict our contacts with 'evil' people and refrain from going to 'evil' places lest we 'lose our testimony' and ruin our witness." What did Jesus do? He spent time with sinners, communicating with them, so that he might lead them to the truth.

Missiological Communication Principles Learned So Far

Based on our study and experience, we can conclude that an adequate communication theory for missiology will need to include the following elements:

Missiological communication starts with the commission given by Christ. The scriptural mandate as well as spiritual foundations must be the starting point for mission. We have a clear goal to communicate the gospel in such a way that people will want to listen, understand, follow, and commit themselves. It is Christ's mission, and we are the agents of that mission. The real challenge of the world is therefore the challenge of Christ who is the Lord of the mission. With him as our model the incarnation is the method and the cross is the price. *Go therefore into all the world and communicate the gospel* (Mk 16:15).

Missiological communication places the person at the center. The final and complete communication of God to humanity was in the form of a human person: the incarnation of Jesus Christ. Similarly, the Christian communicator needs to learn how to communicate as a human being (Kraft 1991a, 38-51).

The commission given by Jesus was a person-based commission: *"When the Holy Spirit has come upon you, you shall be my witnesses . . ."* (Acts 1:8). Jesus gave us the example by becoming a real human being, participating in our affairs (Phil 2:7; Jn 1:14). In him, the message and the medium became one. What gives communication its character is not only the message but the messenger. For example, the credibility of a piece of literature is associated with the way it is distributed and with the person who is handing it out. Often an audiocassette is listened to because a friend has introduced it. The person speaking on radio or through television will be subject to all the dimensions of personal communication if the message is to be trusted.

Missiological communication is receptor oriented. The term *receptor* points to its singular assumption and is preferred by this writer. The term was coined by Kraft, and he uses it extensively in his writings (e.g., 1991a, 67-74, 92, 151-153). The term *audience oriented*, as used by James Engel (1979), could also be used to indicate that there is usually more than one receiver. The "target audience" is usually a people group with individuals who have a certain degree of homogeneity.

Jesus is the prime example of receptor-oriented communication. In John 3 we have the memorable conversation between Jesus and Nicodemus. The receptor, Nicodemus, was a highly educated man, a philosopher, a man with status, someone who would be embarrassed if seen talking alone with Jesus. Jesus showed his acceptance and empathy by sacrificing his sleep to meet with Nicodemus when nobody would see them. The very language Jesus used shows respect for Nicodemus and an understanding of his needs. Jesus aptly entered into that frame of reference and from there led Nicodemus into new discoveries. A similar approach can be seen in the following chapter, John 4, where the receptor was an illiterate, low-status Samaritan woman.

The way Jesus used parables is another illustration. Parables were created out of the everyday life of the people who listened. In a parable, the audience become players, and as such each one discovers new truths and principles.

The sovereignty of the audience is a God-given capacity (Engel 1979, 318). Our missiological communication will therefore always ask questions like, Who is my listener? Where is the person? What are the needs? How can we meet such needs? (Søgaard 1993, 99).

Charles Kraft has given a ten-point outline of what he sees as important regarding receptors (1981). Receptors have felt needs, but they are already part of reference groups to which they are committed. Based on their background, needs, and interests, receptors will also be constructing meanings from the messages received. They will be evaluating the pros and cons of the new ideas as they filter the incoming signals as to relevance, usefulness, and acceptability.

Missiological communication is centered on community. The church is God's primary agent for world evangelization. It is the community of believers that demonstrates the reality of the incarnation (Dyrness 1983). The calling is to mission, and this mission can reach its highest potential if media is rightly used in the context of a local church. It is the local church that best can provide permanency and continuity to our efforts, providing permanent structures for effective communication.

For example, television and radio may bring about dramatic movement in the spiritual growth process of an individual, but they alone cannot provide the basis for development at every stage of the process. They need to be integrated with other ministries, particularly with the outreach of the local churches, if ultimate goals are to be achieved.

Missiological communication is a process. The different mission approaches can be used at different stages in the communication process, depending on the need of the receptor and the capabilities of the channel. For example, radio can be used at several stages of the decision process, and it can be programmed to communicate within a person's limited latitude of acceptance/rejection.

The listener/receptor will be experiencing an ongoing decision-making process, beginning at the time of initial exposure and awareness and continuing through various stages leading to full acceptance of the message. During this process the needs of the audience will change and the communicator must adapt his or her methods and programs accordingly. At each stage the purpose is to elicit cognitive, affective, and behavioral changes. Our communication messages must be designed as a process that corresponds to the needs of a receptor at his or her present position or stage in life and the needs and problems faced at that time.

There have been a number of attempts to describe the spiritual process that people live through (Engel 1979; Søgaard 1975, 1993). It is the communicator who needs to adapt to such a process, so that communication messages are relevant to the receivers.

Missiological communication needs good research and information. Research is like a flashlight. It can guide us through the maze of multiple decisions and lead us through the darkness by throwing light on the path ahead of us. Research does not provide us with the answers but does provide us with the information on which decisions can be based, making receptor-oriented communication possible. Research, in addition to sharpening the vision, also helps monitor and evaluate a ministry by providing effectiveness measures.

We cannot prepare good and relevant messages without basic information about the people and their context, and such knowledge can only be obtained through formal or informal research. For any receptor-oriented approach, for the setting of goals, and for intelligent and effective planning processes, we need good information.

If we do not have relevant information on the audience, we may easily be tempted to turn away from the so-called hard and unresponsive fields and target what appear to be more responsive areas. However, before making such a determination we should attempt to discover the reasons for "unresponsiveness." What are the barriers and how were they created? Have we really taken time to understand our listeners? Are we using a language they readily understand? Have we failed to incarnate the message in flesh and blood?

Though research principles and methodologies are readily available, the concept of research as relevant to ministry has not always been accepted by Christian communicators. Sometimes a theological justification for such a position is given. Research needs to become a nonthreatening daily phenomenon that we all engage in as we seek information from or about each other. In the interest of accountability and good stewardship, we should have no theological problems in viewing research as a legitimate tool of missiological communication.

Missiological communication uses approaches that are based on the cultural context of the receptors. As human beings we are totally immersed in our culture. This limits communication as well as makes it possible. Even though the similarities that unite people are much greater than the differences that separate them, the differences provide the greatest challenge to Christian communicators. Essentially, we use the same symbols of communication, but such symbols may have radically different meanings. An intercultural perspective will always accept the fact that different cultural perceptions give different views of reality.

   Much of our evangelism and mission takes place across cultural boundaries; therefore the question of meaning in communication will need more attention than the specific forms of communication utilized. We must begin with a high view of culture, not prejudging as anti-Christian aspects which God can use or which may even be given by him. God seems to view human culture primarily as a vehicle to be used by him and his people for Christian communication purposes.

   An intercultural understanding will automatically lead us to investigate local and traditional media and art forms. This does not mean that we will be limited to folk media, but that such media will be included. Nor will we, for example, impose a seven-tone musical scale on a people who traditionally sing in a five-tone scale. A number of groups in Asian countries, such as India, Thailand, and Indonesia, have demonstrated the viability of using traditional forms of dance and drama in evangelization. If such ministries are well integrated with local churches, the impact is enormous as the gospel is expressed in the local cultural forms and communication symbols.

Conclusion

   There are many challenges facing Christian communicators. As we are dealing with an applied discipline, it is of utmost importance for all missiological disciplines to integrate communication thinking and courses into training programs and mission activities. We need extensive research to develop appropriate and effective communication approaches.

   One of the primary challenges is the fact that we are living in an increasingly nonreading world. Yet, when we look at Christian ministry, we are primarily looking at linear, literacy-based approaches. We urgently need to develop means of communication for nonreading people. In addition to the nonreading populations of the world, there is a rapidly increasing segment of humanity made up of people who, though officially classified as readers, nevertheless increasingly use sound and visual media as their primary means of nonlinear approaches to communication (Søgaard 2001).

   There is also an increasing number of poor people in the world, people who to a large extent are outside our reach, and who are also nonreaders. Our Bibles are not relevant for them, and their economic situation makes most Christian communication products and programs outside their reach. Yet, the call of Christ was to communicate good news to the poor (Lk 4:18).

7

Negotiating the Gospel Cross-Culturally

The Contributions of Intercultural Communication to Missiology

ROBERTA R. KING

Communicating the gospel in today's global world is complex. It must be bravely and wisely negotiated for persuasive effectiveness. Cultural factors heighten even further the complexity of creating an understanding of the Christian faith. Missiology has long recognized the seminal importance of intercultural communication to the discipline. This chapter addresses the question "What is at present the primary contribution of intercultural communication to missiology?"

I will start with a story that began on the far side of the Ngong Hills. Maasai *manyattas* (homesteads) made of mud and straw boldly stand in the stark, windy, and dry setting overlooking Kenya's Great Rift Valley. Our task was simple that day. We just needed to buy two cowhides from the local Maasai. We were making traditional African harps[1] in the Christian Music Ministry course for Daystar University and cowhide was the required covering. As we approached the *manyatta*, I was struck by the contrast between this rugged area with its lack of running water and electricity and the comfortable city life in the neighboring city of Nairobi.

Our first task was to get someone's attention. Perhaps they were days away with their herds searching for water. After looking around, we found a woman who was willing to talk with us. It turned out that I had some major lessons to learn in bargaining for cowhides; my negotiation skills would involve a steep learning curve. It was not a matter of simply asking to buy the two hides. Rather, there was a long period of greetings, establishing our identities, and building relationship with one another, followed by the explanation of the need for the cowhides. When the initial amount of money was suggested, the woman laughed hilariously at the pitiful amount we were offering. How did we think we could

---

[1]Many East African peoples have their own indigenous harps. In this case we were making *kipugandets*, harps from the Kalenjin people of Kenya. Cowhide is used to cover the sounding chamber.

pay so little? "Don't you know how valuable these are to me and my family?" was the shaming question that came back to us. We backed off, and asked questions about the drought and the state of their cattle. After discussing this for a while, the woman responded with her ridiculously exorbitant price. To which we laughed hilariously! This time, we moved to asking about the woman's life and her family before we raised our offer just a bit higher. To which the woman once again showed her displeasure followed by lowering her price slightly. The negotiation continued with each of the participants changing their price only minimally with each cycle. When we had finally seesawed the amount down to a price agreeable to both parties, we completed the transaction. In the end, each party had learned something about the other: a relationship had been established. I was amazed as I looked at my watch. It had taken two hours to negotiate for two hides! And even then, I was not sure we had gotten an especially good price.

Communication is complex and multifaceted. Popularly thought of as the mere sending of information, communication requires negotiating between peoples for understanding. Such negotiation does not move forward in linear fashion. Just as I experienced in negotiating for cowhides, creating understanding and coming to agreement proceeds in a cyclical, somewhat jigsaw fashion. By moving into the Maasai woman's context, we had found ourselves negotiating on her terms. It was a cyclical process determined by cultural rules. Similarly, communicating the Good News of Jesus Christ is a complex process, one that carries long-term significance for the sake of the Kingdom of God. Although purchasing cowhides does not compare with the grave task of introducing the person of Jesus Christ to the peoples of the world, many parallel principles are at work as people seek to establish relationships and communicate the Christian message. As a process, communication is regulated by cultural norms, perceptions, and expectations. Pervasive at every level, "culture influences communication" (Dodd 1998, 4). The discipline of intercultural communication takes into account the multiple components of communication involved when people attempt to make themselves understood in differing contexts. These dimensions, or arenas of negotiation, are critical to missiology with its goal of making Jesus Christ known and understood in all cultural contexts. In this chapter, we investigate the theories, components, and *praxis* of intercultural communication that contribute significantly to the field of missiology.

Intercultural Communication: Negotiating Differences

Missionaries today find themselves functioning in a global world where there is an increasingly reflexive connectivity with worldwide communities. The ease of the Internet and the widespread use of English and popular culture through the Internet foster a sense of a macro global culture being created. Yet, as scholars note, "local cultural patterns do not simply disappear" (Ott and Netland 2006, 21). Rather than one macro global culture, theorists speak of "glocal" cultures where cultural diversity exists on multiple levels acknowledged both globally and locally (Berger and Huntington 2002). Instead of reducing cultural encounters to a minimum, the impact of globalization is to heighten them on a plethora of levels. Thus, in today's world, missionaries function as " 'inbetweeners,' standing between different worlds, seeking to build bridges of understanding, mediating relationship[s] and negotiating partnerships in ministry . . . Increasingly, missionaries are bridge persons, culture mediators, who stand between different human worlds" (Hiebert 2006, 297).

Missionaries are almost always communicating across cultures. The concept of bridging between cultures and overcoming gaps lies at the heart of intercultural communication (Gudykunst 2004). Kraft takes up this point, noting that "we who specialize in communication theory spend much of our energy seeking to understand how communicational bridges are built and how to cross them" (1991a, 3). Thus, the study of intercultural communication acknowledges the multiple gaps that exist between differing peoples within their unique cultural settings. Recognizing that culture is a primary variable in the communication process, intercultural scholars research "how culture pervades what we are, how we act, how we think, and how we talk and listen" (Dodd 1998, 4). Focusing on "the influence of cultural variability and diversity on interpersonally oriented communication outcomes" (ibid.), we see differences and contrasts between people emerge as a central theme in the discipline (Gudykunst 2004; Rogers and Steinfatt 1999; Dodd 1998; Kraft 1991a).

Ultimately, the major question of particular significance to missionaries is "How do people who differ from one another learn to interact in meaningful and understandable ways?" In order to deal with such questions, scholars have identified major elements that impact the intercultural communication process. Among them are differences in communication and social style, worldview, customs, expectations, rules, roles, and myths. Additionally, a key component to the discipline is experiential and participatory learning. In order to really understand intercultural communication, one must experience it (Rogers and Steinfatt 1999, 69) by entering into new cultural contexts. Learning to negotiate for cowhides among the Maasai, for example, must be experienced and practiced in order to refine such interactions. As Dodd argues, "Intercultural communication indicates what to do when we encounter . . . differences, not just their existence" (Dodd 1998, 8). Studying theoretical models and individual components of communication fosters the possibility of learning to communicate appropriately and effectively within varying cultural contexts.

The Quest for Appropriate Communication: Models

An understanding of how communication works is essential when missionaries move out to "make disciples of all nations" (Mt 28:19 NIV) by initiating relationships with peoples of differing cultural backgrounds. The missiological question is "How does one learn to interact with people in culturally appropriate ways that will earn a hearing for the gospel?" Communication theorists have developed a series of models based on three fundamental components in the process: the sender, the message, and the receptor (Shannon and Weaver 1949).[2] Varying components are emphasized in each model in an attempt to comprehend communication in all its various aspects. Two major categories have emerged and are generally categorized as the code model and the inferential model, or relevance theory (Shaw and Van Engen 2003, 108).

Two code models of communication. The code model lies at the foundation of communication theory. Among the many code models that have emerged, both the interaction and transaction models are of particular significance to missiology. Interaction models emphasize that communication is "a dynamic process whereby human behavior, both verbal and nonverbal, is perceived and responded to" (Samovar and Porter 1972, 272). Note that the modes of communication are expanded from verbal and written to the full multiple set of human means of interconnecting. This model also fosters "feedback" between both the sender and receiver as a critical means for negotiating to a point of understanding. Thus, communication is not unidirectional as in the "hypodermic needle model" of communication (Rogers with Shoemaker 1971). Nor is it is static. Rather, communication is dynamic, ongoing, everchanging, and continuous. Kraft, in *Christianity in Culture,* builds upon this model when he argues that the goal of a communication event is to bring about interaction in such a way that the understanding of the receptor corresponds with the intent of the communicator (1979a, 394). The purpose behind the interaction is to influence people and achieve understanding of the intended message. Significantly, in interaction models, meaning is not in the message, but in people (Berlo 1960, 175). In other words, receptors perceive the content of a message through their own eyes and decide the meaning of a message or communication event. The word *rubber*, for example, can refer to the elastic material consisting of dried sap from various tropical trees, or in Britain, it can refer to a school eraser used to correct written mistakes. The context and language (British English vs. American English) helps determine the meaning. In the end, however, the receptor is "sovereign" (Engel 1979).

The transaction model moves beyond the mere relationships between source, message, and receptor to focus on the process of creating a meaning (Jørgensen 1986, 28). Building on the concept that meanings are in the message-user (Berlo 1960, 175), Barnlund argues that the aim of communication is "not a reaction to something, nor an interaction with something, but a transaction in which (humans) invent and attribute meanings to realize (their) purpose" (Jørgensen 1986, 29). The focus shifts to the sender and the receptor who now become initiator and interactant. Both are interactive participants.

The transaction model includes activity prior to communication and the effects after the communication event. The initiator conceptualizes ideas and determines the intent of the message before encoding and sending the message to the interactant. During communication, the interactant goes through a decoding pro-

---

[2]Shannon and Weaver are credited with developing the basic model that continues to be foundational for the field.

cess that culminates in determining meaning and deciding on the subsequent thought and action to take. Viewing communication as transactional evokes the need to realize that communication is continuous, unrepeatable, irreversible, and involves the total person (King 1989, 59). Meaning is being negotiated between the initiator and the interactant. During worship events, for example, or all-night celebrations such as in Africa, multiple transactions are taking place as all participants (initiators and interactants), dialogue, eat, sing, and dance together. Missiologically, this model affirms the critical importance of interactive relationships in Christian witness that foster a growing involvement with people within their own context.

The inference model of communication. The inference model focuses its attention on the importance of context by emphasizing and developing the notion of a "cognitive environment." Based on work by Sperber and Wilson in the mid-1980s, the model considers "how an audience perceives an author's intent" (Shaw and Van Engen 2003, 110). The model asserts that communicators must make the intention or "ostention" of their communication clear in a way that receptors are able to "infer" what the communicator intended. Furthermore, communication is considered "relevant" when an author's intent matches the recipient's inferences.

This requires an alignment of communication signs that "fit with both the communicator's and the receptor's sense of what, for them, is reality—that is, there is a context that provides understandability of communication" (Shaw and Van Engen 2003, 110). Thus, relevance theory perceives "meaning as originating in the mind of the speaker, but does not perceive that meaning to be fully contained in the verbal stimulus" (Hill 2003, 20). In contrast to early code models, the forms of communication (that is, written and/or verbal), are not the only determinants of meaning. Rather, the audience's contexts, or sets of assumptions and life experiences, influence the interpretation of a message and play as important a role as the text (Hill 2003, ii).[3]

Relevance theory has become particularly significant in Bible translation where the focus is on presenting a message that facilitates the audience's interpreting, or inferring, the intended meaning of the author. Hill's work among the Adioukrou of Côte d'Ivoire (Hill 2003), for example, explored the contextual assumptions of four Gospel texts of the original receptors and then compared them with those of the Adioukrou. Contextual materials were then prepared to compensate for the lack of the original biblical assumptions on the part of the Adioukrou. The purpose of ensuring an understanding of a message lies at the foundation of the inferential model, appropriately asking in the case of Bible translation: "How would it have been communicated using the present context?" (Shaw and Van Engen 2003, 112). Smith argues that *creating understanding* (1992) of a message is the goal of communication; relevance theory purports to do so at a deep, cognitive level.

---

[3]*Context*, also referred to as *cognitive environment*, aligns itself well with worldview, a critical area of missiological study.

Arenas of Intercultural Negotiation

While communication models help us to understand the process of facilitating the understanding of a message, intercultural communication also brings to the discussion the pervasive influence of culture to each component in the process. The nature and characteristics of each component are investigated and significantly expanded. In an attempt to avoid miscommunication or creating barriers to the gospel, each component becomes an arena of intercultural negotiation, ultimately providing missiology with a refined approach to effectively communicate the Good News of Jesus. The following section limits its discussion to five critical arenas that are particularly significant to missiology.

Negotiating the world of the receptor. At the heart of missiology lies the concern to enter into the receptor's world in order to create understanding of the Good News of the Kingdom. In his major work on communication, *Communication Theory for Christian Witness*, Kraft emphasizes the critical importance of the receptor as the key participant (1991a, 68-80). Indeed, if participants are to "create and share information with one another as they move toward a mutual understanding" (Rogers and Steinfatt 1999, 133), missionaries need to understand basic characteristics of receptors and how they function in society. Kraft, for example, posits that receptors have felt needs that are very personal, so personal that "the communicator must gain permission to enter the respondent's private space by dealing with what the respondent permits to be dealt with" (Kraft 1991a, 69). In negotiating the world of the receptor, the communicator must therefore build credibility with the respondent, scratching where it itches before moving to deeper-level issues. He notes, "Felt needs are . . . the touchstones from which life change can be recommended and accomplished. And the Christian message is designed to change life" (Kraft 1991a, 69-70). Learning to identify felt needs directs the paths that missionaries take in bringing people to understand who Jesus Christ is. Intertwined with the felt needs of receptors is the notion that "receptors are active." This includes the "granting or withholding of permission for a communicator to enter what might be termed their communicational space. Since communication is a transaction, it proceeds only at the permission of the transactor" (Kraft 1991a, 72). Despite finely crafted verbal or written messages, communicators often find that their messages have been rejected because permission to be heard has not been granted in the first place. Receptors actively decide what they will do with a message.

Becoming receptor oriented in doing mission lies at the core of missiology. Not only does it require an understanding of the nature and characteristics of receptors, but it also involves learning cultural patterns and cultural systems of communication in order to effectively transmit a message.

Negotiating the message via signal systems. All of life involves communication. We are communicating whether we are speaking or not, for communication employs all five senses: hearing, seeing, touching, tasting, and smelling. As

scholars note, "Human beings . . . draw on a multitude of resources to intercon-
nect with each other and in so doing interactively create their human world"
(Finnegan 2002, 8). These multiple resources are brought together to encode
messages as a means of passing information and intent. Although the verbal and
written systems are the most commonly recognized, intercultural communication
has specialized in recognizing the crucial dynamics of nonverbal communication, taking the analysis to deeper levels. As Kraft argues, "Indeed, often the
verbal symbols conveying the content of the message are to the total message
only what the tip is to the iceberg" (1991a, 94). A minimum of twelve signal
systems are used in the communication process, including those that are less
conscious but of deeper impact. These are systems such as artifactual, audio,
kinesic, tactile, and olfactory (Smith 1992, 144-165). Each system varies culturally in its use, function, and signification, making interpretation of a message
more complex than most people realize. Furthermore, several systems[4] are used
simultaneously to communicate messages with the potential of contradicting their
intent when inappropriately matched (Kraft 1983a, 76). This is due to the fact
that nonverbal communication is less intentional and self-conscious than verbal
or written communication. Whether the communicator is aware of them or not,
these signals influence the meaning of a message at deep levels. In the West, for
example, waving is seen as a friendly greeting. In Uganda, however, a policeman
waving his hand at waist level is a command to stop the car, a command that must
be obeyed or the transgressor will face severe consequences. It is essential for
missionaries to know and understand how the signal systems vary between cultures in order to avoid misunderstandings between people of differing cultures.

Acknowledging the critical impact of the nonverbal components in the communication process has led missiologists to recognize the appropriateness and
profound impact of musical and other art forms in negotiating the gospel cross-
culturally. Indeed, musical and other art forms like dance, drama, and storytelling
serve as foundational communication systems that play central roles in people's
lives. An emerging arena of missiology relates to contextualization. Shaw argues, for example, that "a group may use dance forms that they incorporate into
an all-night ritual. Such holy dance may be the appropriate communication vehicle to associate the vertical and horizontal planes of the communication environment. Scripture is full of such dancing" (Shaw and Van Engen 2003, 115).
Likewise, Kraft views drama as a "combination of codes that should be more
often and more effectively used by Christian communicators [with its unique
ability to] highlight the personal, living, experiential dimensions of Christian
messages" (1991a, 114).

Music is another signal system. Ethnomusicology studies the music in relation to culture by addressing music, dance, and drama in terms of local and global cultural variables, their impact, and significance. As an emerging field of
missiological study that specializes in nonverbal communication, ethnomusicology
is being taken more seriously for Christian witness. When practiced within cul-

---

[4]*Channels* is the more common technical term for signal systems.

turally appropriate parameters, the arts carry great potential for communicating the gospel with profound impact. The key is that these forms must represent God's intention for humanity and remain faithful to the message of Scripture. Such forms have the potential to speak at a deep level within the receptor's perception and are processed through a people's worldview or message filter.

Non-Western arts and music are used in ways that differ from the West. Among the Nyarafolo people of Côte d'Ivoire, West Africa, a Muslim mother dances to the new story songs about Jesus based on the Gospel of Luke. As she dances, she is indicating her willingness to identify with the stories, to relate to them, and ultimately to her Christian son. Rejoicing in the openness to the message, her son eagerly takes the opportunity to continue the dialogue via the song-*cum*-dance. In East Africa, on the other hand, the Maasai *eoko* song form provides an opportunity for a community to flesh out misunderstandings and disagreements within the song performance. Having failed to gain a hearing of the story of the prodigal son with his family, a Maasai theology student discovered that the *eoko* song form fostered reception of the Christian message. Amazed, he exclaimed, "Music and dancing is one of the best avenues of teaching, preaching, and formulating theological thoughts among the Maasai. Music involved my family in the story and opened the door to a good reception" (Pulei 2000, 27).

Negotiating worldviews. Worldview consists of people's beliefs, values, and assumptions that serve as a message filtering system leading to the inferring of meaning. How does the cross-cultural witness negotiate these worldviews that function at deep levels within people's interpretation mechanisms? We limit our discussion here to two key concepts. First, we must realize that worldviews operate at both group and individual levels. Collective cultural consciousness is an important concept defined "as an embedded memory of historical events that are particularly significant to a given cultural group" (Rogers and Steinfatt 1999, 3). Momentous historical events serve as defining moments in a group's development and are automatically interpreted through that group's collective historical and worldview lenses. The holocaust for Judaism, the Christian crusades for Muslims, the history of slavery for African Americans, and the destruction of Native American cultures are examples of collective cultural events that contribute significantly to the interpretation filters of those groups. An awareness of how the major features of these events are understood is required to help shape the Christian message appropriately for each community.

Cross-cultural workers must learn to negotiate values between people of differing cultures at interpersonal levels. Lingenfelter and Mayers, in their book *Ministering Cross-Culturally*, address "the tension and conflict that missionaries, pastors, and laypersons experience when they attempt to work with people who come from different cultural and social backgrounds" (1986, 9). Challenging readers to adapt their personal lifestyles to build effective bridges of communication, Lingenfelter and Mayers help readers to identify their own value biases with the hope of increasing sensitivity to others with differing values. Contrasting value differences are addressed and include (1) time- vs. event-oriented persons, (2) dichotomistic vs. holistic thinking, (3) declarative vs. interrogative lifestyle, (4) task orientation vs. person orientation, (5) status vs. achievement focus, and (6) concealment vs. willingness to expose vulnerability. Learning to recognize and navigate such cultural differences helps cross-cultural Christian workers to avoid misunderstandings and facilitates a closer agreement and understanding.

Negotiating meaning and understanding. Worldviews determine meaning at deep levels. Even though messages are encoded via signal systems and exchanged with an intent to create meaning(s) among receptors, it is the person receiving the message who decides its meaning. Thus, intercultural communication has developed a person-oriented theory of meaning. That is, specific meanings are not housed within particular words or phrases. Rather, they are contained within people. As Berlo argues, "Meanings are not in the message. They are in the message-users" (1960, 175). Thus, meanings are not transmittable between people, only messages are. As Smith explains further, "Meaning is always personal and unique to each individual. Similar meanings are held by different people, but precise meanings are personal. There is no way to transfer meaning directly from teacher to student, from employer to employee, or from preacher to congregation. Meaning is developed indirectly" (Smith 1992, 63).

Therefore, careful communicators of the gospel must not assume that others interpret their messages the same way as they do. To tell a non-Christian financier that "Jesus saves" could be interpreted that Jesus has a savings account in a bank. The message of salvation must be carefully defined and expressed in ways that bring about closer meaning to the intended message. In truth, successful communication occurs when people negotiate the meaning of a statement (Adler and Rodman 2006, 78). Meaning arises out of a dynamic interactive relationship between the actual message transmitted, the signal systems used, the environment in which the message is transmitted, the people who receive it, the relationship between the people, and the manner of transmitting the message. In the end, however, it is the receptors who make the final decision on what the message means to them within their own context and cognitive environment.

Negotiating relationships. Messages do not consist of content only. Scholars assert that messages are made up of both content and relationship dimensions: "The content dimension of messages refers to the information in the messages (e.g., what is said). The relationship dimension of messages is inferred from how the messages are transmitted (including the specific words used), and it deals with how the participants are relating to each other. The way we communicate offers a definition of the relationship between us" (Gudykunst 2004, 10).

A dynamic interaction takes place between the message and the relationships existing between the participants within the communication process. As Dodd explains, "By its nature, intercultural communication assumes not only the message, but the social relationship associated with an interaction" (Dodd 1998, 21). A special relationship, for example, had to be established with the Maasai woman before I and my colleague could negotiate for the cowhides. What relational dynamics were at play in that simple interaction? How did the Maasai woman relate to an Anglo-Westerner and a non-Maasai Kenyan? Did she perceive the Anglo-Westerner as extremely rich and was the Kenyan from a friendly or hostile Kenyan ethnic community? Undoubtedly, relationship played a determining factor in the bargaining process. Hence, an inextricable bond links message with relationship. Such message-relationship bonds operate to determine whether the message is received at all, how it is interpreted and acted upon. In this sense, meaning results not only from what is said, but also from who says it (Dodd 1998, 22).

The gospel is a person-message (Jn 1:1). For the Christian communicator, the link between message and relationship is particularly critical. As Kraft argues, the one who brings the gospel message is the major component of the Christian message that is communicated (1991a, 43). Consequently, the missiological question now centers on how to become personal in order to gain credible and trustworthy relationships that align with the import of the Good News of Jesus Christ. Relationships that make the Christian message a visible, living reality are essential and are reflective of the incarnation where Jesus "lived among us" (Jn 1:14b). Note that God through Jesus Christ did not impersonally communicate God's love and interest in people. Rather, he became involved in the lives of people, communicating himself within the contexts of their daily activities and relationships, speaking their language, making himself vulnerable, identifying personally with individuals (Jn 4), and interacting with people in one specific location on earth. Furthermore, he did not just speak the message; he became the message. Although he occasionally delivered sermons (monologues) and dialogued with persons around him, it was the totality of his life involvement that impacted early believers to follow him. He demonstrated the primary means of communicating God's love by living among the Hebrew people within their local cultural context. Since the essence of the gospel is about relationship with God, it is imperative that the dissemination of information about God not be divorced from the relational reality of knowing God through Jesus Christ and through his witnesses.

Conclusion

Jesus was an intercultural communicator of the gospel. In his incarnation he was fully God and fully human, and thus he modeled a way to witness to the glory of the Father within human social contexts. He participated fully in the lives of his receptors in order to make the Good News available through his death and resurrection. Being God himself, he knew and understood both the spiritual and social dynamics of his earthly encounter. In Jesus Christ, God gave us the supreme example of receptor-oriented missional interaction. The discipline of intercultural communication provides theories, models, and tools of *praxis* that help us to understand our social roles in becoming incarnate in another culture. Intercultural communication fosters dynamic cross-cultural negotiation of the gospel for the sake of the Kingdom of God.

8

Communication Theory in Missiology

Where to from Here ?

KNUD JØRGENSEN

The dynamic of Christianity . . . is not in the sacredness of cultural forms— even those that God once used. The Christian dynamic is in the venturesome- ness of participating with God in the transformation of contemporary cultural forms to serve more adequately as vehicles for God's interaction with human beings. What we seek is a Christianity equivalent in its dynamics to that displayed in the pages of the New Testament. (Kraft 1979a, 382)

In all of this the primary commitment of the church should be to communi- cate the good news of Christ . . . purity in the church is never guaranteed by institutional arrangements. The church is truly itself when it communicates Christ. This therefore must be the emphasis of the liquid church. (Ward 2002, 71)

Let Missiology Challenge Theology!

A Norwegian colleague, Notto Thelle, to whom I shall return later, uses the term "the double conversion of the missionary" to describe his own life and his encounter with people of a different faith in Japan. This encounter changed him as a missionary and made his Christian faith unfold in a larger world. I have experienced something similar in another part of the world: ten years in Ethiopia and many additional years in close contact with China and Latin America have changed my life, my faith, and my theology. And my friendship with Charles Kraft played a key role in my double conversion. When I first met him as one of his doctoral students in 1974, I was a typical European, Lutheran, conservative, evangelical theologian. Kraft became a kind of midwife for transforming me into a missiologist. Other factors along the road of conversion were my meeting with the East-African Revival and its call to live in the light and my encounter with growing and transformed churches and Christians in Ethiopia and China.

Over the years this has made me realize that our Western theology continues in Constantinian bondage. This bondage implies a deep crisis of communication (also noted by Hiebert in this volume). It was Kraft who, together with others, made me understand that the way out of that bondage and into a new future was to let missiology challenge and even replace my Western theology. The Asian missiologist Hwa Yung claims in his book *Mangoes or Bananas?* (1997, 19) that "any authentic indigenous theology—indeed, any theology for that matter—must be missiological and pastoral in its fundamental conception" (ibid.). Missiological means that which relates to the mission of the church, and pastoral refers to the process of nurturing the growth of converts and bringing them and their churches to maturity in faith and witness. This implies that the pastoral is linked to the missiological: "If the above is correct, then every theology must ultimately be judged by its efficacy in enhancing or obstructing the mission of Christ, the *missio Dei*" (ibid.).

I recall being part of a doctoral course with Kraft in 1978 where we gave feedback to a draft of *Christianity in Culture* (1979a). That course made me realize that major parts of the theology I inhaled as a student in Copenhagen in the sixties were quite far from being "authentic indigenous theology." Rather, it was a theology developed within the Constantinian era and therefore characterised by the fact that the church was more preoccupied with "Christianization" than with mission. Today all of us staunch, conservative Lutherans, along with folks from other established churches, need to admit that the *Corpus Christianum*—the idea of a unity made up of state, religion, and culture as the canopy for the church's work—no longer functions. We are at the end of an era that has lasted since Constantine's state church and church tradition in the fourth century. This calls for a dramatic readjustment process. The idea of the *Corpus Christianum* symbolized a wedlock between the church and the holders of power, which, in different ways, turned a missionary church into a pastoral institution. As the state religion of Rome, the Christian faith spread rapidly to the provinces of the empire, but over time it became the established civil religion and the society's administrator of religious meaning. The church's structure adopted the shape of the society's structure, with parochial churches, and a clear division between *clerici* (priests) and *idiotes* (laypeople). Faith was practiced by taking part in the arrangements of the church, and evangelization was replaced with (forced) "Christianization." Breaking with the Constantinian tradition and its access to power and influence is not easy (see, for example, Guder 2000, 113, 140). In other parts of the world a break with the Constantinian forms of the church has already taken place, or it was not present in the first place. To Westerners, especially in Western Europe and Scandinavia, it has in some places and countries become an obstacle to mission because it conceals the fact that we are not, in fact, in a missionary situation. "Constantinianism is a hard habit to break. It is particularly hard when it seems that we do so much good by remaining in 'power.' It is hard to break because all our categories have been set by the church's establishment as a necessary part of Western civilization" (Hauerwas 1991, 18).

With reference to what I mentioned above about the missionary's double conversion, Darrell L. Guder, uses the term the "continuing conversion of the church" (Guder 2000). This conversion is related to rethinking theology, evangelization, worship, leadership, and structures. Most importantly, it demands undertaking measures against the gospel reductionism within the church. The early church went from being a movement to becoming an institution. Constantine's church replaced the understanding of the gospel as an event with the formulation of a defined faith system consisting of truths. The Kingdom of God was conceived as the eternity that awaits a Christian after death. Salvation was given to the individual by the church, particularly through the sacraments. On the basis of these gospel reductions, the organizational structure of the church was transformed into a state religion, and the administrator of religious meaning became the basis for society (ibid., 103). Likewise, according to Guder, the reformation and pietism helped people grasp the grace of God in a new way, but they may also have reduced the gospel to a matter of salvation for the individual only. "The benefits of salvation are separated from the reason for which we receive God's grace in Christ: to empower us as God's people to become Christ's witnesses. This fundamental dichotomy between the benefits of the gospel and the mission of the gospel constitutes the most profound reductionism of the gospel" (ibid., 120). Salvation is a great benefit, but it is not only for our own benefit, but to make us witnesses.

As a university student I was drawn into a Western theology which in many ways was what Hwa Yung calls "unengaged" (1997, 8-9). We were children of the Enlightenment and therefore distinguished between theory and practise. It was my encounter with theologies from the Global South, first in Africa and then as a student under Kraft, that helped me understand that theology cannot and must not be separated from the concrete world. Truth cannot be separated from practice, and orthopraxis is as important as orthodoxy. Theology must therefore be based on missional/missionary experience. The theology of the early church came into being as a theoretical framework of conceptual thinking based on concrete mission experience. Theological thinking must be missiological thinking if it aims at holding together practice and theory.

The New Testament narratives are prime examples of this. As Chuck Kraft often told us, the Bible was not intended to be a textbook in theology, but rather it was to be a casebook about mission: God's mission and our mission. It is composed of narratives about the God who acts in our salvation and therefore equips his people to be sent to the world. Theology is therefore meant to be "an accompanying manifestation of the Christian mission and not a luxury of the world dominating church" (Kähler, cited in Bosch 1991, 16). The Gospels were clearly written to witness about Jesus Christ to diverse target groups in the Greco-Roman world, and the epistles grew out of the pastoral needs of new congregations in mission situations. There was hardly time or space for the kind of theological research done today. Rather, the New Testament came into being "in the context of an emergency situation, of a church which, because of its missionary encounter with the world, was forced to theologize" (Bosch 1991, 16). May we not against this background claim that mission is the mother of theology? Consequently, can we not say that a theology that is not missiological in its intention is an irrelevant theology?

The biblical texts do not suit the unengaged theology of the Enlightenment. For the same reason today and in the future the missiology of the Global South resonates most closely with the biblical texts (see Jenkins 2006). A major problem, however, is that too often the Western unengaged theology was exported to the rest of the world as part of the missionary era since the end of the eighteenth century. Hwa Yung claims that this theology "has become largely speculative, and often irrelevant to the mission and pastoral concerns of the church" (1997, 22). It represents a blind alley and should not be regarded as the norm of Christian theology. Here is a major challenge for those who want to follow Kraft's thinking into the future. Together with the younger churches in the Global South we must protest against this theology. It is inadequate as a model for engagement with the world of the twenty-first century. It is a blind alley in light of the Christian understanding and tradition as we find that in Scripture, in the early church, and in the Reformation.

My thesis is therefore that there can be no authentic theology unless it is based on the pastoral and missional practice of the church. Such an authentic theology will demand a personal engagement by the Christian and by the local congregation. "Just as the church ceases to be church if it is not missionary, theology ceases to be theology if it loses its missionary character" (Bosch 1991, 494).

Different Worlds—Different Languages

To many of Kraft's students his communication principles have become almost second nature. I imbibed these principles both from his *Communication Theory for Christian Witness* (1991a, 47) and from his extensive treatment in *Christianity in Culture* (1979a, 147-169). In my dissertation I took these principles and the underlying theology and theory into the world of media communication (Jørgensen 1986) and worked particularly with the implications of transaction and meaning, and how this in turn calls for a strong receptor-oriented approach involving audience participation.

There can be little doubt that Kraft's work with communication principles and their theological/missiological underpinning in God's incarnational approach to communication is one of his major contributions to a generation of missionaries and communicators. Along the way Kraft also influenced the thinking and even the vocabulary of major missiologists like Lesslie Newbigin. Newbigin wrote,

1) The communication has to be in the language of the receptor culture. It has to be such that it accepts, at least provisionally, the way of understanding things that is embodied in that language . . .
2) However, if it is truly the communication of the gospel, it will call radically into question that way of understanding embodied in the language it uses. If it is truly revelation, it will involve contradiction, and call for conversion, for a radical *metanoia*, a U-turn of the mind.
3) Finally, this radical conversion can never be the achievement of any human persuasion, however eloquent. It can only be the work of God. (Newbigin 1986, 5-6; see also Hunsberger 1998)

This model of cross-cultural communication, based on a theology of cultural plurality, echoes Kraft's thinking and models. The principles, the models, and the concepts developed by Kraft in the area of communication will continue to influence the next generation of missiologists, both directly and indirectly. One field of missiology in particular need of such influence is religious dialogue.[1] Let me in this context call attention to the fact that our major religions also represent different languages and different worlds. A colleague of mine, Notto Thelle, describes this in terms of the "languages" of relation, awareness, and energy (Thelle 2005, 48-62). Relationship characterises the religions of the ear (Judaism, Islam, Christianity, with the focus on the word and on obeying), awareness is the religion of the eye (Buddhism, Hinduism, with the focus on enlightenment and awakening), and energy represents the ancient and modern searches for empowerment, as we find them in animist spiritism as well as in new religious movements and alternative spiritualities where the focus is on vitality, inner power, and life force. It seems to me that this approach to mutual understanding could be a helpful approach in the future. Here the basic communication principles of meaning and receptor orientation are taken seriously in order to understand. Thus, I understand the new spiritual movements much better when I view what they say within a framework of energy, vitality, strength, inner power, and life force. It is somewhat similar to the concept of *qi*—or *ki* in Japanese—as an expression of life force or cosmic energy. In addition to this fascination with the East (Buddhist meditation, Chinese traditions) the contemporary search for strength and energy also finds its background in traditional occult philosophy and its desire to be initiated into the hidden potentials of human existence.

To realize that our religions use different languages with different meanings is important in itself. It may also lead us to ask whether these languages represent incompatible worlds or whether there also could be some degree of complementarity (ibid., 57). For example, the biblical narrative is filled with illustrations of seeing, awareness, and wisdom (Mt 5:8; Jn 8:32; 2 Pt 1:19; etc.). True, these expressions of insight and awareness are relational. "Seeing God" in the biblical tradition primarily expresses relationship. Yet the energy or power aspects are also obvious in connection with biblical relationships. The New Testament has much to say about *dynamis* and *exousia*. So even though Christianity is primarily concerned with the personal aspect of God, biblical symbolism also opens space for a language of seeing and energy.

In the same way Buddhism is not without hearing and relationships. And insight and awareness are expected to result in compassion. Within new spiritual movements with their focus on energy, the same energy is supposed to be the result of insight into the hidden relationships in the cosmos. Although various religious traditions tend to cultivate one of the three categories mentioned, they also give room for all three. The categories are not closed systems. This will pose some major challenges to Christian missiology in the future. How do we develop a deeper, less antagonistic understanding of one another in a world that is grow-

---

[1]See what Kraft says about dialogical interaction in general in Kraft (1991b, 62-65).

ing more and more multireligious and multicultural? Must Christianity continue to "attack" the others? Or are there ways whereby we may develop a new relationship, without losing the gospel focus on Christ as the unique way?

I may affirm that the Christian faith is a public truth and at the same time accept pluralism in the public room, instead of relegating it to a private sphere. In other words, truth about faith is as valid as other truths. From a Christian view we therefore accept pluralism, but we also maintain the right to challenge pluralism. We challenge it because we insist that there is also something called truth in the realm of religion. And for this truth I am ready to dialogue, argue, and debate.

This is what Lesslie Newbigin calls committed pluralism, in contrast to agnostic pluralism (Newbigin 1989). Agnostic pluralism, which Western culture subscribes to, has renounced any talk about knowledge and truth in relation to faith. The committed, engaged pluralism, on the other hand, takes other religions seriously and dares to raise questions about the other's faith. Engaged pluralism dares to reveal the dogmatic background of the rationalistic claims about the world of facts. Committed pluralism will argue for a place in the public sphere, and it will reveal the idols of materialism, consumerism, and individualism. It will call the many spiritualities to account in public discourse, spiritualities which often disguise themselves in the private sphere.

I am committed to believing that every part of the created world and every human being are already related to Jesus. Everything was made through the Logos, he is the life of all, and he is the light that gives light to every person. The presence and work of Jesus are not confined within the area where he is acknowledged. In every human there is not only a moral consciousness (Rom 2:14-15), but also a religious consciousness. This does not imply that everything is light; both Scripture and experience make it abundantly clear that there is also darkness. But the light shines in the darkness. And this light may also shine in the lives of other human beings. My Christian confession does not force me to deny the reality of the work of God in the lives and thoughts and prayers of men and women outside the Christian church. Neither do I deny the dark side of religion. But this dark side does not prevent me from seeing the light of God in the lives of men and women who do not acknowledge him as Lord. Paul's speech at the Areopagos (Acts 17) points to a continuity between our lives and the only God, while at the same time acknowledging confrontation and a call to conversion.

Mission as *Martyria*

When Kraft deals so extensively with communication theory, he does so in the context of Christian witness:

> God himself is the message, and we respond to a person. It is in relation to the person of God, not to some words about him, that we "live and move and have our being" (Acts 17:28 [NIV]). As with human communication at a much lower level, the most crucial dimensions are the results of life rubbing against life to produce and maintain life. The ultimate Christian message is

a person. And anything that reduces that message to mere verbalization is unworthy of the message. (Kraft 1991a, 40-41)

More than twenty years ago, under Kraft's mentoring guidance, I wrote about the media in the mission of the church. My desire was to view the witnessing community as the *Sitz im Leben* for Christian media communication (Jørgensen 1986, 439-440). The media may start a dialogue with an audience, but the continuation of the dialogue requires that the mediated word become flesh and blood in the person as medium. In that connection I used the term the "mediatisation of the laity," exemplified in a major multimedia evangelism project in Japan. This focus on media as extension of ministry will remain on the agenda of Christian media communication and ought to receive increasing attention in a globalized information society in order to counteract the many still-existing electronic church ministries.

Within missiology in both Europe and North America for several years now there has been a strong focus on the *missional church* and on emerging churches. The term missional church is an expression of the fact that the church is not primarily an institution with services and activities whose mission is on the periphery. The task is not to invent a number of mission programs aimed at attracting new churchgoers. Rather, we are challenged to be what the church has always been: people of flesh and blood carrying the reality of the gospel within them, communicating it through missional being and action. For that reason, it is likely that the famous but seldom realized priesthood of all believers will become the basic structure of church and mission in the future. Together with this structure one could hope for a rediscovery of the gifts of the Holy Spirit in a broad biblical conception, as that which equips the missionary congregation in a postmodern reality.

This focus on church as mission also means that our ability to be magnets attracting people to Christ becomes important, as it is in our sister churches of the South and East. Therefore, a missional church should emphasize meditation, spirituality, presence, genuineness, and lifestyle. Modeled on our brothers and sisters in the South and East, we should in a new way become personal carriers of the spiritual reality the world longs for. Along with being centrifugal in our mission outreach, we should also revitalize the centre; we need to live centripetally.

When going out, our primary task is to be witnesses. The missional thinking often and markedly underlines the fact that the church's missional call, according to the New Testament, is to be witnesses. Mission is witness. *Martyria* is the sum of *kerygma*, *koinonia*, and *diaconia*, all three of which constitute important dimensions of the witness for which the church is called and sent (Van Engen 1991). "We are using a missiological hermeneutic when we read the New Testament as the testimony (witness) of witnesses, equipping other witnesses for the common mission of the church" (Guder 2000, 53-55). Thus, testimony becomes a demonstration through the lives and actions of God's people to the fact that the Kingdom of God becomes present in the disciples of Jesus Christ. In this way the testimony of the gospel defines the identity, activities, and communication to which the church has been called since Pentecost.

It would be faithful to Charles Kraft's legacy if missiology in a new millennium were to focus squarely and primarily on mission as witness. Guder expresses this focus in the following way:

> The missional church understands its calling as witness to the gospel of the in-breaking reign of God and strives to be an instrument, agent and sign of that reign. As it makes its witness through its identity, activity, and communication, it is aware of the provisional character of all that it is and does. It points toward the reign of God which God will certainly bring about, but knows that its own response is incomplete and that its own conversion is a continuing necessity. (Guder 2004, 126)

We have already initiated the future with the growing focus on fresh expressions of the church or emerging churches within which "witness" is viewed as a missional vocation and as part and parcel of being incarnational and relational (Archbishops' Council 2004; Gibbs and Bolger 2005; Frost and Hirsch 2003). What missiology needs to do better, however, is to do more research on missional churches in the Global South with the aim of having churches in the North learn from churches in the South. Tormod Engelsviken raises this question in the following way:

> Is one of the most important explanations of the growth among churches in the South that they are missional churches, not only in a theoretical and theological sense, but also in practice? Do they, more than the churches in the North, do and practice what they are ecclesiologically, i.e. God's witnessing people in mission? Is this in turn a major reason for their own growth and for the growing missionary activity that emerges from these churches? And if so, what may we in the churches in the North learn from the churches in the South with regard to mission? (Engelsviken 2004, 80)[2]

Engelsviken's article describes his own research on this question in Malaysia, and one of the characteristics he highlights as part of the DNA of missional churches in the South is spontaneous witness.

Communication through Community

I vividly recall how Kraft cherished the term *dynamic equivalence* and applied it to translation, inspiration, theologizing, transculturation, conversion, leadership—and church.[3] And I remember how he impressed on us that a "contemporary church, like a contemporary translation, should impress the uninitiated observer as an original production in the contemporary culture, not as a badly

---

[2]Translation from the Norwegian is my own.
[3]See Kraft (1979a) with reference to dynamic equivalence churchness, in loco.

fitted import from somewhere else" (Kraft 1979a, 318). To illustrate what he meant, he would often quote Alan Tippett's emphasis on indigenous peoples of a community thinking of the Lord as their own (Tippett 1973b, 158). Kraft also drew on William Smalley's definition of an indigenous church to inform his development of the concept of dynamic equivalent church. Smalley defined the indigenous church as "a group of believers who live out their life, including their socialized Christian activity, in the patterns of the local society, and for whom any transformation of that society comes out of their felt needs under the guidance of the Holy Spirit and the Scriptures" (Smalley 1958, 61-65). At the time I learned the expression from Kraft, I was working in Ethiopia and therefore applied the term to the church within which I served. Upon my return to the West in the 1980s I realized that what I originally—and erroneously—had termed an "imitation-church" in Ethiopia was and is much more a dynamic-equivalent church than the church within which I now struggle in Norway. Actually, the entire enterprise of missional church and emerging churches are attempts to come to grips with the sad fact that our churches in the West are very badly fitted indeed. Pete Ward's *Liquid Church* attempts to give a bold vision of how to be God's people in worship and mission—a flexible, fluid way of being church (2002). He claims that liquid church should replace congregations with communication, and he does so by likening the church to a network with various hubs and with a heavy focus on Internet connections, e-mail, and personal contacts. "The Christian community needs to adopt this and similar kinds of communication as its measure of fellowship in Christ. Meetings are of less significance than the quality and kind of communication that takes place in the church" (Ward 2002, 89).

My heading "Communication through Community" is inspired by Eddie Gibbs, who in his *Church Next* develops this topic. Christian communities should become "meaning-makers"; people need fresh images of how life is meant to be lived, and they need evidence that following Jesus really makes a difference (Gibbs 2000, 192). The solution is obviously not more prime-time television or more colored tracts; our Western culture, like any culture, longs for a positive personal experience with people who have seen and heard and touched (see 1 Jn 1:1-3, the Magna Carta for Christian communication).

I think this means that nonbelievers need to encounter the gospel in another way than sermons from a pulpit. They need to see the story of salvation exemplified in believers being "letters from Christ." The *martyria* of the individual is essential, but even more importantly, it must be incorporated and reinforced by a community that makes sense of the new life. A major factor for emerging churches is living as community (Gibbs and Bolger 2005, 89). It is clear that for these communities, church is a people, a community, a rhythm, a way of life, a way of connectedness, followers of Jesus Christ in a lost and hurting world so loved by God. By their very being they are salt and light.

Engelsviken emphasizes the same in his research on the missional church in Malaysia: the work of the Holy Spirit results in renewal not only of individuals, but of the entire congregation, and it is this renewed congregation that through the ministry of the spiritual gifts attracts newcomers (Engelsviken 2004).

The growth of churches in the Global South and the search for new meanings and new forms of being church in the North make it essential that we create bridges of cross-fertilization between churches in the South and those in the North. We need to develop new models for how churches through their entire being may communicate the biblical message in a new century.

Part III

SPIRITUAL POWER

Introduced by J. Dudley Woodberry

What's in a name? Words bring with them meanings from their past and acquire additional nuances—some positive and some negative—as they travel through new mouths, pens, and computers. This is certainly the case as we have sorted through the potential candidates for a title to this section: Power Encounter or Spiritual Power Encounter, Spiritual Warfare, Spiritual Conflict, Healing, Blessing, Authority, or Dynamics. What is too militant or too anemic? What includes too much or too little? As in many elections the winner is chosen as the electorate weighs candidates' pluses against their minuses. "Spiritual Power" has been chosen in the present context because *power* (*dunamis*) is the quality the Holy Spirit brought the disciples for their witness (Acts 1:8) and can express an encounter and a blessing. "Power" is also the word that Charles Kraft links with "truth" and "allegiance" in his analysis of the three encounters in Christian witness (1991b, 1992a). In this case he took the term *power encounter* that one of his mentors, Alan R. Tippett, used to describe a major encounter between ancestral gods against the biblical God (1971) and broadened it to include other expressions of God's power.

The Bible certainly describes a world that includes Satan, demonic beings, and magic (van der Toorn, Becking, and van der Horst 1995; Unger 1963; Klutz 2003). In the Old Testament demons are associated with idolatry (Dt 32:17). In the New Testament they blind the minds of unbelievers (2 Cor 4:3-4), fight against Christians (Eph 6:12), and will lead rulers to fight against God (Rev 16:14). They enter and dwell within people (Mt 12:43-45). But they submitted to the authority of Jesus (Mk 1:27). Believers in turn are to test the spirits (1 Jn 4:1-4) and fight against them (Eph 6:10-18). Magic was also widely exercised in the Mediterranean world (Arnold 1989; Davies 1969).

In Scripture we also see signs and wonders as God through his servants overcomes the forces of evil—for example, with Moses and the Egyptian magicians (Ex 4-12) and Elijah and the prophets of Baal (1 Kg 18). With Jesus they demonstrated the coming of the Kingdom of God (Lk 11:20) and continued with the apostles (e.g., Acts 3:6-13).

During the time of the apostolic fathers of the second and third centuries, belief in demons and the practice of exorcisms and the gifts of healing and prophecy continued and were widespread. These were practiced in a context where suffering was also expected, transformed lives were seen as a greater witness to the truth of the gospel, and a clear distinction was made between the Spirit's work and that of pagan magic (Smedes 1987, 25-28; Engelsviken 2001b, 18-20).

Stories of miraculous healings and exorcisms continued into the fourth and fifth centuries. Increasingly in the Middle Ages, however, people mixed nonbiblical beings and magical practices with biblical teachings, and relics and shrines were used as means for healing. Yet there are records of "power encounters" in which, for example, Boniface, a missionary to Germany in the eighth century, cut down a holy oak in Geismer, and St. Olva in the eleventh century struck down an idol in Norway. Both were followed by mass conversions (Engelsviken 2001b, 20-21; Smedes 1987, 28).

The Protestant Reformers rejected the intercession of saints and the use of relics and shrines but maintained a sense of confronting a personal devil and evil spirits that could be driven out of people by prayer. In the post-Reformation period the Danish-Norwegian Lutheran Church until 1783 included in the baptismal ritual the words "Depart you evil spirit and give room for the Holy Spirit" (Engelsviken 2001b, 23-25; Smedes 1987, 28-29). And the Anglican baptismal ritual to this day includes the renunciation of the devil and all his works.

By the time of the modern missionary movement from the West there was little emphasis on signs and wonders among Evangelicals. One reason was a common Western worldview that recognized only a seen world and a trans-empirical world (of heaven and hell), while non-Westerners commonly recognize an additional middle world of spirits and magical forces (Hiebert 1982, 35-47). Another reason was that a major percentage of Western Protestant missionaries—especially Evangelicals from the English-speaking world—came from churches, Bible schools, and seminaries of the Reformed or Dispensational traditions where some degree of cessationism was taught. This ranged from the belief that all extraordinary works of God had ceased with the early period of the Church to those who held that they might take place today but were limited to extraordinary situations.[1]

Against this background Peter Wagner in his introductory chapter "Missiology and Spiritual Power" shows how spiritual power entered the missiology curriculum at Fuller and elsewhere. As noted, Alan Tippett, the first anthropologist to join the Fuller faculty, had described the significance of power encounters in the movements to Christ in the South Pacific, where new believers in Christ destroyed their former objects used in worship, thereby challenging their old gods (1971). However, it was the offering of the course on signs and wonders by John Wimber that led to the paradigm shift that Kraft and Wagner both experienced. This shift led to a major new orientation in their ministry and writing, and to considerable discussion and debate within the three schools at Fuller and in the broader world of missiologists and theologians. It has led to the discipline of spiritual power or spiritual dynamics having a significant—though troubled—place in the broader field of missiology.

---

[1]For various Reformed perspectives see Berends (2007).

In the chapter "Power and Blessing: Keys for Relevance to a Religion as Lived," I describe how ill-prepared I was when I arrived in Pakistan to understand the popular Islam of the masses, let alone to ascertain how the gospel met their felt needs. Therefore, I, along with the other School of World Mission faculty, have continued to interact with Chuck in his pilgrimage. The chapter points out how the masses in biblical times also had an animistic worldview that involved a need for power and blessing. This made a bridge for them to see the biblical God as the source of that power and blessing but also raised the danger of the new faith being imbedded with animistic beliefs and practices. The same bridges and dangers exist as we deal with folk religions and/or religious systems as they are lived today. Some missiologists viewed the approaches of Kraft, Wagner, and others as involving syncretism with animism, to which Kraft responded that instead he advocated God-given authority (Rommen 1995, 9-136). One of Chuck's contributions to the field is his highlighting of the interrelationship of a power encounter, a truth encounter, and an allegiance encounter (Kraft 1991b, 1992a). Thus, in his view the power needed to be combined with the truth of God's Word, and both lead to allegiance to God in Christ.

John and Anna Travis are current students of Charles Kraft. Their chapter "Deep-Level Healing Prayer in Cross-Cultural Ministry" comes from their present experience on the field with models that are built with insight from Kraft's actual experience. Herein lies the strength of Kraft as a practitioner-scholar, while many of his missiological and theological critics work without the aid of experience, though they have raised some significant questions for the future. From actual case studies John and Anna have seen the efficacy of deep-level healing prayer both in people giving their allegiance to God in Christ and in their discipling as their deep-level wounds are healed. As such it is earning a place in the field of missiology.

In "Spiritual Conflict: A Challenge for the Church in the West, with a View to the Future," Tormod Engelsviken draws on his experience of interacting with Charles Kraft and other missiologists in various consultations and collaborative publications that have arisen as a result of the teaching and writing of Kraft and others on spiritual power. These collaborative studies have been sponsored by Fuller Theological Seminary (Smedes 1987; Wagner and Pennoyer 1990), the Society of Pentecostal Studies (Robeck 1991), the Evangelical Missiological Society (Rommen 1995), and the Lausanne Committee for World Evangelization (Engelsviken 2001b; Moreau et al. 2002). Engelsviken has indicated areas of agreement and tension and questions for the future. With the rising interest in the spirits and the occult in the West, and the rise of the churches in the Global South with more awareness in these areas, he calls on us jointly to seek biblical guidance that we may experience more fully the power of God's coming Kingdom. Charles Kraft has been one who has helped blaze the way.

9

Missiology and Spiritual Power

C. PETER WAGNER

No one has made a greater contribution toward introducing the dimension of spiritual power to the discipline of missiology than Chuck Kraft. As a colleague for more than thirty years, I have been close enough to Chuck to observe with great admiration his unusual ability to identify an area of importance to the field and then to analyze it, systematize it, teach on it, and publish a cutting-edge article or book on the subject. For example, his *Christianity in Culture* (Kraft 1979a; Kraft with Kraft 2005) and his *Anthropology for Christian Witness* (1996) are missiological textbooks which, in my opinion, have not been surpassed. Likewise, his *Christianity with Power* (1989), more apropos to this chapter, has probably helped more people make the transition from cessationism to embracing the power of the Holy Spirit than any other book.

Early Years at Fuller

Kraft, of course, was not the first missiologist to recognize that power encounter has been a key factor in people movements to Christ. Interestingly enough, however, Donald McGavran, founder of the Fuller School of World Mission, did not seem to grasp the importance of spiritual power in his seminal research leading to *The Bridges of God* (1981) and *Understanding Church Growth* (1990). I cannot recall him ever mentioning it in class when I took my degree under him in the late 1960s. However, much later on, he did introduce a lecture on divine healing in his advanced church growth course shortly before his retirement from teaching in 1981. That opened the door for me to compile those thoughts as a new chapter in the third edition of *Understanding Church Growth*, which he asked me to revise and update in 1990. The chapter is titled "Divine Healing and Church Growth" (144-152).

One of McGavran's closest missiological associates was Melvin Hodges of the Assemblies of God. Hodges participated in the annual Church Growth Lectures in 1962, and he contributed three chapters in *Church Growth and Christian Mission* (McGavran), published in 1965. One might have expected that Hodges, the most respected Pentecostal missiologist of that time, would have focused on spiritual power in his missiological writings. Curiously, he almost seemed to avoid the subject, not even mentioning it in *Church Growth and Christian Mission*. He did include a chapter on the personal baptism of the Holy Spirit in his textbook *A Theology of the Church and Its Mission: A Pentecostal Perspective* (1977), as well as a 3-page section (out of 185 pages) on miracles. Proportionally, however, spiritual power as a component of mission strategy seemed incidental rather than central in Melvin Hodges' writings.

Meanwhile, McGavran, realizing that he could not build a strong missiological faculty at Fuller without due regard to anthropology, partnered with Alan Tippett of Australia/Fiji, who assumed that role. Tippett observed the crucial dynamic of power encounter in movements to Christ in the South Pacific. For example, in his analysis of the conversion of animists, Tippett postulated that the first step in the process must be a rite of separation from old ties and loyalties. He wrote,

> This step is often a very spectacular ritual—fetishes are burned, sacred totemic taboo fish are eaten, idols are stripped of their decorations and thrown into a fire . . . These are symbolic acts, with their focus on the *locus of power* of the rejected religion. They are *power encounters* in which converts show their change of faith and demonstrate that they no longer fear the old gods . . . They have rejected the supernatural resources on which they once relied, and are challenging the old power to harm them . . . The conversion of animists is not a passage from nonfaith to faith. It is a passage from wrong faith to right faith, from the false god to the true God. (Tippett 1987, 82-83)

Alan Tippett's introduction of power encounter into missiological theory was rooted in his social scientific approach to describing and analyzing people movements. While he was an accurate observer of this phenomenon, he never became a *participant* observer. His Methodist theological underpinnings allowed little room for what might have been perceived as Pentecostal-type activities. Tippett, unlike his protégé and successor Chuck Kraft, leaned toward caution against stepping outside of the traditional theological box. Kraft, on the other hand, was never characterized by such inhibitions. This allowed Kraft to become not only an observer of spiritual power, but a participant observer as well.

Shortly I will describe how Chuck Kraft was introduced to spiritual power, casting much of my narrative in the first-person plural because I myself was going through the paradigm shift with him. First, however, I think it would be good to lay a bit of biblical foundation to this concept.

A Biblical Foundation

Looking back, it is difficult to comprehend how most of us who were Bible-believing, Evangelical missiologists could have ignored for so long the essential, not just optional, role that spiritual power has in biblical missiology. For us, a motivational starting point for our lives and ministries was Jesus' Great Commission: "Go, therefore and make disciples of all the nations, baptizing them in the name of the Father and of the Son, and of the Holy Spirit, teaching them to observe all things that I have commanded you" (Mt 28:19-20, NKJV). Let me make two related observations:

First, Jesus' words leading up to this classic statement of the Great Commission were "All authority has been given to me in heaven and on earth" (Mt 28:18, NKJV). The word *authority* is *exousía*, frequently translated "power," as it is in Matthew 10:1. There the Bible says that Jesus gave his disciples "power," namely spiritual power, when he sent them out to spread the good news of the Kingdom of God for the first time. Jesus was so insistent that this power was necessary to accomplish his purposes that, when he finally left the earth, he told his disciples not to go out and begin spreading the Good News, but rather to go to Jerusalem. Why? Before they began preaching the Kingdom of God, they needed to "tarry in the city of Jerusalem until [they were] endued with power from on high" (Lk 24:49, NKJV).

Jesus was also quite specific as to the divine source of this power from on high. His very last words on earth were "But you shall receive power when the Holy Spirit has come upon you; and you shall be witnesses to me in Jerusalem, and in all Judea and Samaria, and to the end of the earth" (Acts 1:8, NKJV). It goes without saying that the coming of the Holy Spirit on the day of Pentecost provided the necessary infusion of spiritual power for the mission assignment with which Jesus had entrusted his disciples.

My second observation relates to Jesus' mandate that those who become his disciples be taught to "observe all things that I have commanded you." Prominent among the numerous things that Jesus had explicitly commanded his disciples to do was to minister, hands-on, with spiritual power. Let's go back to Matthew 10 where Jesus gave his disciples *exousía*, clearly commanding them to "heal the sick, cleanse the lepers, raise the dead, cast out demons" (Mt 10:8, NKJV). This is not an isolated proof text. Time after time he commanded them to use spiritual power as they preached the gospel. He even said, "And these signs will follow those who believe: In my name they will cast out demons; they will speak with new tongues; they will take up serpents; and if they drink anything deadly, it will by no means hurt them; they will lay hands on the sick and they will recover" (Mk 16:17, 18, NKJV). Chuck Kraft and I were not the only professional missiologists who, for a long time, managed to ignore or attempt to explain away texts like these.

Consider as well the experience of the apostle Paul. Paul's ministry in the city of Athens turned out to be one of his most disappointing evangelistic endeavors. He made the mistake of assuming that declaring the truth of God would open the way for the activation of the power of God. He was operating out of the same paradigm that Kraft and I had been assuming in our missiological theory and practice. We had not realized that we had the order reversed. We now are convinced that a demonstration of the power of God is the most effective means for opening individuals and groups to the truth of God.

Paul used his intellectual abilities to research the religion and philosophy of Athens, coming up with the concept of the Unknown God. He crafted what professors of homiletics often regard as his finest sermon. He gathered an audience on Mars Hill and began speaking to them, but never finished his speech. Instead, he experienced a public speaker's worst nightmare—his audience ridiculed him and left before he was finished. He planted no church in Athens, and won only a few converts.

Fortunately, Paul was the kind who learned from his mistakes. He decided that he would no longer attempt evangelism through intellectual brilliance but rather through spiritual power. How do we know this? We know it from Paul's personal description of how he undertook the evangelization of Corinth, the city he visited right after Athens. Here is what Paul said, along with some of my comments:

> And I, brethren, when I came to you, did not come with the excellence of speech or of wisdom [as I did in Athens] . . . And my speech and my preaching were not with persuasive words of human wisdom [as was my sermon on Mars Hill], but in demonstration of the Spirit and power, that your faith should not be in the wisdom of men but in the power of God. (1 Cor 2:1, 4, 5, NKJV)

Signs and Wonders at Fuller

Along with most other missiologists whom we knew, neither Kraft nor I had ever taken much time to process the words of Jesus or the experience of Paul that I have just cited. For us, spiritual power was important for conversion and living a good Christian life, but healing and miracles and prophecy and casting out demons and things like that were not on our radar screen. That is, until John Wimber came along. Wimber was the innovator who guided us into the radical paradigm shift which ended up with incorporating spiritual power into our missiological teaching and practice.

Previous to a radical conversion to Christ, John Wimber had experienced success in the music industry as manager of the Righteous Brothers. He transitioned into pastoral ministry, and he was pastoring a Quaker church when he enrolled in a Fuller Doctor of Ministry course on church growth which I was teaching. Over the two weeks of class we bonded, and he soon resigned from his pastoral position and joined the staff of the Fuller Evangelistic Association which I was leading at the time. We consulted with churches across the country, with me serving as the church growth theoretician and John as the practitioner. During this time neither of us had any concept of how spiritual power might influence the growth of churches.

After a time, John asked my permission to plant a small church in nearby Orange County. I agreed, assuming it would be a weekend diversion while he continued working for me. It turned out to be Anaheim Vineyard, one of America's most notable mega-churches. From the outset, Wimber began experimenting with incorporating supernatural signs and wonders into his congregational ministry. Many sick people were healed, miracles started occurring, and demons were frequently cast out. I often attended the Vineyard services.

Because of Wimber's extraordinary aptitude for church growth, I began to invite him to be a regular guest lecturer in my annual Doctor of Ministry Church Growth II course. In 1981, when we were planning the course, he suggested that he try a new session on how supernatural signs and wonders could influence the growth of the church. I agreed and I invited our School of World Mission dean, Paul Pierson, to sit through the class with me. At lunch that day, we told Wimber that we were fascinated by the content of his lecture. He responded by telling us that he had collected enough material on the subject to teach a whole course.

Pierson and I related this to the School of World Mission faculty, and for six months we debated whether we should break some new missiological ground and experiment with a course focused on spiritual power. We finally decided to do it. I would serve as the professor of record. John would be a visiting lecturer. We would list the course as "MC510 Signs, Wonders and Church Growth."

Both Chuck Kraft and his wife, Meg, and my wife, Doris, and I attended the initial course in 1982. Not only did Wimber teach, but he demonstrated the validity of spiritual power through hands-on times of ministry. Numerous physical healings and demonic deliverances, some notably dramatic, were witnessed by all. That sparked our paradigm shift. By the end of the quarter Kraft and I had become disciples of John Wimber and proponents of introducing spiritual power into our missiological teaching.

We were not quite prepared, however, for the unusual interest that the course would stimulate, not only in the School of World Mission, but in Fuller's School of Theology and across the nation. For example, Bob Walker, editor of *Christian Life* magazine, flew across the country, visited the class, interviewed key figures throughout the seminary, ran a cover story on the phenomenon, and broke all sales records for a single issue of the magazine (1982, 18-76). Attendance in subsequent offerings of the course reached 250 students, the largest classes ever at Fuller. Ironically, the notoriety of MC510 was what actually precipitated its demise.

While Chuck Kraft and I, supported by Dean Paul Pierson and most of the School of World Mission (SWM) faculty, were encouraged by the prospect of introducing a subject like spiritual power into our seminary curriculum, this sentiment was not shared broadly by the other faculties and administration. The administration was aware that a number of financial supporters had begun expressing some apprehension that Fuller might be leaning toward becoming charismatic. Some professors in the School of Theology were convinced that gifts such as prophecy and healing and tongues and deliverance and miracles had largely ceased with the early church and the canonization of Scripture. Their classroom situations were becoming more and more uncomfortable for them, with many of their students who had taken MC510 testifying of healings and deliverance and asking professors for theological explanations.

Their growing discomfort reached a breaking point in 1985 when the issue of signs and wonders finally surfaced in a School of Theology faculty meeting (Kraft 2005a, 169). Several expressed the opinion that the actual healing of the sick and casting out demons had no place in a seminary classroom. Others were embarrassed by the fact that John Wimber, only a visiting lecturer, was being regarded by some as a national spokesperson for Fuller Seminary itself. Some felt that the theology underlying MC510 was deviant enough from Fuller's Reformed tradition to merit censure. As a result, the School of Theology faculty passed a motion no longer to allow their theology students to receive academic credit for MC510.

We on the School of World Mission faculty, yielding to institutional loyalty, felt we had no choice but to cancel MC510. Sadly, John Wimber carried to his grave the wounding he received from this rejection.

The decision to cancel MC510 was not well received by the student body, many of whom had been deeply influenced by Wimber's teaching and personal ministry. In order to work toward a solution, the provost organized a twelve-member study commission to examine the issues related to teaching spiritual power in a theological seminary. The commission was required to meet weekly for a period of time in order to produce a statement that would represent the position of the seminary. Both Kraft and I were disappointed at the composition of the commission. I was the only member of the committee who was a proponent for incorporating signs and wonders into the curriculum.

The resultant document, published as *Ministry and the Miraculous: A Case Study at Fuller Theological Seminary* (1987), was edited by Lewis Smedes. It sought to weave together perspectives that could be broadly affirmed. While the book never became an official seminary policy manual, it did help reduce the tension resulting from the cancellation of MC510.

Meanwhile, Chuck Kraft and I, both tenured professors, desired to move ahead with incorporating new courses on spiritual power into our School of World Mission curriculum. The Faculty Senate gave permission to offer a substitute course, over which I would preside as professor of record. Kraft and I were to lecture one week each, and the other eight were to be given by other members of the study commission so that all points of view could be fairly represented.

Seminary president David Hubbard had managed to keep at arm's length from the controversy. While he was not an advocate of MC510, neither was he an outspoken opponent. When the impasse seemed to be at its peak, Hubbard convened an unofficial meeting of several major players for an evening of "pie and coffee" in his home. I came with my guns loaded, so to speak, ready for a major battle. No triggers needed to be pulled, however. The meeting turned out to be frank and open, but courteous, harmonious, and peaceful. The Holy Spirit was present in such a powerful way that it seemed like a meeting of a church home cell group. Since that watershed event, teaching spiritual power, signs and wonders, prophecy, demonic deliverance, and related subjects has been permitted, according to the inclinations of each faculty member, in the seminary curriculum. Not all agree with it, but the faculty now agree to disagree.

During this process, and in the providence of God, Chuck Kraft and I each developed different specializations derived from what we had learned from Wimber. Kraft developed expertise in the fields of deliverance and inner healing, while I concentrated on physical healing, signs and wonders in mission strategy, and strategic-level spiritual warfare. As we taught our courses over the years, we were able to develop a body of literature which helped introduce aspects of spiritual power to church leaders as well as to some colleagues in other academic institutions.

Kraft's works included *Christianity with Power* (1989), *Deep Wounds, Deep Healing* (1993), *The Rules of Engagement* (2000), and *Confronting Powerless Christianity* (2002a). Among mine were *Spiritual Power and Church Growth*

(1986), *Signs and Wonders Today* (1987), *The Third Wave* (1988b), *How to Have a Healing Ministry in Any Church* (1988a), *Warfare Prayer* (1992), and *Confronting the Powers* (1996).

One of the most influential books of the time was *Wrestling with Dark Angels* (Wagner and Pennoyer 1990). As word began circulating that Fuller was teaching areas of spiritual power previously relegated only to Pentecostals and charismatics, we began getting reports that a number of our evangelical colleagues were either also beginning to teach it themselves or wanting to know more about the field. In response, the School of World Mission agreed to sponsor an invitation-only academic symposium on power evangelism in 1988. One of the outcomes was *Wrestling with Dark Angels*, which missiologist Douglas Pennoyer, then of Seattle Pacific University and now of Biola University, agreed to help me edit. Contributors included missiologists such as Chuck Kraft, Timothy Warner, Grant McClung, Dudley Woodberry, Donald Jacobs, and others, as well as John Wimber. This book went into eleven printings and circulated as a missions textbook for many years.

Spiritual Power's Inclusion in Missiology

We are now more than two decades this side of MC510. For the most part spiritual power, in differing degrees and with differing areas of emphasis, is an accepted area of missiological curricula. With the worldwide growth of the Pentecostal, the Charismatic, and, more recently, the apostolic movements, it could not be otherwise. Philip Jenkins's writings have substantiated the fact that those who have chosen to follow Jesus' command to heal the sick, cast out demons, and raise the dead, as well as those who follow Paul's axiom of demonstrating the power of God rather than leading off with human wisdom, are advancing the Kingdom of God much more notably in the world today than those who do not (see, for example, Jenkins 2002). David Barrett's research has shown that for many years the only megablock of world Christianity growing faster than the world population and faster than Islam is the megablock which regularly practices supernatural signs and wonders (see Barrett and Johnson 2001, 302; 2003, 25). Chuck Kraft says,

> As evangelicals we are committed to practicing and proclaiming a fully biblical Christianity. If we are to be true to that commitment, however, we need to get beyond what passes for normal evangelical Christianity and into the forefront of demonstrating biblically balanced spiritual power . . . I took a powerless Christianity to Nigeria—a Christianity that offered only secular answers to spiritual problems . . . I regret this deeply and wish with all my heart that I had been led before 1957 into the kind of Christianity that I now know. Now that I am experiencing more of what Jesus promised us and seeing people regularly blessed, healed and freed, I am determined to finish with this kind of Christianity rather than the kind on which I cut my teeth. (2002a, 239)

10

Power and Blessing

Keys for Relevance to a Religion as Lived

J. DUDLEY WOODBERRY

Many missionaries arrived in Pakistan ill-equipped to deal with issues of power such as the demonic—a major concern of local people. I, in addition, arriving with a Ph.D. in Islam as taught, found that I did not understand Islam as lived. A key that I was lacking was an understanding of the importance, in the popular Islam of most of the Muslims I encountered, of the concept of *baraka*—an Arabic and Hebrew word which connotes both blessing and power. This power and blessing comes from God in the Bible and the Qur'an, but in popular belief and practice it also is derived from certain people, objects, and utterances (see Lenning 1980).

It is the strong desire of religious devotees to acquire this power and blessing, and it is the biblical role of God through Christ and his Spirit in providing them that make their understanding so important for the missionary. But it is the often blurred distinction between their divine and magical acquisition that raises the dangers of syncretism. Although I shall draw my examples from Muslim contexts, many of the same phenomena are evident among Hindus, Buddhists, and others. As Jesus made the reception of divine power a prerequisite for local and global witness (Acts 1:8), I will look for guidelines for its expression in the ministry of Jesus and Paul, who lived in a similar context. Finally, I will turn to the issues raised and their implications for missiology. At every stage we are indebted to Charles Kraft who has been so instrumental in bringing the study and exercise of power and blessing ministries back into evangelical mission awareness and practice. And these overlapping concepts of power and blessing express the overlapping foci of his ministry of power encounter and inner healing.

From the Academy to the Street

I had been privileged to study under a who's who of scholars, such as Sir Hamilton Gibb researching the teaching of the Qur'an and major Muslim theological texts. Yet in Pakistan people were wearing miniature Qur'ans around their necks or arms that were too small to read, and many of the people were illiterate anyway; so obviously they were wearing them not for their conceptual content but their protective power or blessing. The sacred texts indicate that humans can pray directly to God, but many Muslims were going to shrines of a holy person to pray because they wanted someone closer to God than they were or someone closer to them than God seemed to be. If a grave of a saint was there, they would touch it to get *baraka* from it. Yet we lived in the outskirts of Islamabad (literally, the place of Islam) in Pakistan (literally, the pure land), a country founded so Muslims would be free to live according to their consciences.

The average Muslim I met blended both the formal Islam of the mosque and the popular faith and practice of the shrine. He or she might meditate on the ninety-nine names of God as a form of worship or might also recite those same names to magically ward off various types of misfortune (see, for example, Frielander 1978). The prophet Amos asks, "Can two walk together unless they are agreed?" Obviously the "high" and "low" forms of Islam make an uneasy alliance for many common people. In a rice ritual of the Maranaos of the Philippines the leader enjoins, "Praise to Allah! Pray that we will not sin in inviting the *tonong* [spirits]. Yet he created the *tonong*." The devotees then ask the *tonong* to be intermediaries and "pray to Allah that all farmers will have a beautiful harvest." Finally the leader again admonishes the farmers to pray to God that they might not sin in inviting the *tonong*, but God created them and, the leader adds, "gave them power" (Madale 1974, 76-77). This desire for power leads them even to risk offending God.

From the earliest period of the Qur'an we see a concern for God's protection against harmful forces like the "evil eye" from those who are envious (113:5), curses that bind people through occult practices (113:4), and harmful spirits (114:4-6). Yet elements of magic creep into Orthodox sources. The Qur'an condemns sorcery (2:102), and authoritative traditions (*hadith*) ascribed to Muhammad condemn magical practices like divinations, but then allow certain forms of it (*Mishkat al-Masabih*, n.d., Bk. 22, chap. 3, par. 1). The pre-Islamic pilgrimage was reinterpreted and made the fifth pillar of Islam but retained the Black Stone in the corner of the Ka'aba and the Zam Zam water, both of which are touched by pilgrims to acquire *baraka*.

Subsequently, Islam was often spread by syncretistic Sufis and thus often adopted additional elements from, for example, Javanese Mysticism or African indigenous religions. Islamicists in turn decry these additions to what they consider pure Islam. Orthodox/Othoprax Muslims are concerned about power and blessing but see the source as God. Followers of African traditional or indigenous religions might pray to ancestors for blessing. As they are being Islamized they might pray through the ancestors to God. When they become more Islamized, they will pray to God for the ancestors that they might be blessed.

The worldview of those with a mixture of formal Islamic and folk beliefs tends to be a power encounter between helpful, harmful, and neutral beings and forces with names and categories drawn from formal Islam and traditional religions. Thus, other-worldly beings and forces would include God, angels, Satan, divine decrees, and harmful fate. Various beings and forces extraordinary to this world would include good spirits, apostles, prophets, living and dead saints, ancestors, harmful spirits, *baraka*, amulets, sacred objects, the "evil eye," and curses. In the ordinary arenas of this world we see natural forces and folk medicine. Dreams are a point of contact between the extraordinary and ordinary realms of this world. A major concern of devotees is to find ways to acquire helpful *baraka* and helpful beings to ward off those forces and beings which are harmful (see Hiebert 1989, 52-54; Musk 1989, 192). This belief system shows the relevance of power and blessing ministries to their felt needs. It can be a bridge for witness where God is identified as the source, but it also raises the danger of facilitating "Christian magic" and syncretism. These divergent tendencies lead to the need to learn guidelines from Jesus and Paul as they ministered with power in similar contexts.

Guidelines from Jesus[1]

In the world of popular Islam there are many phenomena associated with power and blessing. These include spirit beings (called *jinn* and angels), objects (the Black Stone and amulets), places (*mazars* and *ziarats*), times (*mawlids*), rituals (incantations and sacrifices), and persons (*walis*, *pirs*, and sorcerers). Jesus lived in a similar world—one of spirit beings (demons—Lk 9:37-43, angels—Mk 1:13), objects (the hem of his garment—Lk 8:41-56), places (the pool of Bethesda—Jn 5:1-47), times (when the waters of the pool were troubled), rituals (anointing with oil—Mk 6:13), and persons (himself—Lk 5:17-26).

Jesus' sending out of the disciples in a teaching and power ministry in Luke 10 suggests guidelines for us in similar contexts today. We read that "the Lord . . . sent them . . . two by two" (vs. 1). The *first* guideline we see is that in such ministries *we should go in partnership*. Although he originally faced his adversary alone, he developed an approach of partnership. The powers are real, and discernment and support are needed. A very effective team ministry developed in Pakistan, for example, where each member had a different gifting: teaching, discerning of spirits, and counseling (Stacey 1989, 296-297).

The passage in Luke 10 goes on: "The Lord . . . sent them ahead of him . . . into every . . . place where he . . . was about to come" (vs. 1). *Second, our task is to prepare the way for Jesus*. The major advances of the church have normally had a period of preparation, of pre-evangelism. The dramatic harvest of Iranians today is based on the previous service of people like William Miller, who said he did not think they were even plowing the soil but merely removing the rocks. Paul noted a sequence of tasks when he said, "I planted, Apollos watered, but God gave the growth" (1 Cor 3:6). Chuck Kraft, in turn, as has been noted, indi-

---

[1]This section and the subsequent one, "Guidelines from Paul," are a revision of what I previously called with less justification "How Jesus Would Encounter Power in Folk Islam" and "How Paul Would Encounter Power in Folk Islam" in my chapter "The Relevance of Power Ministries for Folk Muslims" in *Wrestling with Dark Angels* (1990, 313-331); used by permission.

cates a sequence of power encounter leading to truth encounter leading to an allegiance encounter with Jesus. The disciples were here sent out especially for the power and truth encounters ("heal the sick . . . and say, 'The kingdom of God has come near you' "—Lk. 10:9).

Jesus continues, "Pray . . . the Lord of the harvest to send out laborers" (Lk 10:2). *Third, prayer and divine commissioning are essential*—obvious prerequisites for spiritual encounter. "I send you out as lambs in the midst of wolves," Christ said (Lk 10:4). *Fourth, we enter the encounter with a power that is expressed by vulnerability, by the cross.* Our Lord conquered the cosmic powers on the cross (Col 2:15), and we can expect to be "partakers of Christ's sufferings" (1 Pet 4:13). We are not to adopt the weapons of the enemy. Instead, we are to convey a message of forgiving love. We must convey a theology of suffering that not only rejoices when God delivers us or others but which recognizes the grace and comfort that God gives in suffering (2 Cor 1:7) and the character he develops in us through it (Rom 5:3-5). Christ's instructions included, "Carry no purse" (Lk 10:4). Yet elsewhere the disciples are told to take one and even to get a sword (Lk 22:35, 36). This suggests, *fifth, that we may be expected to alter our approach according to the timing and the context.* We note historical cycles in the more extraordinary signs and wonders, with the greatest number occurring when there are major expansions of the Church into new areas prior to the additional witness of the Bible and the confessing Church.

Jesus goes on to tell the disciples, "Whenever you enter a town and they receive you, . . . heal . . . and say . . . 'The Kingdom of God has come near to you' " (Lk 10:8-9). We are told later (Lk 10:17) that the demons submitted to them in Jesus' name. Thus apparently at least some of the healing included deliverance from the demonic. Thus, a *sixth* guideline is that *we are to bear witness by deed (power encounter and healing) and word (truth encounter).* They are told to leave any place that does not receive them but still announce that "the kingdom of God has come near" (Lk 10:8, 10-11). *Seventh, although we are to focus on the receptive, we still are to leave a witness with those who are not.*

The unresponsive are told, "Woe to you . . . for if the mighty works done in you had been done in Tyre and Sidon, they would have repented" (Lk 10:13). *Eighth, ministries of power and proclamation lead to opposition as well as faith.* This was certainly true of our Lord's experience, whose preaching and healing led to increasing numbers of disciples on the one hand and opposition that led to chants of "crucify him" on the other.

When the disciples returned and reported that "even the demons are subject to us in your name," Jesus responded, "I saw Satan fall like lightning from heaven" (Lk 10:17-18). *Ninth, our worldviews need to be expanded to include the spirit world and the cosmic battle there.* This lack in Western worldviews is what Paul Hiebert has called "the flaw of the excluded middle" (1982, 35-47).

Jesus gave the disciples authority over "serpents and scorpions and over all the power of the enemy" (Lk 10:19). *Tenth, Jesus had delegated to those he has commissioned authority in both the physical and spiritual realms.* The disciples are warned, "Do not rejoice in this, that the spirits are subject to you; but rejoice that your names are written in heaven" (vs. 20). *Eleventh, our salvation (and thus apparently a gift of evangelism) should be prioritized over a gift of exorcism.* Some have found that involvement with the demons has so monopolized their time that they have lost balance in other areas of their Christian life.

In the latter part of Luke 10, Jesus addresses God as "Father, Lord of heaven and earth" (Lk 10:21). *Twelfth, we should demonstrate that rather than fearing potentially harmful beings and forces, Christians may be confident that the universe is under the control of a personal, loving Father.* For the masses of Muslims concerned about harmful beings and forces, this is often the first revolutionary message of the gospel.

Christ's prayer then recognizes that God has "hidden these things from the wise and understanding and revealed them to babes" (Lk 10:21). *Finally, for understanding such spiritual realities, simple faith and teachableness are more important than erudition.* Most of us in academia or in foreign missionary service have had to learn about the spirit world and spiritual warfare from the common people we served. Richard De Ridder observed how unprepared his formal training in traditional Reformed theology left him for dealing with the spirit world in which his people lived. He concluded, "This is a chapter of Reformed Theology that has still not been written, and perhaps which cannot be written by the West" (1975, 222).

Guidelines from Paul

Ephesus in Paul's day, as described in Acts 19, contained the major elements found in popular Islam. It had spirit powers (Acts 19:11-20), power objects in the silver shrines of Artemis (vs. 24), and the sacred stone that fell from heaven (Acts 19:35), a meteorite like the Black Stone in the Ka'aba in Mecca. It had a power place, the temple of Artemis (Acts 19:27), and power times when there were celebrations in honor of the goddess. There were power rituals, the Jewish exorcists who tried to use the name of Jesus as a power word (Acts 19:13). Other rituals would have been used by those who practiced the magic arts (Acts 19:18-19). We shall seek to derive guidelines from what Paul said and did in this context: the center of magic for the Mediterranean world.

In Ephesus "he entered the synagogue and for three months spoke . . . about the kingdom of God." Then he "argued daily in the hall of Tyrannus. This continued for two years, so that all . . . heard the word of the Lord" (Acts 19:8-10). The *first guideline is that we should engage in power ministries in the context of teaching.* The power encounter and the truth encounter need to go together: the word announcing the Kingdom and the power demonstrating its presence even though it is not fully consummated.

We read that "when some were stubborn and disbelieved, speaking evil of the Way before the congregation [of the synagogue], he withdrew" (Acts 19:9). The *second guideline, already seen in Luke 10, is that we should focus on the receptive.*

The account continues, "God did extraordinary [literally, not the ordinary] miracles [literally, powerful deeds] by the hands of Paul" (Acts 19:11). *Third,*

God may use us in performing the miracles, but God will be the One accomplishing the task. Conversely, common devotees tend to focus on the human instrument as the power person. *Fourth, the word extraordinary reminds us that there are also ordinary ways that God works.* We need to remember that the God who does extraordinary things is also the One who established and works through the laws of nature which he established, laws such as those governing healing through medicine. Even the gift of grace to endure suffering unchanged is a work of God.

The extraordinary works are described: "handkerchiefs and aprons were carried away from his body to the sick, and diseases left and the evil spirits came out of them" (Acts 19:12). *Fifth, he might let objects convey the power, but the power would be God's, not that of the objects.* As Jesus used saliva in enabling eyes to see, a Coptic Orthodox priest in Egypt whom I knew would send some of his saliva in a bottle to the sick who could not come to him, and God would sometimes heal them. It is in this area that teaching must be clear so observers make the distinction between healing from God and magic.

"Itinerant Jewish exorcists," we read, "undertook to pronounce the name of the Lord Jesus over those who had evil spirits" (Acts 19:13). Attempts at exorcism play a significant role among Muslims.[2] *Sixth, real evidences of the power of God are often accompanied by counterfeits.* Christian contexts such as speaking in tongues are also found among Muslims. Thus discernment is needed to decide between (1) what is real and what is illusion, (2) what is of God and what is demonic, and (3) what are the physical or psychological or spiritual causes, or any combination of these. Here we need the help of medical doctors and psychologists, but ones who have room for the demonic as a possible cause of the phenomena observed.

The evil spirit answered the exorcists, "Jesus I know, Paul I know, but who are you?" (Acts 19:15). *Seventh, spirits recognize the authority of Jesus and those in whom he resides.* Folk Muslim practitioners try to appease or threaten spirits, but the Christian can speak with authority because Christ has authority over all such powers (Eph 1:20-21).

The Acts 19 passage continues, "The man in whom the evil spirit was leaped on them, mastered all of them, and overpowered them" (Acts 19:16). *Eighth, spirits have real power, using the bodies they inhabit.*

The result in Ephesus was that "fear fell upon them all" (Acts 19:17). *Ninth, evidences of power elicit fear which can only be balanced when God is seen as a loving Father.* As has been demonstrated previously, the mood of folk Muslims is that of fear.

The verse continues, "and the name of the Lord was extolled" (Acts 19:17). *Tenth, signs of the power of Kingdom should lead to the exalting of the King.* This is often not the case since folk Muslims just want healing and usually do not care from where it comes. In Mindanao the sick may go to the Muslim shaman, the Catholic priest, the government hospital, and the Protestant missionary. Thus, as

---

[2]Besides videos in my possession from East Africa and Indonesia, see Philips (1997), Bali (2006a, 2006b), al-Ashgar (1998), and Kim (2004).

has been noted, ministries of healing and exorcism must be accompanied by teaching about God as the source of healing, and comfort and grace when he does not give physical healing.

In Ephesus many new believers confessed their practices of magic and burned their books of magic (Acts 19:18-19). *Eleventh, since Christian converts often continue magical practices, materials associated with magic need to be destroyed and warnings must be given to avoid substituting Christian magic.* If a former Muslim sorcerer in an African country had not burned his paraphernalia, it has been said, he probably would have used it to discover and curse those who stole his boat and fishing net, his only means of support for himself and other converts who had lost their jobs and homes. In Faisalabad (formerly Lyalpur) in Pakistan people cast off their Muslim amulets at an evangelistic meeting and then outside bought St. Christopher's medals for stronger Christian amulets. I knew a Christian holy woman in the capital city of Islamabad who wrote Bible verses, rather than quranic verses, for amulets.

The result in Ephesus was that "the word of the Lord grew mightily" (Acts 19:20). *Twelfth, the demonstration of God's power should lead to the increase of the message rather than be an end in itself.* This is why lasting church growth has normally only resulted when power ministries have been combined with teaching.

The story concludes with the silversmiths, with their economic interests, stirring up the populace by appealing to the religious concerns and civic pride of the people. Then the legal and governmental institutions were identified as a means of expressing complaints or redressing wrongs (Acts 19:24-39). *Thirteenth, the "powers" with which the Christian must contend are not only individual spirits but the demonic behind human institutions, be they commercial, religious, legal, or governmental.* These are included in the biblical definition of the "powers" (Wink, 1984).

Today, the Temple of Artemis, one of the seven wonders of the ancient world, has been dismantled and the remains have sunk into the marsh except one pillar, which bears witness to the glory that had once existed there. Nearby stands the Isa (Jesus) Khan Mosque representing the Orthodox faith that has replaced the old paganism. Yet the mosque is surrounded by homes in which are hung glass replicas of blue eyes (*nazars*) to ward off the "evil eye"—reminders of the folk beliefs and practices that are mixed with the Orthodox ones. Like the temple before, these too will pass away. All that will be left is the name on the mosque—Jesus—since, as the previous residents of the city were told, he sits "far above all . . . power" (Eph 1:21).

Implications for the Present and the Future

There are a number of implications of this overview of power and blessing as keys for relevance to a religion such as Islam as lived by the common people. First, we see parallels with the context which the Bible describes. In Numbers 22 Balak thought that Balaam had power within himself to curse the Israelites so they could be defeated. Instead he learned that the power comes from God so the Israelites were blessed. We see a similar contrast between divine power and that of parishioners of magic in the Qur'an, where in surahs 113 and 114 Muhammad seeks protection in God from curses and practitioners. These parallels can be bridges for interpretation. Second, the felt needs of the people can lead to the devotees finding answers to their ultimate needs. Their fear of unseen beings and forces, powerlessness, sickness, and crises can lead them to salvation, wholeness, and reconciliation. God then is seen as the source of power, healing, and the grace to endure suffering. Rather than turn to divination, one can trust in the wisdom of God; instead of consulting the zodiac one looks to the Creator of the planets. Christ is understood not only as Savior and Lord but also as the healer, the exorciser, the blesser, and the authority concerned with the issues people face in their worldviews.

The Kingdom of God has entered human history. This means that the power of the new age is here for healing, and the promise of its consummation with Christ's return gives hope for complete healing where it is not yet experienced today. Meanwhile, for the pain that continues here and now, we have in Christ the companionship of one who understands our suffering (Phil 3:10; Heb 2:18).

The shift of the center of gravity of the church worldwide to the Global South where there is much more recognition of spiritual beings and forces means that attention will continue to be given to issues of power and blessing. And it should be. Since the need for healing can be the result of physical, emotional, and spiritual problems such as sin, or the demonic, there will need to be more collaboration between practitioners, biblical scholars and theologians, medical doctors, and psychologists. All must be open to the insights from the other fields, with special attention to practitioners, since so much has been written by those without experience with the phenomena of the demonic.

Where Scripture is silent or not clear, there is need for guidelines and humility on all sides in areas of experimentation and ministry concerning the demonic. At the same time we need to be open to the unexpected and surprising actions of the Holy Spirit. Though we "look through a glass darkly," we look to the day when our faith will be confident sight. So Paul reminded the Ephesians that Christ sits at God's right hand "far above all rule and authority and power and dominion" (Eph 1:21).

It is noteworthy that the rise of Christianity in Southwestern Arabia is attributed to power ministries by the oldest extant biography of Muhammad (d. 632), Ibn Hisham's recension of a work by Ibn Ishaq (d. 767). It tells of a Christian construction worker who cursed a snake that died, prayed for a blind boy who was healed, and then in God's name cursed the local sacred palm tree which was uprooted by a wind ([Hisham] 1955:14-16). Perhaps in the providence of God Christianity's spread in Arabia once again will be through the demonstration of his power.

11

Deep-Level Healing Prayer in Cross-Cultural Ministry

Models, Examples, and Lessons

JOHN AND ANNA TRAVIS

Charles Kraft, a pioneer in the field of inner healing and deliverance, has introduced thousands worldwide to this type of ministry, which he calls "deep-level healing."[1] We studied under Chuck Kraft at the Fuller School of Intercultural Studies a number of years ago and immediately began applying the principles of deep-level healing in our cross-cultural work in Asia. Through travel and training outside our region, we are also having the opportunity to pray with people from a variety of different ethnic and religious backgrounds in Africa, the Middle East, and various parts of Asia. John is presently doing doctoral studies exploring ways in which inner healing and deliverance can be an important part of cross-cultural ministry. We are finding that deep-level healing can be a valuable means of obtaining God's grace for those yet outside of Christ, for those being discipled, as well as for those being developed as leaders.

Why the Need for This Kind of Prayer

Since the 1980s we have worked among a particular unreached Asian people group. We have been challenged as to how to encourage deep character transformation in new believers and emerging leaders. Too often we have failed to get to the roots or deep heart issues holding people back from reaching maturity in Christ. Our frustration led us to seek additional means for character transformation to supplement what was already taking place through study of the Word,

---

[1] *Deep-level healing* is the term Kraft uses to describe the ministries of inner healing and deliverance. Kraft's model of deep-level healing is described in detail in *Deep Wounds, Deep Healing* (1993) and *Defeating Dark Angels* (1992b), and somewhat in *I Give You Authority* (1997), and is taught by Kraft in Fuller's School of Intercultural Studies (SIS) courses and training seminars. Throughout this paper, we will use the terms *deep-level healing* and *inner healing* interchangeably.

prayer, service, and fellowship. Over time we have observed that most who have failed to grow in Christ were not stumbling over theological issues per se, but rather over areas such as unresolved problems of the past (unforgiveness, rejection, haunting fears, emotional hurts), interpersonal conflicts, or occult involvement. One episode from the early days of our ministry illustrates this.

A new believer in a particular unreached community was a violent, powerful shaman. He came to Christ through the amazing love shown him by Tazim,[2] a follower of Jesus from the same ethnic group. One night, shortly after coming to faith, the shaman went into a violent rage.[3] Tazim, a Bible college graduate, had never encountered such behavior directly, but from his familiarity with Gospel accounts of deliverance, he assumed that it was demonic. He commanded, "In the name of *Isa* (Jesus) the Messiah, come out!" The shaman instantly fell to the floor and for the next two hours one demonic presence after another was expelled. I (John) arrived after the deliverance was over and found him sitting peacefully on the floor of his bamboo house, seemingly in his right mind. He then willingly surrendered to us all of his occult paraphernalia; together we prayed over the objects, smashed them with a hammer, then burned and buried them. Over the ensuing months the former shaman continued to be discipled by Tazim, and through his witness, several other families believed. A while later, the shaman had a dispute over money with another believer, and he suddenly cut himself off from any kind of fellowship, refusing to be reconciled. He finally sold his land and moved out of the area; we have not seen him since. We later learned that although this shaman had truly believed, was baptized, and was showing some fruit of the Spirit, he still had much bitterness, envy, and unforgiveness toward a number of people. It was clear the light of the gospel was not reaching certain parts of his will and emotions. Tazim himself, it turned out, was also in need of inner healing related to childhood emotional wounds that prevented him from effectively relating to and developing teammates, thus hampering the ministry of this otherwise gifted leader. From what we know now, we are convinced that deep-level healing could have greatly helped both these men and their families.

A Basic Model

After training and mentoring by Kraft, studying the related works of other evangelical scholar-practitioners,[4] receiving prayer ourselves, and praying with

---

[2]A pseudonym. Throughout the remainder of this paper, all names used in case studies are pseudonyms as well.

[3]We find this extreme behavior uncommon; however, it can occur, especially in cases of extensive occult involvement. Kraft teaches that those leading prayer sessions should order demons in Jesus' name to remain quiet and not harm the person receiving prayer.

[4]Besides *I Give You Authority* (1997), *Deep Wounds, Deep Healing* (1993), and *Defeating Dark Angels* (1992b) by Kraft, those we found particularly helpful were Wimber with Springer (1987), MacNutt (1974), Anderson (1990), Murphy (1992), Smith (1996), and Arnold (1997). Stacey (1989) offers a model of prayer specifically for use in ministry among Muslims.

a number of believers from various backgrounds and ethnicities, we began to form a basic working model for this type of ministry in our cross-cultural setting. Knowing some of the controversy surrounding inner healing and deliverance prayer,[5] we wanted to make sure that our model was both biblical and practical (i.e., appropriately contextualized and reproducible). This contextualized model, based largely upon the work of Kraft, is explained in the *Undivided Heart Prayer Manual* (Travis 2002)[6] and has been used for a number of years in various cross-cultural contexts. It consists of three types of prayer[7] heuristically referred to as breaking prayer, healing prayer, and deliverance prayer.

Breaking prayer (term borrowed from Neil Anderson's *Bondage Breaker* [1990]) deals with breaking spiritual bondage and is characterized by renunciation and repentance. It covers areas such as occult involvement (Dt 18:9-14), generational bondage (Lam 5:7; Ps 79:8, 9), ungodly "soul ties,"[8] judgments of self or others (Mt 7:1, 2; Jas 4:11, 12; Rom 14:4), vows made outside of God's will (Prov 20:25; Mt 5:33-37; Lv 5:4-6), curses (Ps 62:4; 109:28; Jas 3:9-10; Prov 26:2; Gal 3:13; Rom 12:14), and any other sin or activity that may have given Satan an open door into one's life. Renouncing and repenting is referred to and illustrated often in Scripture (e.g., Ez 14:6; Dn 4:27; Prov 28:13; 2 Cor 4:2; Acts 19:18-19). Breaking prayer is helpful in starting the process of inner healing, or in resolving issues which present themselves once the process of prayer for healing is under way.

Healing prayer occurs when the Lord heals deep emotional pain. This generally takes place as the one seeking healing (the prayee) and the one leading the prayer time (the pray-er) go together before the Lord in prayer, asking God to remind the prayee of any incident(s) where the prayee's heart was wounded. As the prayee remembers (see Ps 42:4; Lam 3:19-20),[9] he or she verbally describes

---

[5]Searching the Web for articles on inner healing and deliverance will show many articles both for and against inner healing. Among Christian writers (non-Christian groups also use the term) cautions are raised, for example, against the misuse of visualization, an overemphasis on "words of knowledge," the fear of producing false memories, and the concern of calling something "demonic" which in fact is not.

[6]The term *undivided heart* comes from Psalm 86:11 and Ezekiel 11:19, based upon the principle that in this type of prayer God makes the heart whole, free to be fully devoted to him. Since the term *heart* (*leb* in Hebrew; *kardia* in Greek) is often mentioned in Scripture in terms of healing of our inner selves (e.g., Ps 34:18; 147:3; Is 61:1) we often use the term *heart healing* interchangeably with inner healing and deep-level healing.

[7]These three types of prayer are alluded to in Kraft (1993, 1997) and *Defeating Dark Angels* (1992b), as well as in other works such as Wimber (1987) and MacNutt (1974).

[8]Unhealthy bonds with others, caused by such things as sexual involvement outside of marriage, submission to shamans, or overdependence on a parent or other authority figures into adulthood. Both healthy human ties and unhealthy soul ties are alluded to in Scripture (e.g., Gn 2:24; Lv 26:13; Col 2:2; Eph 5:21-25; 6:1-4; Gal 1:10; Prov 29:25; Jg 14 and 16 [Samson's soul ties with women]; 1 Cor 6:15-17).

[9]The emphasis in this model is not on the details of the memory (endeavoring to avoid the possible problem of "false memories"); the emphasis is on the negative emotions which surface, and waiting on God to bring healing and freedom.

(pours out; Ps 64:1; 62:8; 38:9; Mt 26:36-44) to God the emotions connected with the incident, being honest about even the worst reactions. He or she then asks God to show something of himself at the point of pain (Ps 34:18; 69:17), trusting that even at the darkest moment, God was actually present (Ps 139:7-16). The pray-er and prayee wait before God until he does what only he can do: heal the wound and lift the pain (Ps 94:19; 147:3). (If the healing does not seem to come, we have found it helpful to return to breaking prayer, asking God to highlight any area where repentance and renunciation are not yet complete. Often this clears the way for healing.) We have witnessed God's healing communication with the prayee[10] come in various forms: a still small voice (1 Kg 19:12), a mental picture or vision,[11] a Scripture verse recalled, a physical sensation (Mk 5:29), miraculous peace (Dn 10:18, 19), a sense of God's presence (Ex 33:14).

During the days of Jesus' earthly ministry we see numerous cases of inner healing as he touched and restored people's troubled hearts, emotions, and souls through his powerful, loving words and deeds. Jesus brought about inner healing in the restoration of the guilt-ridden Peter (Jn 21:15-19), the socially ostracized woman at the well (Jn 4:4-42), the despised Zacchaeus (Lk 19:1-10), the grateful prostitute honored by Christ (Lk 7:36-50), the rescued adulteress (Jn 8:2-11), the blind man emboldened by Christ (Jn 9:1-41), the ceremonially unclean hemorrhaging woman (Mk 5:25-34), and the tormented, feared wild man freed of myriad demons (Lk 8:26-39). In each of these touching encounters with Christ, we see Jesus healing more than physical bodies: he heals broken hearts and shattered lives; he takes away rejection, shame, and sorrow. Essentially, this is what healing prayer is: helping people, in a context of prayer, listen to God and spiritually experience his love and healing power, similar to the way people experienced it when Jesus walked on earth.

---

[10]One objection to inner healing is the overuse of the gift of the "word of knowledge" (1 Cor 12:8), where the pray-er receives knowledge from God about the prayee's situation, thus bringing God's healing to the prayee via the pray-er. The undivided heart model being described emphasizes instead the direct communication of God with the prayee, and encourages the pray-er to keep waiting and praying silently until the prayee receives directly from God.

[11]Just a few of the many pictures in the Scriptures: still waters, a valley, a table before enemies (Ps 23); Jacob's stairway (Gen 28); the captain of God's army (Josh 5); hills full of horses and chariots of fire (2 Kings 6); God's angel of judgment (1 Chron 21); the train of God's robe (Is 6); a figure like that of a man, an idol of jealousy, the idols of Israel portrayed on a wall (Ezra 8); one who looked like a man (Dn 10); fire on the heads of the believers (Acts 2); a sheet and animals (Acts 10); lampstands, scrolls, horses, bowls, incense, and a Lamb (Rev 1-22); the face of Christ (2 Cor 4:6). We view "visualization" as problematic not due to the fact that mental pictures are involved, but due to the fact that in some forms of inner healing, the pray-er creates or suggests the mental pictures for the prayee. Suggestion and visualization are not part of the undivided heart prayer model. (We find that pray-ers may have discernment or a "word of knowledge" which they purposely do not share, and often prayees then receive from God a very similar message. Later, the pray-er may share what he or she sensed, in order to confirm what God already spoke to the prayee.)

How can this occur when Jesus, though alive, is not present in body with us? The answer is that wherever we are gathered in his name, until the end of the age he is with us, and spiritually we can hear our Shepherd's voice (Mt 18:20; 28:20; Jn 10:4-16, 27).

Humans, even today, are hardwired to experience the Lord's presence, but not all take advantage of this (Ps 16:11; 91:1; 139:7). Experiencing the presence and healing of Christ is, of course, highly subjective, yet prayees seem to know when he has touched them in a special way. Tears often follow as they then effortlessly forgive the one who offended them (Mt 6:12-15; 18:21-35), renounce blaming God (Jb 40:8), and repent of sin (Prov 28:13; 1 Jn 1:9, 10) often committed as a wrong reaction to pain (Eph 4:26, 27). A new sense of joy (Ps 28:6, 7), either then or shortly thereafter, can be expected. Some may need this type of prayer repeatedly over a short period of time or on different occasions throughout their lives. Interestingly, from what we have seen up to this point, although images and messages people receive from God may in some way be context-culture specific, this Spirit-to-spirit healing between God and humans seems to be a fairly supra-cultural experience.[12]

Deliverance prayer or simply deliverance is the ordering out of demons from the life of the prayee with the authority given us in Christ (Eph 6:12; Mt 10:8; 28:18). If sufficient breaking prayer and healing prayer have occurred,[13] this process of ordering demons to leave can be quite simple and straightforward. At other times, the demons resist expulsion and a struggle takes place. We have observed both types of reactions during prayer sessions. The literature on the topic seems to confirm this as well. It is also important to note that many conservative Evangelical scholars and leaders today believe that the deliverance ministry may be needed by some who know Christ as well as those who do not yet know him.[14] We have seen many cases where committed followers of Jesus needed deliverance and experienced very significant change in their lives afterwards.

A final word on this basic model is to note the importance of Kraft's formulation of the three encounters of power, truth, and allegiance in Christ-centered ministry (Kraft 1991b). In fact, it is seeing deep-level healing as a form of power encounter, and power encounter as a part of evangelism, discipleship, and leader-

---

[12]Kraft discusses the universal or supra-cultural aspects of deep-level healing prayer in chapter 22 of *Appropriate Christianity* (2005b).

[13]We notice that if breaking and healing prayer are emphasized in the beginning, this lessens the possibility that issues which are not necessarily demonic will be assumed to be demonic. However, we notice that often "the world, the flesh, and the devil" are all involved in a particular issue that needs healing.

[14]This has been controversial; this chapter is too brief to deal with this topic. Well-known Evangelical scholars and professors who believe that a Christian can be "demonized" (*daimonizomai*, or "under the influence or inhabited by a demon") would include Merrill Unger, Chuck Swindoll, Ed Murphy, Neil Anderson, Clinton Arnold, John Wimber, Peter Wagner, and Charles Kraft, to name a few. For an excellent treatment of this topic see Arnold (1997).

ship development,[15] that makes this kind of prayer so valuable in cross-cultural ministry. One underlying principle is that in much of the world, God's truth is not expressed or understood primarily in propositional theological statements. Rather, truth is understood, and allegiance to God often only finally comes about, when one experiences God's power as well. Western Christians have too often wrongly assumed that verbal proclamation of God's truth is enough. Yet this is not the way Jesus and the disciples ministered, nor how the early church was birthed and expanded as recorded in the Gospels and Acts. In Scripture, we see truth proclaimed and allegiance called for, largely in the context of powerful signs, wonders, and healings (e.g., Acts 2:1-41; 3:6-26; 4:29-31; 8:4-8; 2 Cor 12:12; Rom 15:17-19). In short, deep-level healing is not an end in itself; rather, it is part of the larger divine plan of seeing biblical truth and allegiance to God made real in every human life.

Case Histories of Deep Healing Prayer

The following examples are shared with a number of safeguards. No real names are used, countries are not given, and identifying details are changed.

Jasmine came from a traditional Muslim family and was raised in a majority Muslim city. As a young teen, a Christian visited her home and shared the gospel with her. She immediately believed and silently prayed to receive Jesus as Savior. Out of fear of persecution from family and friends she told no one of her decision. For three years she grew little in her faith and had virtually no fellowship or discipleship. Then one day at high school she ran into a young woman from a campus Bible study. Jasmine and Jana began a discipling relationship. For three months they met for Bible study, but Jasmine, who was normally an alert student, simply could not concentrate and kept falling asleep. Whether they met in the morning, noon, or evening, the result was the same. Finally Jana suggested they meet for special prayer one morning. Jana prayed over Jasmine, "Anything preventing Jasmine from understanding the Word of God, I come against you in the name of Jesus." The normally quiet Jasmine screamed and ran for the door. Jana tackled her and kept praying. Finally Jasmine felt a presence leave her. Immediately she was able to concentrate and understand God's Word. On that very day she also received some inner healing as she read from Scripture words of Jesus' love for her. She received inner healing prayer for various issues on two subsequent occasions, and today she has an outreach to a number of close Muslim friends and prays inner healing for them. One has come to faith in Christ.

Hassan was a relatively new follower of Jesus from North Africa, but he simply could no longer feel the presence of Christ the way he did when he first believed. He was about "to give up on Jesus," convinced he didn't really care

---

[15]Kraft (1989) refers to three stages of spiritual development in a believer's life where he or she increasingly experiences more power, truth, and allegiance to God. These three phases of spiritual development correlate roughly with evangelism, discipleship, and leadership development.

about him. When I (John) met to pray with him, we read Psalm 139:7-18 together, which speaks of God's omnipresence, and then asked what his greatest pain in life was. He said it was over a broken relationship with a young lady. As we prayed, however, it became clear that he was troubled by something else: it was his hatred for Mustofa, whom he had resented bitterly for many years. Years ago when Hassan was in grade school, Mustofa picked a fight with Hassan's little brother. This happened during Ramadan, a time when fighting was strictly forbidden. Hassan stepped in to defend his brother, but Mustofa beat up Hassan badly, leaving him on the ground with dust and dirt covering his prized blue jeans. Hassan said he felt like a failure; he couldn't defend his brother, he couldn't defeat a younger boy in a fight, he was lying on the dirty ground, and no one watching him even cared enough to come to his aid. He hated Mustofa, he hated the onlookers, he despised himself. I prayed, "Lord, you are all-knowing and all-powerful, in fact you were there when this happened all those years ago, as your Word says in Psalm 139. Please show something of your love to Hassan in the midst of his most painful memory." I waited; nothing happened. Five minutes, ten minutes . . . no reaction, no sense of the presence of the Lord. Finally Hassan said he saw a figure dressed in white standing next to him, but he did not seem to be helped by this. Then suddenly right in front of me Hassan started crying, then sobbing. I asked what was happening. More tears, more crying. His nose was running. For ten minutes he kept wiping his nose and eyes. Finally he gained composure and told me what happened. The powerful figure standing tall next to him, whom he identified as Jesus, had suddenly bent down, picked Hassan up, put him on his knee and started brushing the dust off his blue jeans and comforting him. That was all. But this meant the world to Hassan. Someone knew of his shame and pain and defeat, yet cared for even the small details of his life. Since God is not bound by time, he gave Hassan the healing he needed during prayer, the healing he had missed when the event happened so many years ago. (I found out later that in the local culture it is especially shameful to be in dirt, have dust on your clothes, or lose a fight to someone younger. Also, had the crowd and his friends been honorable, they would have broken up the fight.) Over the next few minutes Hassan said over and over again how wonderful and caring Jesus is. He then, with all his heart, forgave Mustofa, forgave the crowd, and reaffirmed his allegiance to God through Christ.

Vedika, a woman from South Asia who had been hearing the gospel from several friends, listened intently as the concept of breaking prayer was explained to her. In her country there is a version of the ouija board where spirits are invited to move a coin to spell out answers to questions like "Where does the man I will later marry live now?" Though she was not yet in the Kingdom, she realized the childhood ouija-type games she had played displeased God. Vedika and I (Anna) had a chance to pray together, while a friend prayed diligently for us in the next room. God revealed to Vedika during prayer that in addition to the ouija games, idolatry practiced by her ancestors, the everyday practice of numerology, and her visits to a spiritual guide grieved his heart as well. The Lord not only convicted her of sin, which she freely confessed and repented of, but he also comforted her over the sorrow it brought into her life. When her name was measured by the numerology system, it was viewed as unlucky. The Lord showed his tender care for her, as if he was cleansing her name from what was bad and giving her name a new meaning. At last the Lord whispered in her heart that he was displeased with a power object she wore, which she had received from the spiritual guide she often visited. At first she could not believe the object was connected to evil power. "But I thought it brought peace and joy into my life!" she said. (From the brief stories I heard during the time of inner healing, her life did not seem characterized by peace and joy.) We decided to ask God specifically what he thought of her power object. Seconds later she looked up and said, "I see a black snake." That settled it; the object had to go. As she tried to remove it from her body, a force pulled the other direction. At last she removed it and gave it to a friend for safe keeping until she could dispose of it in a permanent way. We heard later that she, together with another family member, did dispose of it and that she had come into the Kingdom.

Mariha's husband was a Muslim follower of Christ,[16] yet Mariha was still outside the Kingdom. This lovely couple from the Middle East welcomed us into their beautiful home, and Mariha and I (Anna) had the chance to start praying right away. She had much pain related to her relationship with her mother, who had died a number of years before. The Lord showed Mariha vivid scenes from her childhood, all revolving around the theme of her mother. When the intense pain would surface (she could feel it physically in her body) she would pour out her heart to God, not holding anything back. Over and over Jesus would make himself known in each memory, taking away the pain from when she was a little girl, and showing his victory over the demons also present in many of the scenes in her mind. At last she sighed, "O God, did my mother ever love me at all, even just a little bit?" We waited. There was nothing, no memory of love or nurture, just bellowing tears of emptiness. But then the tears seemed to change. Mariha could barely get the words out, "I see his face! Love beams are shining from his face into my heart, filling the emptiness . . . I am stepping back a bit . . . I see the full picture now . . . He is hanging on the cross and I am at the foot of his cross." When we ended the time of prayer, Mariha asked me, "So what does the cross mean?" God was revealing one of the truths so difficult for most Muslims to accept: the cross of Christ. Mariha was so blessed over what God did for her, she arranged for another family member, who had had emotional difficulties for several years, to also receive prayer. His first question to me (John) when we met for prayer was "What does the cross mean?" Both Mariha and her relative later came to Christ through the witness of faithful friends.

Lessons Being Learned

Most people are prayees before they become pray-ers. There seems to be something "contagious" about this kind of prayer; it is usually more "caught"

---

[16]Mariha's husband is a true follower of Christ, yet has remained socioreligiously a part of the Muslim community and freely shares with others the new life he has in Jesus. This type of Jesus Muslim is alluded to by Kraft (1996, 210-214).

than taught. Note how Jasmine is now praying for others. We have seen this pattern in our own lives, and frequently in the lives of others.

Deep-level healing prayer is a very direct means to help a person connect with God. Even with prebelievers we are finding it is usually easy to bring up a conversation about deep-level healing. It rings true with most people that the God who created us would also provide means to heal us. It can be a good place to begin introducing Jesus as healer: healer of body, soul, and spirit. This can lead to a knowledge of Jesus as Savior and Master as well (recall Kraft's three encounters). Both Vedika and Mariha moved much closer to Jesus as a result of inner healing prayer.

A relationship of trust between pray-er and prayee is crucial. For people to want to pray with us, we must be known as people who are trustworthy. This may take place when a trusted friend introduces us to friends (as in the case of Mariha and Hassan). Or it may occur as we build meaningful relationships, which in a cross-cultural setting will mean having an excellent grasp of the heart language of the prayee, and the culture and sentiments of the people. We must also understand the socioreligious factors that shape the prayee's life so that we know contextually appropriate ways to share truth (i.e., truth encounter) and contextually appropriate ways to bring people into relationship with God through Christ (i.e., allegiance encounter).

Deep-level healing should be an essential component of discipleship. As we have now watched dozens of new believers go through discipleship, we are convinced that this model of prayer (or something like it, with its essential components) is necessary to get to the deepest roots and wounds of the heart (e.g., the case of Hassan). In some societies where overt occult practices are routine, it is likely most new believers will need deliverance from demons (recall the cases above of the shaman and Jasmine). In fact, in our own work we emphasize four basic ministry skills in training: how to contextually share Christ with the lost, how to disciple new believers, how to lead a small group Bible study, and how to pray for inner healing and deliverance. We are also seeing some new believers receive prayer and then shortly thereafter pray for someone else.

Receiving deep-level healing is a crucial part of leadership development. Since unhealed leaders tend to hurt others, it is essential that leaders receive healing. It would be especially effective if ministries had a systematic practice of administering deep healing as a routine part of leadership development. In cultures where saving face and avoiding conflict and shame are paramount, it seems this type of prayer would be culturally appropriate and missionally effective.

We are greatly indebted to the theoretical as well as practical instruction of Charles Kraft in his courses, seminars, and books. Through his keen understanding of religion and culture, he firmly places deep healing prayer in the context of overall cross-cultural ministry (see, for example, the three encounters model:

1996; 2005b; with Kraft and Kraft 2005). Through reports of his students world-wide, as well as his own experience in praying with hundreds of persons, Kraft writes with the authority of a scholar-practitioner. Yet, Kraft's work does not end here! We must now learn how to appropriately contextualize and widely apply deep-level healing in all cultures and segments of society: in Africa, Asia, and the postmodern West; in Hindu, Buddhist, and Muslim milieus; among young and old, educated and less educated, men and women, rich and poor. Many more chapters describing how healing occurs in these varied contexts must one day be written.

12

Spiritual Conflict

A Challenge for the Church in the West with a View to the Future

TORMOD ENGELSVIKEN

This chapter will trace my own pilgrimage from seeing the need for equipping missionaries for spiritual conflict, to interacting with other missiologists and reflecting on Scripture on related issues, to seeing the challenges these pose for Western churches.

Personal Experiences

I went to Ethiopia to teach systematic theology at the Mekane Yesus Theological Seminary in 1971, almost immediately after having finished my own theological education in Norway. I started teaching the usual subjects that I had myself studied as part of the ordinary theological curriculum in a Western Lutheran seminary. Very soon, however, the students raised questions that I was not prepared to answer. I remember particularly when a bright student asked for my advice on how to deal with people who were possessed by evil spirits. How should the demons be cast out? Neither the teaching on Satan and evil spirits nor the practice of casting them out of possessed people had been part of my theological training. Fortunately, my confidence in the authority of the Scriptures and my respect for the spiritual experiences of the Ethiopian Christians led me to study the biblical accounts and compare them with the contemporary Ethiopian experience. This study resulted in a book, *Besettelse og åndsutdrivelse* which was published in Norwegian in 1978 (Engelsviken). My point here is that the encounter with challenges and experiences in the church of the Global South that were very different from those of my own Western church background forced me to question traditional Western theology and start to reflect on new issues.

In the same year, 1978, I participated in the Lausanne consultation on Gospel and Culture in Willowbank, Bermuda, where I had the privilege of meeting Dr. Charles Kraft for the first time, and actually stay with him in the same room! This consultation, as well as later postdoctoral studies at Fuller Theological Seminary in 1983 and 1987, was a real eye-opener as far as the understanding of the relationship between Christianity, culture, and contextualization were concerned. The direction and content of my own missiological interest and thinking have been deeply influenced by these encounters with Kraft and other Fuller professors.

To close the circle, more than a generation after my first encounter with spiritual conflict in the form of possession and exorcism in Ethiopia, I encountered the same reality in China in February 2007 in the testimony of a female leader in a house church. She related how she had been able to help a young woman who showed signs of possession during a prayer meeting, and how the woman had finally been set free after having turned over a necklace that had been given to her by her boyfriend who had had it blessed in a Buddhist temple for good luck.

The Consultation "Deliver Us from Evil"

The leading Malaysian theologian Hwa Yung in *Mangoes or Bananas* has argued convincingly that a truly contextual theology in Asia "would necessarily involve the practice of 'power encounters' in the healing and exorcism ministries" (1997, 75-76). He places relevance for "the evangelistic and pastoral tasks of the church" as one of four criteria of a contextual mission theology together with relevance for the sociopolitical concerns, inculturation, and faithfulness to the Christian tradition (ibid., 69, 123). Included in these evangelistic and pastoral tasks are the ministries of healing and exorcism.

But this concern for spiritual conflict is of course not limited to Asia. As we have seen it is highly relevant in Africa, and it also is very important in Latin America. When the Lausanne Theology and Strategy Working Group considered the need for a consultation in the late 1990s, an overwhelming majority of those asked for their opinions with regard to topics to be dealt with in a consultation answered that the question of spiritual conflict was on the top of their agenda. This almost unanimous show of interest in the questions of spiritual power led to the consultation named "Deliver Us from Evil" in Nairobi, Kenya, in August 2000. The consultation brought together a broad spectrum of views and experiences, yet all participants were committed to evangelical Christianity. Twelve plenary papers and ten case studies were presented, and the consultation was also able to produce a "consultation statement." The consultation resulted in two books, a shorter Lausanne Occasional Paper (LOP) named *Spiritual Conflict in Today's Mission* (Engelsviken 2001a) and the full consultation report with all the papers, *Deliver Us from Evil: An Uneasy Frontier in Christian Mission* (Moreau et al. 2002). Among the participants at the consultation who also wrote papers were Charles Kraft and his wife, Marguerite, with the titles "Contextualization and Spiritual Power" (Kraft 2002b, 276-289) and "Spiritual Conflict and the Mission of the Church: Contextualization" (M. Kraft 2002, 290-308).

I would like to highlight a few points in the consultation statement adopted unanimously by the participants.[1] The statement takes its point of departure from the Lausanne Covenant (1974), the Manila Manifesto (1989), and the LCWE Statement on Spiritual Warfare (1993).

There is a severe difference in worldview and understanding of the spiritual realities and spiritual conflict between the church's ministry in the Western world and that of the Two-Thirds World. The thirty participants at the conference came from all parts of the world, including the West. It was noted with interest that "most of the consultation participants from Western societies had come to recognise the realities of the unseen or spiritual realm as a result of their cross-cultural experience. Those from the Two-Thirds World frequently reported their experiences with Western missionaries, who were unaware of these spiritual realities, and were thus unable to minister to the spiritual realities that Two-Thirds World people experience on a day-to-day basis" (Engelsviken 2001a, 82-83). Spiritual conflict seems to be an area where the theological and practical differences are the greatest between the Western churches and the churches in the Global South. One might ask how this untenable difference can be equalized. It is obviously not possible to maintain that "spirits exist" in the South and not in the West! This view would presuppose a view of the spirits as cultural phenomena without ontological reality. This view is quite common in the West, and some even assume that as modernization spreads to larger areas of the world, also in the South, the belief in the ontological reality of the spirit world will eventually disappear, to be replaced by psychological or other rational explanations of the phenomena associated with belief in the spirit world. The consultation statement, however, has an opposite view. The faulty understanding of the spiritual realities is not to be placed in the Two-Thirds World but in the West. It may have many causes, not least the influence of Enlightenment thought and the development of Western science and empiricism. We will come back to the question of whether there is a postmodern change taking place in the West that will lead to more openness to the reality of the spiritual world. The whole theological and missiological area of spiritual conflict may be one where the church in the West has most to learn from the churches in the Global South.

The statement indicates areas of common agreement, and also areas of unresolved tensions, warnings, and areas needing further study and exploration. While it is imperative to speak openly about the differences, it is remarkable that it is possible to reach such a degree of agreement on a topic that has been so controversial in recent years, even among Evangelicals and Pentecostals.

What are the main areas of agreement? The most important seems to be the fundamental agreement that the "powers and principalities" cannot be reduced to mere social and psychological phenomena, but that they are "ontologically real beings." "Satan is a real, personal, spiritual and created being" who seeks to "actively oppose God's mission and the work of God's church" (ibid., 85). This may seem like a very obvious statement to some, but in the academic and theological world of the West it is quite radical and controversial.

---

[1]The statement is found in both Engelsviken (2001b, 82-96) and Moreau et al. (2002, xxvii-xxviii).

The work of Satan and "the spiritual forces of evil" is varied, and includes deceiving; tempting to sin; afflicting the body, emotions, mind, and will; and taking control of persons (possession, demonization). The work takes place in the realm of the occult as well as in false religions. However, the statement emphasizes that the work of the evil one cannot be isolated to the individual or merely spiritual or religious realm. The statement rejects, on the one hand, the conception of the world as a "closed universe governed merely by naturalistic scientific laws." On the other hand, it also rejects "a dualistic system in which Satan is understood to be equal to God": "Because we reject a dualistic worldview, the blessings of God and the ministrations of the angelic host, as well as the consequences of sin and the assaults of Satan and demons cannot be isolated solely to a spiritual realm." Satan also distorts the role of social, economic, and political structures; legitimises violence; and promotes self-interest, injustice, oppression, and abuse (ibid., 85-87). This emphasis on a more comprehensive understanding of the work of Satan and of spiritual conflict is in my opinion one of the main contributions of the consultation.

The fight against the evil one and his forces in spiritual warfare or conflict must also be varied. It is based on the victory of Jesus on the cross and through the resurrection, and on the work of Jesus through prayer, righteousness, obedience, and setting the captives free. The spiritual conflict involves also more than one enemy. Not all sin or wrong can be attributed directly to the devil. The conflict must engage the flesh and the world as well. Christians share in Christ's victory and are given authority to stand against the attacks of Satan in the victory they have in Christ.

The statement also emphasizes the eschatological character of the spiritual struggle. While the victory was won on the cross and through the resurrection, "the return of Christ and the ultimate consummation of his victory over Satan gives us confidence today in dealing with spiritual struggles and a lens through which we are to interpret the events in the world today" (ibid., in loco). The fact that the final victory is still future also means that a triumphalistic attitude in which an absolute and final victory is proclaimed here and now is excluded. Christians live in the tension between the "already" and the "not yet" of the coming of the Kingdom of God, and this tension will also have consequences for the application of the victory of Christ in spiritual conflict.

An Empiricism of Evil?

The acceptance of the statement from the Deliver Us from Evil Consultation, and the wider involvement in spiritual conflict as it is understood in the statement and in numerous books on the topic, has as a basic premise the acceptance of the ontological reality of Satan and his host, the whole spiritual realm, and the possibility that Satan and his demons can in various ways influence the lives of people, Christian believers as well as nonbelievers. While this premise is taken for granted in the Evangelical and charismatic/pentecostal churches in the Global South and by most Evangelicals and Pentecostals in the West, it is rejected by much of the academic theology in the older, mainline churches in Europe and in North America, as well as by the intellectual elite of Western society. In Western theology, it is just not credible to engage in spiritual warfare against personal evil forces. I think it is worthwhile to critique this view as being hardly tenable from both an empirical and a theological perspective.

One might be tempted to relegate the whole question to a matter of theological choice, a mere faith decision. Does faith in the reality of Satan and demons, and all that is connected with this, fall into the category of a mere faith decision? In my opinion it does not, and I would like to forward some arguments in favour of viewing it differently.

First, it has to be admitted that God's existence cannot be proved. The attempts at proving God's existence are not theoretically binding. Yet, the evidence many have provided may make it probable that God exists. As far as truth is concerned I adhere to a theory of coherence where a theory that can include and account for all the evidence in a coherent and consistent way is more likely to reflect the truth than one which does not.[2]

Second, the evidence for the existence of the spirit world and the activity of the evil forces is of two kinds, general and uniquely Christian. Let us first look at the general evidence. It can hardly be denied that people all over the world, in all cultures and religions, do believe in a spirit world and that spiritual personal beings can influence the lives of humans. This is particularly true of non-Western cultures, but also to a certain extent of Western cultures. This is readily accepted by historians of religion and social anthropologists alike and does not need any further documentation. In addition to this belief, there are also claims of experiences of the spirit world, of concrete manifestations of or contacts with spirits. There are both a cognitive worldview dimension and a personal, individual and social, experiential dimension to this belief. Yet, there are enormous varieties as to exactly what is believed and experienced.

I would like to focus especially on one belief and experience that is particularly relevant for our theme, namely, the belief in and experience of demonic possession, or as it is most often called in the New Testament, demonization. Possession is known in many cultures and is therefore not a particularly "Christian" phenomenon. It is, however, often described in relation to Christianity. It is described in the New Testament, the history of the church, and in today's mission. It is especially relevant because it represents "the tip of the iceberg" of demonic activity, both in the sense that it only represents a tiny fraction of what Satan is doing in the world and in the sense that it is a visible and manifest activ-

---

[2]See Gravem (2005, 181-211). In the English abstract it is said, "This article discusses the concept of truth, based on L.B. Puntel's explicative-definitional theory of truth. The question that forms the background of the discussion is how one can understand theoretically the claims to truth of various religions and world-views . . . The author attempts to demonstrate the philosophical strength of Puntel's theory by showing how it is more holistically coherent and more understandable than alternative theories" (ibid., 181). Peder Gravem is professor of philosophy of religion at MF Norwegian School of Theology in Oslo.

ity that may give us information of the vast and more invisible—and possibly even more dangerous—demonic activity below the surface.

In the stories about possession in the Gospels[3] we see that the demons are intelligent beings with a will that implies that they can move, speak, and act.[4] They know their own future and who Jesus is. They are personal, invisible, spiritual beings. It is characteristic of the exorcism narratives, in contrast to the healing narratives, that there is a conflict between Jesus and the spirits. There are three or more personalities involved, Jesus, the possessed, and the demon(s), while in the healing narratives there are only two, Jesus and the sick person. Jesus' attitude and words are different; he speaks stern words of judgment and expulsion to the spirits, but kind words of encouragement to the demonized person (and to the sick). The demon aims to destroy the person as a human being and to disrupt his or her relation with God. Although both the sick and the demonized are said to be "healed" because the end result is health and well-being, the symptoms of sickness and demonization are essentially different.

Even though there are only a few exorcism narratives in the New Testament, the various categories of symptoms are clear: there are bodily or somatic symptoms, psychological symptoms, supernatural or parapsychological symptoms, moral symptoms, and religious symptoms. We cannot go into detail about all the various symptoms, but only emphasize the "supernatural": that the demons have a knowledge they have not been able to acquire in a natural way about who Jesus is, and who his disciples are (Acts 16; 17; 19:15). They show their enmity against Jesus, yet must be obedient to his command. They also know their own future (Mk 1:24; Lk 8:31). That the demons are not mere subjective mental phenomena is also evidenced by the demons' ability to influence the environment of the demonized (Mk 5:13). It is important to notice that it is the total pattern that is indicative of demonization. It is not isolated phenomena but the total expression of a personal spiritual being that has come into the demonized person and dominates his or her actions, words, and total behavior that shows that a demonization has taken place. This is also shown by the fact that the only adequate reaction of Jesus or his disciples to demonization is to expel the demons from the demonized. It is exorcism. This expulsion takes place by a word of authority by Jesus. He expels the demons by a simple command, not by any material means or in anyone's name. The disciples also expel demons by a command, but in Jesus' name, that is, on behalf of and with the authority of Jesus (Acts 16:18; Lk 10:17-20).

If we look at church history we find that possession and exorcism were well known in the ancient church. Several of the church fathers refer to it in their writings (see Skarsaune and Engelsviken 2002, 65-72). The early church theologians were convinced of the existence of the demons, as, for example, expressed

---

[3]The most important references are Mk 1:21-28; 5:1-20; 9:14-29. There are also references to demonization and exorcism in the summaries in Mk 1:32; 3:10-11; Mt 4:24; 8:16-17. There are two important narratives in Acts: Acts 16:16-18; 19:11-20.

[4]The analysis of the exorcism narratives is based on Engelsviken (1978, 24-25).

by Tertullian. "And we affirm indeed the existence of certain spiritual essences; nor is their name unfamiliar. The philosophers acknowledge there are demons" (Tertullian, *Apologeticum* 22, 1980, 36). The evidence shows that the pagan gods were regarded as demons, and that those who were possessed by them when confronted with the message of Christ had to confess that "the wicked spirit, bidden to speak by a follower of Christ, will as readily make the truthful confession that he is a demon, as elsewhere he has falsely asserted that he is a god" (Tertullian, *Apologeticum* 23, 1980, 37). The Christians not only can force a confession from the demons, but also can drive the demons out in the name of Christ: "All the authority and power we have over them is from our naming the name of Christ, . . . Fearing Christ in God, and God in Christ, they become subjects to the servants of God and Christ. So at our touch and breathing, overwhelmed by the thought and realization of those judgment fires, they leave at our command the bodies they have entered . . ." (ibid., 38). This power over the evil spirits and the expulsion of them is also seen as instrumental in the mission of the church. "It has not been an unusual thing, accordingly, for those testimonies of your deities to convert men to Christianity" (ibid.). Similar statements are also found in other fathers. Justin Martyr (ca. A.D. 160) in his *Dialogue* refers to the exorcisms as the very evidence of the fact that Jesus has risen from the dead and now sits at the right hand of the Father (Justin, *Dialogue with Trypho* 85, 1981, 241-242).

It is not possible to explain the different symptoms of possession (including supernatural knowledge) and the reaction to Christian preaching and to Jesus in a purely rational or scientific way. Whenever that has been attempted the result has been a reduction of the phenomena associated with possession in such a way that only a few isolated features have been "explained," but not the total pattern. Whenever phenomena do not fit the theory they have been ignored or denied. This approach to truth violates the principle of coherence where all observable facts have to be accounted for in the theory. The only theory that is able to explain the phenomenon of possession is the religious one, although this theory is not a rational theory in the scientific, immanentistic sense. Only a biblical understanding of demonization is able to both explain the phenomena in a way that does not ignore or deny any of them and lead to a treatment of the possessed that is effective, leading to health and wholeness. Thus, a biblical understanding recommends itself as probable by the truth criterion of coherence.

It is impossible to "prove" the existence of evil spirits and the spiritual realm. It remains ultimately a matter of faith. However, on the empirical evidence of the New Testament, the history of the church, and the contemporary experience of the church, one may conclude that it is possible to draw some conclusions about the nature and activities of demons as well as how they are to be driven out from demonized people. Demonic possession may be seen as a relatively common phenomenon in the history of religion. From a Christian theological point of view it may be seen as giving information about the spiritual realm under the category of general revelation. It is a revelation that in principle may be accessible apart from faith in Christ, although often distorted by the different religious frameworks in which it occurs. Although general revelation primarily is a revelation of God and his will, it may also be seen as including the fall and its consequences (see Rom 1:18; 2:14-16). However, an understanding of the demonic based on experience, although valid to a certain extent for the practice of the church, can never achieve the status of normative Christian teaching. The concept is too fraught with danger of error, and it lacks clear biblical words, conditions for Christian doctrine.[5] This was one of the areas of tension during the Deliver Us from Evil Consultation, and it is expressed in the following way:

> Tension exists concerning the extent to which we can learn and verify things from the spiritual realm from experiences not immediately verifiable from Scripture, in contrast to limiting our understanding of the spiritual realm from Scripture alone . . . We are not agreed as to whether or how the truths about spiritual realities and spiritual conflict methodologies can be verified empirically. Some engage in active experimentation in spiritual-conflict ministry as a means of developing generalities concerning spiritual conflict, while others are not convinced of the validity of this way of learning. (Engelsviken 2001a, 93-94)[6]

The Teaching of Jesus

From a Christian point of view it is, however, possible to take a step further. The experiential evidence itself may inform a Christian understanding of possession and expulsion of evil spirits, but even more important are the words of Jesus contained in the Scriptures. Jesus not only practiced exorcism, but also interpreted it by explaining the significance of it. In his speech about Beelzebub in Matthew 12:22-29, Jesus answers the accusation by the Pharisees that he drove out demons by Beelzebub, the prince of the demons. The answer first points out the improbability that Satan would drive out demons, since that would mean that his kingdom would be divided against itself and therefore would be destroyed. This argument assumes that Satan has a kingdom and a deliberate strategy and that he holds people captive (Mt 12:29). With this option excluded, Jesus can present his own interpretation, "If I drive out demons by the Spirit of God, then the Kingdom of God has come upon you" (Mt 12:28 NIV). Jesus places the exorcisms in an eschatological context. They are irrefutable evidence that the time of salvation has come.[7]

---

[5]Here the Protestant principle of the Scriptures being the source and norm for Christian teaching, the *sola scriptura*, has to be applied.

[6]On this issue Professor Kraft insisted on learning from empirical experience. He expresses this forcefully in the book *The Rules of Engagement* (2000, 23): "We intend . . . that this be a step toward developing a 'science' in the spirit realm parallel to the sciences already developed to deal with human and material aspects of God's creation." It seems to this author that we indeed can and must learn from experience, as in most areas of practical theology, yet have to be careful when it comes to developing authoritative doctrine or "ground rules" (Kraft) apart from Scripture.

[7]See Lk 4:18-19. The proclamation of freedom for the prisoners and setting the captives free belong to the "year of the Lord's favor," to the "good news," that is, to the time of salvation.

Jesus' exorcisms, his practice of absolute authority over the evil powers, his expulsion of them with a mere word, his interpretation of what the exorcisms imply in terms of the coming of the Kingdom of God, and his own victory over the evil power belong to the area of special revelation. Therefore, they can form the basis for authoritative Christian doctrine. It can be documented that Jesus' exorcisms, in which demons know and confess that Jesus is the Son of God and obey him totally, are quite unique in the history of religions. For Christians who believe in the authority of revelation as contained in the Bible there is no option but to accept the ontological reality of Satan and his demons as well as the obligation to engage in spiritual conflict. It is indeed possible to develop a basic Christian understanding of the spiritual realm based on Scripture.

Future Challenges for the Western Churches

Before drawing the final conclusions, I would like to come back to one of the questions that was raised initially. It is often assumed that Western culture and most of the churches in the West under the influence of Enlightenment thought have discarded the spiritual realm. However, some remarkable new developments are taking place in the West that question this assumption. In a recent poll in Norway, one of the most secularized countries in Europe, twenty-two percent expressed the belief that it is possible to get in contact with the spirits of deceased persons. This is an increase of six percent from 1998. Women and young people (thirty percent) are more likely to believe in spirits than men and older people. In Sweden, regarded as possibly more secularized than Norway, sixty-one percent (among youth, seventy-four percent) say they believe in the "spiritual dimension" (Sjödin 2001, 35). Associated with this belief is a deep anxiety. My colleague, professor of history of religion Arild Romarheim, has coined the term *universe of anxiety* to describe it. In a recent article (Romarheim 2007, 23-27) he argues that at least in the Nordic European countries we may observe a return to a premodern religiosity. "We are talking about a worldview which is humankind's most important religious common denominator: belief in spirits." He suggests that the epoch we are entering may be called the "trans-modern." While modernity is with us in the form of the outward lifestyle based on enormous technological advances, the inner life of humans seeks something that transcends this reality.

In Denmark and Norway a prime-time TV program called *Åndenes makt* ("The Power of the Spirits") has gained popularity. It deals with "haunted houses" and people suffering from the influence of spirits or ghosts. Different kinds of people are called in to deal with the problems. Pastors in the Lutheran church in Norway are frequently called to houses with "unrest" to pray and expel evil or bothersome forces. A special liturgy has been developed for this procedure. The Danish pastor Ole Skjerbæk Madsen says that this openness to the spirit world has also led to a new openness for the message of the church. He has developed a "user's guide" for the many Danish people who seek the help of the church in this connection (Romarheim 2004, 61-62).

German missiologist Theo Sundermaier says, "We cannot escape from our Western thinking, but we have to recognize that the globalization of our world is not merely an economic problem, but also a spiritual phenomenon. A mutual interpenetration of different worldviews and strategies for coping with the world takes place whether we like it or not" (Sundermaier 2004, 64). I do not agree with the almost fatalistic view of the impossibility of escaping from our Western culture, but concur wholeheartedly with Sundermaier's view of spiritism as a theological and pastoral challenge to the Western churches.

It seems quite clear that spiritual conflict is an urgent task for the church and its pastoral leaders both in the Global South and in the West. This comes as no surprise. If Satan and his demons and the whole spiritual realm have ontological reality and can actively influence the lives of people, cultures, religions, and political and economic structures, they cannot be relegated to a premodern time or to specific ("animistic") cultures. They are real and active. The increase of interest in spirits and occult activity will undoubtedly also make spiritual conflict even more relevant in the Western churches. In this regard the churches in the West need the help of the churches in the Global South. All churches need a renewed study of the biblical worldview and the practice of spiritual conflict. They also need to draw on the experience of people ministering in this area.

Spiritual conflict has at least three important major dimensions: the christological as it proclaims and realizes the victory, power, and lordship of the living Christ; the diaconal as it helps people suffering under the attack and influence of evil spiritual forces and fights structural evil in the world; and the missiological as it draws people to Christ in faith, sets captives free, and gives a foretaste of the coming Kingdom.

Part IV

SUMMING UP

13

An Overview of the Work
of Charles H. Kraft

ROBERT J. SCHREITER

The language of "paradigm shift" is often overused. There is a tendency at times to trumpet every change or adjustment in a field of study as a fundamental shift in how we perceive and interpret the data before us. Or, alternatively, when someone is puzzled by certain events or phenomena encountered, there is a call for a new paradigm. As a result the language of paradigm shift has become rather shopworn for many scholars.

But to speak of paradigm shift in terms of the work of Charles Kraft, which is being celebrated in this volume, is completely apropos. In the three distinctive areas explored here—anthropology, communication, and spiritual power—he has indeed shifted perspectives within missiology and brought new methods of interpretation to bear upon our understanding of Christian witness. His work has been profoundly influential for Evangelical missiologists, and also for many others of us who are laboring in the Lord's vineyard.

In this concluding chapter, I would like to cull some of the insights that have been offered here by Kraft's colleagues and students and revisit each of these three areas as they pertain to missiology today. This is done to serve as a basis— to the extent possible—to discern where God might be leading us in our next steps as we continue to seek to refine our capacity to bring his Good News to all peoples.

Cultural Anthropology

The relationship between anthropologists and missiologists has been a variegated one, as both Darrell Whiteman and Robert Priest point out. A significant amount of the first anthropological writing was done by missionaries, and a surprising number of anthropologists were missionary kids (although often soured by their parents' religious faith). Religion—something so central to the worlds of the peoples studied by anthropologists—also got a range of different treatments as the descriptions were filtered through the models regnant at any given time. (Michael Rynkiewiech notes how U.S. anthropologists have rewritten their genealogy at one point.)

Charles Kraft was by no means the first to bring anthropological insights and method to bear on missiology, but he has been among the most influential. This influence flowed not only from his books, but also from the generation of doctoral students he has trained at Fuller. Indeed, a number of them have contributed to this volume. Because of his own missionary experience in Nigeria, he has had a keen sense of just where in mission work anthropological insights could have the most effect. Although his contributions met formidable opposition from an older generation of Evangelicals (portrayed in this volume by Paul Pierson), Kraft's work has largely prevailed over those voices. His work in this regard has had considerable impact on a generation of missiologists in mainline Protestant and Roman Catholic circles as well.

Where do we stand with cultural anthropology's contribution to missiology today, and where might that relationship be going? Priest notes the rise and decline of programs in cultural anthropology in Evangelical college and seminary programs. He laments also the relative paucity of fully trained anthropologists working in missiology across the theological spectrum. How is this to be accounted for, given the importance that cultural understanding plays in mission work, and the importance attributed to it by so many experienced missionaries?

There is probably no single answer to this question. Certainly theological politics within mission agencies and schools and seminaries plays a significant role. Ethnocentrism, especially in a powerful nation such as the United States, cannot be discounted either. The part I would like to explore here is the uncertain status of both disciplines—cultural anthropology and missiology. Paul Hiebert sets forth here the epistemological foundations of cultural anthropology's self-understanding as a discipline as, what he terms, positivist, relativist, and cultural realist. He shows how the positivist attitude in an important way imprisoned missiological thinking in a certitude that played to the worst instincts of theological pride and intolerance. The relativist position of what he terms the postmodern helped missiology distance itself from such un-Christian attitudes, but was itself problematic theologically, especially on matters of truth claims. The critical realism Hiebert proposes as post-postmodern may be only partially realized in anthropological writing today, but does seem to be a sane way for missiologists to follow.

Here lies an implication about cultural anthropology that is important for missiologists to think about. Whiteman charts some of the changes in anthropology historically as Hiebert does epistemologically. What strikes this nonanthropologist about both of these narratives is how much cultural anthropology has been a discipline struggling to be recognized as scientific or legitimate alongside the other disciplines in the university. In its earlier phases, it was taking its cue from the natural sciences. In its postmodern manifestations (as relativist, constructivist, and contested) it has its eye on the humanities, especially English and culture studies. Its quest for legitimation has always been sought within the environs of the academy, more so than in the field. The academic forum has also tended to relegate the study of religion as something that will evolve away or remain as an epiphenomenon of other social aspects of society. This neglect of religion as a serious object of study is reflected today in the scramble in the study of international relations, for example, to develop models for understanding the resurgence of religion. Rynkiewich points out at the end of his study areas such as urbanization and globalization as objects of study that have still not been adequately addressed by anthropology. The best studies of these areas that I have seen are being done by nonanthropologists (see, for example, Thomas 2005).

To suggest that developments in anthropology are driven by this quest for academic legitimation, and that the academy shows little interest in religion, is not to say that anthropology should be abandoned by missiologists. It is still the best conversation partner in the social sciences that missiologists have. It is only to point to the inherent limitations of the discipline for missiology, a discipline that is also unsure of itself.

Whether missiology is a discipline in its own right or whether it is a field of work where the use of different disciplines converge (anthropology, communication theory, spiritual power, history, theology) continues to be debated. This is especially acute in Northern Europe, where chairs of missiology are disappearing from theological faculties at a steady pace.[1] Bringing together two sets of uncertainties does not add up to certainty. Here is where some of the malaise seems to lie.

Rynkiewich notes that "missiology is stuck in the 1960s." He apparently makes this comment in view of missiology's relationship to anthropology. That missiology would seem to be that dependent upon anthropology is testimony to the influence of Charles Kraft's work. Let me conclude this first section with some thoughts as to how things might go in this relationship.

Rynkiewich asks us to listen for the new voices. One of these, to my mind, is shifting from a fairly exclusive attention to the otherness of the Other to a more cosmopolitan point of view, as is now arising in the discussions about living in a pluralist world.[2] That is to say, we need more focus on the interaction of these "others" in order to see both similarity and difference.

Second, we need to say farewell to the cult of postmodernism as an academic fashion. To focus on the arbitrary, the constructed character of things, and the inherent instability of all signification is not helping us live in an unstable world: either in developed countries or especially in poor countries that find themselves veering into anomie. People continue to be seeking the whole, that is, a coherent view of the world in which they live (see Schreiter 2007, 47-57). Paul Hiebert's critical realism addresses this. The message of Jesus Christ is about that coherence, not about an arbitrary play of the signifiers. Such a view as the latter only works where fundamental stability of a society is not challenged.

Third, we must attend to the fact that perhaps the majority of missionaries today are not emanating from Europe and North America. The missiology we construct must be attuned to the worlds they bring with them into mission set-

---

[1]Jan Jongeneel's two-volume *Missiologie* (1991) perhaps best reflects the attempt to present missiology as a university discipline standing on its own.

[2]There is a considerable literature growing around this topic. See, for example, Appiah (2006), Benhabib (2006), and Cheah (2006).

tings. Here the work of people like Hwa Yung (quoted frequently in this volume) will help lead the way. A corollary of this is attending to the anthropological writing that deals with phenomena that do not fit into Western thinking or the disciplines that Western thinking has created. I am not referring here to what the West may have deemed "exotic" but what the West has found "unacceptable." I will return to this in the third part.

Communication

Kraft's efforts to make communication, in all its aspects, a central part of missiology is the second of his achievements. As Viggo Søgaard affirms in his contribution to this volume, communication is now an integrated function in all parts of missiology. His listing of the seven principles learned from communications theory for missiology sums up aptly where we have come. Roberta King's contribution of some recent theoretical developments in models of communication complements Søgaard's list.

Perhaps the two single greatest contributions of Kraft's work in communication theory to missiology have been the concepts of orientation and dynamic equivalence. To take the primacy of reception in communication as a principle has proven important not only for effective communication, but also as part of a deeper theological understanding. If God is receptor oriented in his communication, that says a great deal about how we should construe our reception of the Bible and how we shape theology in cross-cultural settings. Indeed, when paired with the concept of dynamic equivalence (itself a consequence of receptor-oriented communication), then the program not only for communicating God's Word in new settings, but also for the theology that emerges in those settings has to be judged by a different set of theological standards than merely correspondence to what is already known as the sole criterion for evaluating the adequacy of those newer theologies. Certainly one task still to be completed is working out the consequences of what theology would look like if developed consistently from a receptor-oriented position.

There are other insights in the contributions here pointing to the future role of communication in missiology that need to be noted. Søgaard remarks that much of our theory still reflects linear thinking in a world where the non-linear still has pride of place, especially in oral cultures. There is perhaps another site of nonlinearity that will also need to be explored: the unassimilated ethnic populations in the urban conglomerates of the world. I am referring here to those peoples immigrating to the metropolitan sites where they maintain (at least in the first generation) their linguistic and cultural identities, even as they interact with other, similar groups and with the dominant language and culture of the city. Related to that is an observation made years ago by Notto Thelle that Knud Jørgensen expands upon here, namely, the differences between the religions of the ear, eye, and of energy. Much communication theory, developed in cultures with monotheistic religious traditions, has focused attention on speech and the ear. The importance of thinking about communication in the encounter between traditions that give priority to different sensory functions is something that remains to be worked out in more detail. Its importance for the dialogue among religions is of special note here. King expands on this in a slightly different way by emphasizing other forms of communication than speech: dance, music, drama, and the like.

Another insight important for the development of missiology is a point Jørgensen makes at the beginning of his article, namely, that theology is inherently missiological. Recent attempts to develop theologies more attuned to communication theory are already taking this cue. Making those so-called communicative theologies more attuned to their missiological implications and consequences will not only enhance the quality of those theologies, but also situate missiology itself more in the heart of contemporary theological developments (see, for example, Scharer and Hilberath 2002).

And a final word needs to be said about an enduring element in communication as it is found in the power of narrative. The inclusion here of a collection of stories from Eugene Nida makes that point more eloquently than any theory of narrative. In those stories, one captures the embeddedness of God's message in the vagaries and foibles—as well as the depth and intricacies—of human language, and culture will always stand as witness to the *pleroma* of God's creation.

Spiritual Power

The third area where Charles Kraft has led the way to a shift in missiological thinking is also the most controversial: that of spiritual power. The authors in this section refer to it in various ways: as spiritual conflict, spiritual power, divine healing, deep-level healing. The fact that it is still known under so many different names indicates that thinking about this phenomenon is not yet settled.

C. Peter Wagner's chapter presents a historical picture of how Kraft became involved in this form of healing and the controversy it has aroused in Evangelical circles. And controversial it indeed is. As Wagner notes, it blurs the line between Evangelicals and Pentecostals. For mainline Protestants it is almost beyond the pale. Yet, as Wagner also notes, the rapid growth of Pentecostal and Charismatic faith in the last decades makes this a phenomenon that cannot be so easily dismissed. That there have been serious and thoughtful consultations on this in Evangelical circles, as Tormod Engelsviken describes, underscores Wagner's point.

Belief in the reality of Satan and the possibility of exorcism and deliverance is part of Roman Catholic and Orthodox thought, although not necessarily held by some individuals in these traditions (especially in the West). All missiologists need to take this topic seriously and see where it fits in our contemporary discussions of spreading the gospel today.

For that to be done, there are a number of issues that need to be examined. First of all, the nature and presence of evil in the world. European Enlightenment views of the world, with their commitment to continual progress and optimism about human emancipation, leave very little room for belief in the ontological reality of evil, let alone its personification in the figure of Satan. What we perceive as evil, they say, is only the good still working itself out or areas where reason has not yet dispelled the darkness. In a highly individualist culture, there is even less room for the reality of evil; for in such a culture, every individual is expected to construct himself or herself. The autonomy of the individual is foregrounded, and optimism about the individual and the individual's progress precludes a strong sense of evil. If there is evil in the world, it is to be found in social structures that are unjust and can be changed. Paul's musing about not being able to do what he wants to do, and doing what he does not want to do (Rom 7:15) has no place here.

In the United States, our capacity to control so much in our surroundings because of the wealth and resources we have can insulate us from unpleasant realities around us. We may think, too, that if people without these resources only had them that then they, too, would think like us. But if we look carefully even at our own situation, we can detect those intractable elements that are connected with an evil beyond human construction and control.

My own work in recent years in social reconciliation, especially in working with societies that are trying to rebuild after civil conflict, has made me think differently about the nature of evil. The devastation one encounters—not only the physical destruction, but the deep-level human suffering that one observer has termed "sociocide" (Doubt 2006)—cannot be accounted for as the sum of individual wrong acts. Moreover, the insidious character of evil that has undone erstwhile good individuals, and made them into killers and torturers, indifferent to the terrible suffering they inflict, cannot be explained away simply as "sometimes good people do bad things." To speak of evil as banal, as Hannah Arendt did a generation ago, misses the point as well. Banal people can do evil, to be sure, but the depths to which those persons sink belie any ordinary sense of banality (Arendt 1964).

The insidious character of evil cannot be dismissed as mere chance. What I have called elsewhere the "narrative of the lie," that insinuates itself into authoritarian and oppressive societies, has a deliberate character to it (Schreiter 1992). The sowing of confusion, the perversion of truth, and the creating out of such acts a coherent and oppressive narrative about societies and the world around them cannot be happenstance. That is caught in the New Testament Greek word for the devil, *diabolos*—"the confuser."

Kraft's engagement with these powers calls us back to a phenomenon that most Western Christians see as a vestige of an older, less enlightened time. But the light of our reason has not entirely extinguished the darkness in which the phenomenon of evil dwells. I will return to this below.

A second aspect of this phenomenon has to do with culture, a point that Travis and Travis dwell upon in their chapter in this section. The presence of the spirit world is a self-evident fact in most cultures outside the West. For all the importance of medicinal substances and technologies in the curing of illness, healing is also an eminently cultural phenomenon, as missionaries and anthropologists well know. It has a significant psychic component. Western medical technology has made great strides in the last century, and certain kinds of illness—such as some mental disorders like schizophrenia and bipolar disorder—we now know are caused by neurochemical imbalances in the brain and can be treated pharmaceutically. Evidence is growing that even the inability to overcome acute traumatic experiences may fall in the same category.

While such medical developments may lead to the hope that one day all mental and emotional states might be dealt with chemically, we are certainly not there yet. My own Roman Catholic tradition believes that, in cases of supposed demonic possession, medical diagnoses and treatments must be exhausted before turning to ritual exorcism. But there remain those phenomena that can only be treated by prayer, ritual, and fasting.

Many cultures of the world attribute suffering in some mental and emotional states as problems arising from the spirit world, be it witchcraft or spirit possession. Western readings of those conditions tend to ascribe descriptions of encounters with the spirit world to something more material. Yet Westerners who have worked in those non-Western contexts sometimes experience phenomena they cannot explain by the categories provided them by their own culture or scholarly disciplines. A few Western anthropologists have begun exploring this territory, albeit cautiously.[3] For those in the West, there are still no adequate categories. Yet in Pentecostal circles in both the West and elsewhere, in the power encounters in which Kraft and his colleagues have engaged, the phenomena are there notwithstanding.

Missiology must take these phenomena seriously, and not fall back timidly because of what other disciplines in the academy may think of it for treading onto this risky ground. That it should be surrounded by caution is important, and people need continual reminding of this. What Kraft has done is open the door to a part of the world once thought closed to regular investigation or superseded by rational thought. What I think missiology must do in regard to these forms of encounter and healing is to help stipulate the conditions under which these forms are engaged, and establish critical reflection on the practices that emerge.

The chapters of the Travises and of Engelsviken work toward doing that. The Travises care about circumscribing these practices, so that, for example, false memories are not created by suggestion and not everything is immediately attributed to the spirit world, and this is very much on the mark. Engelsviken's reminding us that this kind of spiritual healing is not an end in itself, but rather is a means to come to know Jesus Christ and salvation is theologically indispensable. I would like to add two further considerations for a more thoughtful engagement of missiology with spiritual dynamics.

One consideration is an epistemological one. The use of language of warfare, while not within Scriptural warrant, carries with it a hazard. The struggle between good and evil can lead to a dividing up of the world into dualism. It particularly hardens the boundary between Christian faith (or better, our understanding of the message of Jesus; not the message itself) and anything different from it. It creates oppositional identity formation that always carries with it the potential

---

[3] A leading figure in this regard is Canadian anthropologist Jean-Guy Goulet. See Young and Goulet (1994), and Goulet and Miller (2007).

for violence. Thus, anything associated with another religious tradition is automatically considered demonic. Here the insights of cultural anthropology and intercultural communication with which Kraft has so well equipped us have to be brought to bear on our understanding and practice of this kind of healing. We cannot simply allow ourselves to set aside everything else we have learned about the human condition in the face of these encounters.

The second consideration is a more theological and spiritual one. I had spoken above of the insidious character of evil, of the devil as the one who confuses. We must realize that the sheer fact of our engagement with overcoming evil makes us vulnerable to evil's own designs. I have seen this in reconciliation work, where good people are gradually turned into compromising themselves and even others for the sake of reaching some goal, where people have eliminated the complexity and in so doing have done others harm. Confronting evil head-on means that evil can strike at us as well. We are invoking the name of Jesus and his power, but we are still vessels of clay bearing that message (see 2 Cor 4:7). Our spiritual preparation and the spiritual discipline we maintain must reach beyond the moments of encounter to include those times when that same evil will find the opportunity to insinuate itself into our lives and relationships. The fact that such power has been entrusted to us must not inflate our sense of our personal self-worth or (worse) the sense of our own power.

Conclusion

One of the great contributions of the authors in this volume is to allow us to see how these three elements in the thought and work of Charles Kraft have come together to enhance missiology, but more importantly, to advance the work of God's Reign. Looking at these three elements in consort—cultural anthropology, intercultural communication, spiritual power and deep healing—gives us a picture of what will be needed in a special way as we continue into the twenty-first century. No one has captured this better than Paul Pierson in the concluding words of his contribution to this volume: "I suggest that the consistent thread in Chuck's life has been the passionate desire to help men and women come to know and follow Jesus Christ in ways that are authentic in their own contexts and consistent with Scripture, and for them to experience the fullness of the Gospel of forgiveness, reconciliation, and power in their lives." That is clear testimony about a man who is a great Christian and an outstanding missiologist.

The Published Works of Charles H. Kraft

Compiled by Dean Gilliland

This bibliography does not include articles published in denominational periodicals, forewords, and prefaces to books. An earlier version of this listing, featuring Charles H. Kraft's 1958-2001 publications, appeared in Charles H. Kraft, *Culture, Communication and Christianity: A Selection of Writings* (Pasadena, Calif.: William Carey Library, 2001), 474-488.

1958   "Missionary Interpersonal Relations: Younger versus Older." *Practical Anthropology* 5 (January-February): 33-37.

1960   Review: *Must We Introduce Monogamy? A Study of Polygamy as a Mission Problem in South Africa*, by Gunnar Helander. Pietermaritzburg: Shuter & Shooter, 1958. In *Practical Anthropology* 7 (March-April): 91-93.

1961   "Correspondence Courses in Anthropology." *Practical Anthropology* 8 (July-August): 168-75.

1963a   *A Study of Hausa Syntax*. Volumes 8, 9, 10. Hartford Studies in Linguistics.

1963b   "Christian Conversion or Cultural Conversion." *Practical Anthropology* 10 (July-August): 179-87.

1963c   Review: *Social Change in Modern Africa*, by Aidan Southall. London: Oxford University Press, 1961; *Man in Rapid Social Change*, by Egbert DeVries. Garden City, N.Y.: Doubleday, 1961; *The Churches and Rapid Social Change*, by Paul Abrecht. Garden City, N.Y.: Doubleday, 1961. "Mission in a World of Rapid Social Change." In *Practical Anthropology* 10 (November-December): 271-79.

1964a   "A New Study of Hausa Syntax." *Journal of African Languages* 3, 66-74.

1964b   Review: *Dictionary of the Hausa Language*, by Roy C. Abraham. London: University of London Press, 1962. In *Modern Language Journal* 68, 252.

1964c   Review: *Manual of Articulatory Phonetics*, by William A. Smalley. Pasadena, Calif.: William Carey Library, 1963. In *Practical Anthropology* 11 (July-August): 191-92.

1964d   "The Morpheme *na* in Relation to a Broader Classification of Hausa Verbals." *Journal of African Languages* 3, 231-240.

1964e   Review: *Zur Tonologie des Hausa*, by Hans H. Wangler. Berlin: Akademie-Verlag, 1963. In *Language* 40, 504-7.

1965   *An Introduction to Spoken Hausa*. African Language Monographs 5A, 5B. African Studies Center: Michigan State University.

1966a   *Cultural Materials in Hausa*. African Language Monograph 6A. African Studies Center: Michigan State University.

1966b   *Where Do I Go From Here? A Handbook for Continuing Language Study in the Field*. With Marguerite G. Kraft. Washington, D.C.: U.S. Peace Corps.

1966c   *Workbook in Intermediate and Advanced Hausa*. African Language Monograph 6B. African Studies Center: Michigan State University.

1969   "What You Heard Is Not What I Meant." *World Vision Magazine* 13 (April): 10-12; reprinted in *Messenger* 118, no. 16 (1969): 20-22.

1970a   "Hausa *sai* and *da*—A Couple of Overworked Particles." *Journal of African Languages* 9, 92-109.

1970b   Review: *Zur Tonologie des Hausa*, by Hans H. Wangler. Berlin: Akademie-Verlag, 1963. In *African Studies* 29, 129-39.

1971a "A Note on Lateral Fricatives in Chadic." *Studies in African Linguistics* 2, 271-81.

1971b "The New Wine of Independence." *World Vision* 15, no. 2 (February): 6-9.

1971c "Younger Churches—Missionaries and Indigeneity." *Church Growth Bulletin* 7, 159-61.

1972a Review: *Biblical Revelation and African Beliefs*, ed. Kwesi Dickson and Paul Ellingworth. London: Lutterworth Press, 1969. In *Evangelical Missions Quarterly* 8, 244-47.

1972b "The Hutterites and Today's Church." *Theology, News and Notes* 18, no. 3 (October): 15-16.

1972c "Spinoff from the Study of Cross-Cultural Mission." *Theology, News and Notes* 18, no. 3 (October): 20-23.

1972d "Theology and Theologies I." *Theology, News and Notes* 18, no. 2 (June): 4-6, 9.

1972e "Theology and Theologies II." *Theology, News and Notes* 18, no. 3 (October): 17-20.

1973a *A Hausa Reader*. Berkeley, Calif.: University of California Press.

1973b Review: *Church and Culture Change in Africa*, ed. David J. Bosch. In *Evangelical Missions Quarterly* 9, 249-52.

1973c "Church Planters and Ethnolinguistics." In *God, Man and Church Growth*. Edited by A. R. Tippett, 226-49. Grand Rapids, Mich.: Eerdmans.

1973d "Dynamic Equivalence Churches." In *Missiology* 1, no. 1 (January): 39-57. Reprinted in *Readings in Dynamic Indigeneity*. by C. H. Kraft and T. N. Wisley, 87-111. Pasadena, Calif.: William Carey Library.

1973e "God's Model for Cross-Cultural Communication—The Incarnation." *Evangelical Missions Quarterly* 9, 205-16.

1973f "The Incarnation, Cross-Cultural Communication—The Incarnation." *Evangelical Missions Quarterly* 9, 277-84.

1973g *Introductory Hausa*. With Marguerite G. Kraft. Berkeley, Calif.: University of California Press.

1973h "North America's Cultural Challenge: Pluralism's Challenge to Evangelism." *Christianity Today* 17 (January 19): 6-8.

1973i *Teach Yourself Hausa*. With A. H. M. Kirk-Greene. London: English Universities Press.

1973j "Toward a Christian Ethnotheology." In *God, Man and Church Growth*. Edited by A. R. Tippett, 109-26. Grand Rapids, Mich.: Eerdmans.

1973k Review: *Yoruba Names: Their Structure and Their Meanings*, by Modupe Oduyoye. In *Missiology* 1, no. 3 (July): 389-90.

1974a "An Anthropologist's Response to Oden." In *After Therapy What?* Edited by Neil C. Warren, 136-59. Springfield, Ill.: Charles C. Thomas.

1974b "Christian Conversion as a Dynamic Process." *International Christian Broadcasters Bulletin* (Second Quarter): 8-9, 14.

1974c Review: *Concise Dictionary of the Christian World Mission*, ed. S. Neill, G. H. Anderson, and J. Goodwin. Nashville, Tenn.: Abingdon Press, 1971. In *Missiology* 2, 142-44.

1974d "Distinctive Religious Barriers to Outside Penetration." In *Media in Islamic Culture*. Edited by C. Richard Shumaker, 65-76. Wheaton, Ill.: International Christian Broadcasters.

1974e "Extent and Limitations of Media among Muslims." In *Media in Islamic Culture*. Edited by C. Richard Shumaker, 166-69. Wheaton, Ill.: International Christian Broadcasters.

1974f "Guidelines for Developing a Message Geared to the Horizon of Receptivity, Part 1 and 2." In *Media in Islamic Culture*. Edited by C. Richard Shumaker, 17-33. Wheaton, Ill.: International Christian Broadcasters.

1974g "Ideological Factors in Intercultural Communication." *Missiology* 2, no. 3 (July): 295-312.

1974h "Psychological Stress Factors among Muslims." In *Media in Islamic Culture.* Edited by C. Richard Shumaker, 137-44. Wheaton, Ill.: International Christian Broadcasters.

1974i "Reconstructions of Chadic Pronouns I: Possessive, Object, and Independent Sets—An Interim Report." In *Third Annual Conference on African Linguistics.* Edited by Erhard Voeltz, 69-94. Bloomington, Ind.: Indiana University Publications.

1974j "Why Have You Come"; "Why Go to the Mission Field?"; "What If I Hadn't Gone?" (3 lectures). *Missions Week Lectures 1974.* Eugene, Ore.: Northwest Christian College Missions Committee.

1975a Review: *A World to Win: Preaching World Missions Today,* ed. Roger S. Greenway. Grand Rapids, Mich.: Baker Book House, 1975; *The Making of a Missionary,* by J. Herbert Kane. Grand Rapids, Mich.: Baker Book House, 1975; *Discipling the Nations,* by Richard R. DeRidder. Grand Rapids, Mich.: Baker Book House, 1975. In *Christian Scholars Review* 7, 225-27.

1975b Review: *Man and Woman among the Azande,* by E. E. Evans-Pritchard. London: Faber and Faber. In *Missiology* 3, 390-93.

1975c "Toward an Ethnography of Hausa Riddling." *Ba Shiru* 6, 171-24; reprinted in *Folia Orientalia* 17 (1976): 231-43.

1976a "An Ethnolinguistic Study of Hausa Epithets." In *Studies in African Linguistics, Supplement 6: Papers in African Linguistics in Honor of Wm. E. Welmers.* Edited by L. M. Hyman, L. Jacobsen, and R. G. Schuh, 135-46. Los Angeles, Calif.: Department of Linguistics, University of California.

1976b "Communicate or Compete?" *Spectrum* (Spring-Summer): 8-10.

1976c "Cultural Concomitants of Higi Conversion: Early Periods." *Missiology* 4, no. (October): 431-42.

1977a Editorial: "Bible Translation and the Church." *Theology, News and Notes* 23 (March): 2.

1977b "Biblical Principles of Communication." *The Harvester* 56, 262-64, 275; edited and reprinted in *Buzz* (December 1977): 17, 19.

1977c "Can Anthropological Insight Assist Evangelical Theology?" *Christian Scholar's Review* 7, no. 2/3, 165-202.

1977d Review: *So Many Versions? Twentieth Century English Versions of the Bible,* by Sakae Kubo and Walter Specht. Grand Rapids, Mich.: Zondervan, 1983. In *Theology News and Notes* 23, 20-21.

1977e "What Is God Trying to Do?" *Theology, News and Notes* 23 (March): 9-11; reprinted in *Notes on Translation* no. 72 (December): 20-26.

1978a "An Anthropological Apologetic for the Homogeneous Unit Principle in Missiology." *Occasional Bulletin of Missionary Research* 2, no. 4 (October): 121-26.

1978b "Christianity and Culture in Africa." In *Facing the New Challenges—The Message of PACLA,* 286-91. Nairobi: Evangel Publishing House.

1978c "The Church in Western Africa: Response #2." In *The Church in Africa 1977.* By Charles R. Taber, 166-75. Pasadena, Calif.: William Carey Library.

1978d "The Contextualization of Theology." *Evangelical Missions Quarterly* 14, 311-36.

1978e "Interpreting in Cultural Context." *Journal of the Evangelical Theological Society* 21 (December): 357-67.

1978f "Strategies for Reaching Africa's 300 Million Lost." In *Facing the New Challenges—The Message of PACLA,* 490-500. Nairobi: Evangel Publishing House.

1978g "What Is an Indigenous Church?" In *Facing the New Challenges—The Message of PACLA,* 304-7. Nairobi: Evangel Publishing House.

1978h "Worldview in Intercultural Communication." In *Intercultural and International Communication.* Edited by Fred L. Casmir, 407-28. Lanham, Md.: University Press of America.

1979a   *Christianity in Culture: A Study in Dynamic Biblical Theologizing in Cross-Cultural Perspective.* Maryknoll, N.Y.: Orbis Books.

1979b   *Communicating the Gospel God's Way.* Pasadena, Calif.: William Carey Library. Mandarin trans., 1983.

1979c   "The Credibility of the Message and the Messenger." *Ashland Theological Bulletin* 12, no. 1 (Spring): 17-32.

1979d   "Dynamic Equivalence Churches in Muslim Society." In *The Gospel and Islam: A 1978 Compendium.* Edited by Donald M. McCurry, 114-28. Monrovia, Calif.: MARC.

1979e   "God's Model for Communication." *Ashland Theological Bulletin* 12, no. 1 (Spring): 3-16.

1979f   "Measuring Indigeneity." *In Readings in Dynamic Indigeneity.* By C. H. Kraft and T. N. Wisley, 118-52. Pasadena, Calif.: William Carey Library.

1979g   "The Power of Life Involvement." *Ashland Theological Bulletin* 12, no. 1 (Spring): 43-60.

1979h   *Readings in Dynamic Indigeneity.* With Tom Wisley. Pasadena, Calif.: William Carey Library.

1979i   "What Is the Receptor Up To?" *Ashland Theological Bulletin* 12, no. 1 (Spring): 33-42.

1980a   Review: *Christianity in Independent Africa*, by E. Fasholé-Luke, A. Hastings, and G. Tasie. Bloomington, Ind.: Indiana University Press, 1978. In *Theology Today* 36 (January): 618.

1980b   "The Church in Culture—A Dynamic Equivalence Model." In *Down to Earth: Studies in Christianity and Culture.* Edited by John Stott & Robert Coote, 211-30. Grand Rapids, Mich.: Eerdmans.

1980c   "Conservative Christians and Anthropologists: A Clash of Worldviews." *Journal of the American Scientific Affiliation* 32 (September): 140-45.

1981a   *Chadic Wordlists.* 3 vols. Berlin: Verlag von Dietrich Reimer.

1981b   "The Place of the Receptor in Communication." *Theology, News and Notes* 28, no. 3 (October): 13-15, 23.

1982a   "My Distaste for the Combative Approach." *Evangelical Missions Quarterly* 18, 139-42.

1982b   Review: *Toward an African Theology*, by J. S. Pobee. Nashville, Tenn.: Abingdon Press, 1979; *African Theology en Route: Papers from the Pan African Conference of Third World Theologians*, by Kofi Appiah-Kubi and Sergio Torres. Maryknoll, N.Y.: Orbis Books, 1979; *African Godianism: A Revolutionary Religion for Mankind through Direct Communication with God*, by K.O.K. Onyioha. New York: Conch Magazine, 1980. "Theology from African Perspectives." In *Journal of Psychology and Theology* 10 (Summer): 161-62.

1983a   "Can Anything Good Come Out of a Condensed Bible?" With R. Daniel Shaw. *Eternity* 34, no. 2 (February): 28-29.

1983b   *Communication Theory for Christian Witness.* Nashville, Tenn.: Abingdon Press.

1983c   Review: *The Theology of Change: A Christian Concept of God in an Eastern Perspective*, by Jung Young Lee. Maryknoll, N.Y.: Orbis Books, 1979. In *Journal of Psychology and Theology* 11, 74.

1983d   Review: *Third-Eye Theology: Theology in Formation in Asian Settings*, by Choan-Seng Song. Maryknoll, N.Y.: Orbis Books, 1979. In *Journal of Psychology and Theology* 11, 75.

1984   Review: *Doing Theology across Cultures*, by Morris Inch. Grand Rapids, Mich.: Baker Book House, 1982. In *TSF Bulletin* 7 (May/June): 24, 25.

1985a   Review: *Beliefs and Self-Help: Cross Cultural Perspectives and Approaches*, by G. H. Weber and L. M. Cohen. New York: Human Sciences Press, 1982. In *Journal of Psychology and Theology* 13 (Spring): 68-69.

1985b   "Cultural Anthropology: Its Meaning for Christian Theology." *Theology Today* 41 (January): 390-400.

1985c   "Gospel and Culture." In *Christianity in Today's World*. Edited by Robin Keeley, 274-75. Grand Rapids, Mich.: Eerdmans. British ed., 1985.

1985d   " 'The Third Wave' in the Covenant Church." *Narthex* 5, no. 1, 5-15.

1985e   "Why the Vineyard Should Move into Crosscultural Ministry." *First Fruits* 2, no. 8 (November/December): 15-19.

1986a   "Evangelicals Rediscover the Gifts." *Renewing Australia* (December): 12-13.

1986b   "Five Years Later." In *Signs and Wonders Today: The Remarkable Story of the MC510 Signs, Wonders and Church Growth at Fuller Theological Seminary*. Edited by C. Peter Wagner, 115-24. Wheaton, Ill.: Christian Life Magazine.

1986c   "Let's Fight Staticosis." *Worship Times* (Summer): 5.

1986d   "Missiology and SIL." In *Current Concerns of Anthropologists and Missionaries*. Edited by Karl J. Franklin, 133-42. Dallas, Tex.: Summer Institute of Linguistics.

1986e   "Sing *About* or Sing *To*?" *Worship Times* (Fall): 4.

1986f   "Supracultural Meanings via Cultural Forms." In *A Guide to Contemporary Hermeneutics*. Edited by Donald K. McKim, 309-43. Grand Rapids, Mich.: Eerdmans.

1986g   "The Question of Miracles." *The Pentecostal Minister* (Winter): 24.

1986h   "Worldview and Bible Translation." *Notes on Anthropology* no. 6/7 (June-September): 46-57.

1986i   "Worldview and Bible Translation." In *Anthropological and Missiological Issues*. Edited by Karl J. Franklin. Dallas, Tex.: Summer Institute of Linguistics.

1987a   "A Shaky Stage?" *Worship Times* (Winter): 1-2.

1987b   "Organ or Guitar?" *Worship Times* (Summer).

1987c   "Shifting Worldviews, Shifting Attitudes." *Equipping the Saints* (September-October).

1987d   "Shifting Worldviews, Shifting Attitudes." In *Riding the Third Wave*. Edited by John Wimber and Kevin Springer, 122-34. England: Marshall Pickering.

1987e   "The World Needs More Spiritual Power." *AD2000* (May): 3.

1987f   "World View and Worship." *Worship Times* (Spring).

1987g   "Worship Is Up to the Worshippers." *Worship Times* (Fall): 4.

1988a   "Follow the Leader?" *Worship Times* 2, no. 4 (Winter): 4.

1988b   "The Lord's Supper: A Live or Dead Ritual?" *Worship Times* (Spring): 3.

1989a   *Christianity with Power: Your Worldview and Your Experience of the Supernatural*. Ann Arbor, Mich.: Servant Publications. British ed., 1989. German trans., 1989. Philippine ed., 1990. Mandarin trans., 1991. Korean trans., 1992. Japanese trans., 1994.

1989b   "Contextualizing Communication." In *The Word among Us*. Edited by Dean Gilliland, 121-38. Dallas, Tex.: Word Books.

1989c   "Don't Worry about Ignorance: It's Our Knowledge That's the Problem." *Missions Tomorrow* (Spring/Summer): 27-34.

1989d   "The Hymnal Is Not Enough." *Christianity Today* 33, no. 6 (April): 8.

1989e   "Who Was This Man: A Tribute to Alan Tippett." *Missiology* 17 (July): 269-81.

1990a   *Communicate with Power*. Manila, Philippines: OMF Literature. Korean trans., 1992.

1990b   "Response to F. Douglas Pennoyer." In *Wrestling with Dark Angels*. Edited by C. Peter Wagner and F. Douglas Pennoyer, 271-79. Ventura, Calif.: Regal Books.

1990c   "Shifting Worldviews, Shifting Attitudes." In *Conflict and Conquest: Power Encounter Topics for Taiwan*. Edited by Kenneth D. Shay, 15-19. Taiwan: O. C. International.

1991a   "A Third Wave Perspective on Pentecostal Missions." In *Called and Empowered: Pentecostal Perspective on Global Mission*. Edited by Murray W. Dempster, Byron D. Klaus, and Douglas Peterson, 299-312. Peabody, Mass.: Hendrickson Publications.

1991b   Review: *The Church and Cultures: New Perspectives in Missiological Anthro-*

pology, by Louis J. Luzbetak. Maryknoll, N.Y.: Orbis Books, 1988. In *International Bulletin of Missionary Research* 15, no. 1 (January): 37-38.

1991c   *Communication Theory for Christian Witness*. Rev. ed. Maryknoll, N.Y.: Orbis Books.

1991d   "It's What We Think We Know—That's the Problem." *Renewing Australia* (December): 14-15, 37.

1991e   "Receptor-Oriented Ethics in Cross-Cultural Intervention." *Transformation* 8, no. 1 (January-March): 20-25.

1991f   "What Kind of Encounters Do We Need in Our Christian Witness?" *Evangelical Missions Quarterly* 27, no. 3 (July): 258-65.

1992a   "Allegiance, Truth and Power Encounters in Christian Witness." In *Pentecost, Mission and Ecumenism, Essays on Intercultural Theology*. Edited by Jan A. B. Jongeneel, 215-30. New York: Peter Lang.

1992b   "Changing What We Know." *Renewing Australia* (June): 19-21, 29.

1992c   "Conversion in Group Settings." In *Handbook of Religious Conversion*. Edited by H. Newton Malony and Samuel Southard, 259-75. Birmingham, Ala.: Religious Education Press.

1992d   *Defeating Dark Angels*. Ann Arbor, Mich.: Servant Publications. British ed., 1993. Mandarin trans., 1994. German trans., 1995. Korean trans., 1995. Russian trans., 2000.

1992e   "Do We Depend Too Much on Worship Leaders?" *Worship Leader* (December-January): 7.

1992f   "Fear of Change Is Like Acting on a Shaky Stage." *Worship Leader* (October-November): 9, 39.

1992g   "How Our Worldview Affects the Way We Worship." *Worship Leader* (June-July): 10, 53.

1992h   "Hymns vs. Praise Songs: Which Shall We Sing?" *Worship Leader* (April-May): 7, 44.

1992i   "Traditions Too Often Lose Meaning Over Time." *Worship Leader* (August-September): 8, 53.

1992j   "Worship: Tradition, or Just 'Follow the Leader?' " *Worship Leader* (February-March): 7, 29.

1993a   "Are We Really Communicating What We Intend?" *Worship Leader* (August-September): 6, 8.

1993b   "Communicating and Ministering the Power of the Gospel Cross-Culturally: The Power of God for Christians Who Ride Two Horses." With Marguerite G. Kraft. In *The Kingdom and the Power*. Edited by Gary S. Greig and Kevin N. Springer, 346-56. Ventura, Calif.: Regal.

1993c   "Communication in Worship: To Whom Do We Sing?" *Worship Leader* (February-March): 7-8.

1993d   *Deep Wounds, Deep Healing*. Ann Arbor, Mich.: Servant Publications. British ed., 1994. Japanese trans., vol. 1, 1995. Philippine ed., 1995. Korean trans., 1995. Japanese trans., vol. 2, 1997. German trans., 2000.

1993e   Review: *Facing the Powers: What Are the Options?* by Thomas H. McAlpine. Monrovia, Calif.: MARC, 1991. In *Missiology—An International Review* 21 (April): 226-27.

1993f   "How Acts of Worship Help Defeat the Devil." *Worship Leader* (June-July): 8, 44.

1993g   "Organ/Guitar Preference Reflects View of God." *Worship Leader* (April-May): 7.

1993h   "Organs vs. Guitar Question a Matter of Context." *Worship Leader* (October-November): 9, 34.

1993i   "Shouldn't We Be Teaching People How to Worship?" *Worship Leader* (December-January): 4, 11, 30.

1993j   "Understanding and Valuing Multiethnic Diversity." With Marguerite G. Kraft. *Theology News and Notes* 40, no. 4, 6-8.

1994a   "Alan Tippett." In *The Australian Dictionary of Evangelical Biography*. Edited by Brian Dickey, 373-74. Sydney: Evangelical Historical Society.
1994b   "Church Growth Needs to Be for the Right Reasons?" *Worship Leader* (September-October): 10.
1994c   "The Concept of Power Encounter." *CMS Bulletin* 3, no. 2, 1-2.
1994d   Condensation of "The Power of God for People Who Ride Two Horses." With Marguerite G. Kraft. *CMS Bulletin* 3, no. 2, 9-13.
1994e   "Dealing with Demonization." In *Behind Enemy Lines*. Edited by Charles Kraft, 79-120. Ann Arbor, Mich.: Servant Publications.
1994f   Review: *Models of Contextual Theology*, by Stephen Bevans. Maryknoll, N.Y.: Orbis Books, 1992. In *International Bulletin of Missionary Research* 18, no. 21 (July): 131.
1994g   "Our Youth Need to Know That Worship Is Warfare." *Worship Leader* (May June): 8.
1994h   "Spiritual Power: Principles and Observations." In *Behind Enemy Lines*. Edited by Charles Kraft, 31-62. Ann Arbor, Mich.: Servant Publications.
1994i   "Taking Out the Garbage and Exterminating the Rats." *Renewal News for Presbyterian and Reformed Churches* (Summer).
1994j   "Two Kingdoms in Conflict." In *Behind Enemy Lines*. Edited by Charles Kraft, 17-29. Ann Arbor, Mich.: Servant Publications.
1994k   "What Are We Communicating about Worship?" *Worship Leader* (April): 8.
1995a   " 'Christian Animism' or God-Given Authority." In *Spiritual Power and Missions*. Edited by Edward Rommen, 88-136. Pasadena, Calif.: William Carey Library.
1995b   Review: *Defeating Dark Angels*, In *Reformation & Revival* 4 (Winter): 153-56.
1995c   "Media Are to Serve, Not to Be Served." *Worship Leader* (May-June): 22, 42.
1995d   "Worship Isn't Very Important." *Worship Leader* (January-February): 10.
1996a   *Anthropology for Christian Witness*. Maryknoll, N.Y.: Orbis Books.
1996b   "Beneath Our Words." *Worship Leader* (September-October): 17.
1996c   Review: *Roots of Acceptance: The Intercultural Communication of Religious Meanings*, by William E. Biernatzki. Rome: Pontificia Universitas Gregoriana, 1991. In *Missiology* 24 (January): 131-32.
1997a   "Feel First, Think Later." *Worship Leader* (September-October): 16.
1997b   *I Give You Authority*. Grand Rapids, Mich.: Chosen Books. British ed., 1998, 2000. German trans., 1998. Japanese trans., 2 vols., 1999. Korean trans., 2000.
1997c   "Information vs. Stimulus." *Worship Leader* (January-February): 14.
1997d   "The Rule That Breaks All Rules." *Worship Leader* (May-June): 14.
1998a   "Communication Happens." *Worship Leader* (May-June): 14.
1998b   Review: *Culture Confrontation and Local Mobilization: Essays in Honour of Sigbert Axelson*, ed. Veronica Melander. Uppsala: Swedish Institute of Missionary Research, 1997. In *Missiology* 26, no. 3 (July): 378-79.
1998c   "Meaning by Association." *Worship Leader* (January-February): 16.
1998d   "My Pilgrimage in Mission." *International Bulletin of Missionary Research* 22, no. 4 (October): 162-64.
1998e   "Source or Receptor?" *Worship Leader* (September-October): 14.
1999a   *Communicating Jesus' Way*. Pasadena, Calif.: William Carey Library.
1999b   "Culture, Worldview and Contextualization." In *Perspectives on the World Christian Movement*. Edited by Ralph D. Winter and Steven C. Hawthorne, 384-91. Pasadena, Calif.: William Carey Library.
1999c   "In with the Old, In with Two New." *Worship Leader* (January-February): 16.
1999d   "Three Encounters in Christian Witness." In *Perspectives on the World Christian Movement*. Edited by Ralph D. Winter and Steven C. Hawthorne, 408-13. Pasadena, Calif.: William Carey Library.
2000a   "Anthropology"; "Cultural Conversion"; "Culture Shock"; "Curse, Curses"; "Divination, Diviners"; "Dynamic Equivalence"; "Interpersonal Communication"; "Po-

lygamy and Church Membership"; "Power Encounter"; "Witchcraft and Sorcery." In *Evangelical Dictionary of World Missions*. Edited by A. Scott Moreau, Charles Van Engen, and Harold A. Netland. Grand Rapids, Mich.: Baker Book House.

2000b   *The Rules of Engagement: Understanding the Principles That Govern the Spiritual Battles in Our Lives*. With David M. DeBord. Colorado Springs, Colo.: Wagner Publications.

2001a   "Anthropological Perspectives on American Women's Issues." In *Culture, Communication and Christianity*. By Charles H. Kraft, 85-95. Pasadena, Calif.: William Carey Library.

2001b   "The Bearing of the Passages in 1 Timothy and Titus on the Matter of Church Leadership in Polygamous Societies." In *Culture, Communication and Christianity*. By Charles H. Kraft, 415-26. Pasadena, Calif.: William Carey Library.

2001c   "God, Human Beings, Culture and the Cross-Cultural Communication of the Gospel." In *Culture, Communication and Christianity*. By Charles H. Kraft, 19-43. Pasadena, Calif.: William Carey Library.

2001d   "Let's Be Christian about Polygamy." In *Culture, Communication and Christianity*. By Charles H. Kraft, 403-14. Pasadena, Calif.: William Carey Library.

2001e   *Culture, Communication and Christianity: A Selection of Writings by Charles Kraft*. Pasadena, Calif.: William Carey Library.

2002a   "The Believer's Authority over Demonic Spirits." In *Ministering Freedom from Demonic Oppression*. Edited by Doris M. Wagner, 43-63. Colorado Springs, Colo.: Wagner Publications; reprinted in *How to Minister Freedom*. Edited by D. M. Wagner, 50-59. Ventura, Calif.: Regal Books.

2002b   *Confronting Powerless Christianity*. Grand Rapids, Mich.: Chosen Books.

2002c   "Contemporary Trends in the Treatment of Spiritual Conflict." In *Deliver Us from Evil*. Edited by A. S. Moreau et al., 177-202. Monrovia, Calif.: MARC Publications.

2002d   "Contextualization and Spiritual Power." In *Deliver Us from Evil*. Edited by A. S. Moreau et al., 290-308. Monrovia, Calif.: MARC Publications.

2002e   "Generational Appropriateness in Contextualization." In *The Urban Face of Mission*. Edited by H. Conn, M. Ortiz, and S. Baker, 132-56. Phillipsburg, N.J.: R&R Publishing.

2004   *Defeating Dark Angels*. Ventura, Calif.: Regal Books.

2005a   "Appropriate Contextualization of Spiritual Power." In *Appropriate Christianity*. Edited by Charles H. Kraft, 375-96. Pasadena, Calif.: William Carey Library.

2005b   "Appropriate Relationships." In *Appropriate Christianity*. Edited by Charles H. Kraft, 325-40. Pasadena, Calif.: William Carey Library.

2005c   *Christianity in Culture: A Study in Dynamic Biblical Theologizing in Cross Cultural Perspective*. With Marguerite G. Kraft. Revised 25th year ed. Maryknoll, N.Y.: Orbis Books.

2005d   "Contextualization and Time: Generational Appropriateness." In *Appropriate Christianity*. Edited by Charles H. Kraft, 255-74. Pasadena, Calif.: William Carey Library.

2005e   "Contextualization in Three Crucial Dimensions." In *Appropriate Christianity*. Edited by Charles H. Kraft, 99-116. Pasadena, Calif.: William Carey Library.

2005f   "The Development of Contextualization Theory in Euroamerican Missiology." In *Appropriate Christianity*. Edited by Charles H. Kraft, 15-34. Pasadena, Calif.: William Carey Library.

2005g   "Dynamics of Contextualization." In *Appropriate Christianity*. Edited by Charles H. Kraft, 169-82. Pasadena, Calif.: William Carey Library.

2005h   "Is Christianity a Religion or a Faith?" In *Appropriate Christianity*. Edited by Charles H. Kraft, 83-98. Pasadena, Calif.: William Carey Library.

2005i   "Meaning Equivalence Contextualization." In *Appropriate Christianity*. Edited by Charles H. Kraft, 155-68. Pasadena, Calif.: William Carey Library.

2005j "Spiritual Power: A Missiological Issue." In *Appropriate Christianity*. Edited by Charles H. Kraft, 361-74. Pasadena, Calif.: William Carey Library.

2005k "Why Appropriate?" In *Appropriate Christianity*. Edited by Charles H. Kraft, 3-14. Pasadena, Calif.: William Carey Library.

2005l "Why Isn't Contextualization Implemented?" In *Appropriate Christianity*. Edited by Charles H. Kraft, 67-80. Pasadena, Calif.: William Carey Library.

2005m *SWM/SIS at Forty: A Participant/Observer's View of Our History*. Pasadena, Calif.: William Carey Library.

2006 "Christianity in Three Crucial Dimensions." In *Speaking of Mission*. Edited by Michael Frost. Sydney, Australia: Morling Press.

2007 *Worldview for Christian Witness*. Pasadena, Calif.: William Carey Library.

Edited Works

1994 *Behind Enemy Lines*. Ann Arbor, Mich.: Servant Publications. Korean trans., 1996. Japanese trans., 1997.

2001 *Culture, Communication and Christianity: A Selection of Writings*. Pasadena, Calif.: William Carey Library.

2002 *Behind Enemy Lines*. Ann Arbor, Mich.: Servant Publications.

2005 *Appropriate Christianity*. Pasadena, Calif.: William Carey Library.

Bibliography of Works Cited

Adler, Ronald B. and George Rodman. *Understanding Human Communication*. 9th ed. New York: Oxford University Press, 2006.

al-Ashgar, Umar Sulaiman. *The World of the Jinn and Devils*, translated by Jamal al-Din M. Zarabozo. Boulder, Colo.: Al-Bashir Co., 1998.

Allen, Roland. *Missionary Principles*. London: Roxburghe House, 1913.

Anderson, Neil T. *The Bondage Breaker*. Eugene, Ore.: Harvest House Publishers, 1990.

Appiah, Kwame Anthony. *Cosmopolitanism: Ethics in a World of Strangers*. New York: W.W. Norton, 2006.

The Archbishops' Council. *Mission-Shaped Church: Church Planting and Fresh Expressions of Church in a Changing Context*. London: Church House Publishing, 2004.

Arendt, Hannah. *Eichmann in Jerusalem: A Report on the Banality of Evil*. Rev. ed. New York: Penguin, 1964.

Arnold, Clinton E. *Ephesians, Power and Magic: The Concept of Power in Ephesians in the Light of Its Historical Setting*. Cambridge: Cambridge University Press, 1989.

———. *3 Crucial Questions about Spiritual Warfare*. Grand Rapids: Baker Books, 1997.

Arnold, Dean. "Why Are There So Few Christian Anthropologists? Reflections on the Tensions between Christianity and Anthropology." *Perspectives on Science and Christian Faith* 58, no. 4 (December): 266-282, 2006.

Bali, Wahid Abdussalam. *The Cutting Edge: How to Face Evil Sorcerers*, translated by Haytham Kreidly. Beirut: Al-Kitab al-Alami lil Nasher, 2006a.

———. *Man's Protections against Jinn and Satan*, translated by Haytham Kreidly. Beirut: Dar al-Kotob al-Ilmiya, 2006b.

Barbour, Ian G. *Myths, Models and Paradigms*. New York: Harper & Row, 1974.

Barrett, David B. and Todd M. Johnson. *World Christian Trends AD 30—AD 2200: Interpreting the Annual Christian Megacensus*. Pasadena, Calif.: William Carey Library, 2001.

———. "Annual Statistical Table of Global Mission: 2003." *International Bulletin of Missionary Research* 27, no. 1 (January 2003): 24-25.

Barrett, Lois Y., et al., eds. In *Treasure in Clay Jars: Patterns in Missional Faithfulness*, The Gospel and Our Culture Series. Grand Rapids: W. B. Eerdmans Publishing Co., 2004.

Bavinck, Johan H. *The Impact of Christianity on the Non-Christian World*. Grand Rapids: Eerdmans, 1948.

Benedict, Ruth. *Patterns of Culture*. Boston: Houghton Mifflin, 1934.

Benhabib, Seyla, with Jeremy Waldron, Bonnie Honig, and Will Kymlicka. *Another Cosmopolitanism*. The Berkeley Tanner Lectures. New York: Oxford University Press, 2006.

Berends, Willem. "Cessationism." <<http://www.pastornet.net.au/rtc/cessatn.htm>>. Accessed May 16, 2007, 2007.

Berger, Peter L. and Samuel P. Huntington. *Many Globalizations: Cultural Diversity in the Contemporary World*. Oxford: Oxford University Press, 2002.

Berlo, David K. *The Process of Communication: An Introduction to Theory and Practice*. New York: Holt, Rinehart and Winston, 1960.

Black, Matthew and William A. Smalley, eds. *On Language, Culture and Religion*: *In Honor of Eugene A. Nida*. The Hague: Mouton, 1974.

Boas, Franz. *Race, Language and Culture*. New York: The Macmillan Co. Second ed., 1982, by University of Chicago Press, 1940.

Bodley, John H. *Victims of Progress.* Menlo Park, Calif.: Cummings Publishing Co., 1975.

Bonk, Jonathan J. *Missions and Money: Affluence as a Western Missionary Problem.* New ed. Maryknoll, N.Y.: Orbis Books, 1991.

Bonsen, Roland, Hans Marks, and Jelle Miedema, eds. *The Ambiguity of Rapprochement: Reflections of Anthropologists on Their Controversial Relationship with Missionaries.* Nijmegen, The Netherlands: Focaal, 1990.

Bosch, David J. *Transforming Mission: Paradigm Shifts in Theology of Mission.* Maryknoll, N.Y.: Orbis Books, 1991.

Brown, Arthur. *The Foreign Missionary.* London: Fleming H. Revell, 1907.

Burke, Kenneth. *A Grammar of Motives.* New ed. Berkeley: University of California Press, 1969. Original ed., 1945.

Burridge, Kenelm. *In the Way: A Study of Christian Missionary Endeavours.* Vancouver: University of British Columbia Press, 1991.

Bush, Luis, ed. *Transformation: A Unifying Vision of the Church's Mission.* Printed for the Thailand gathering of Lausanne in September 2004. Thailand: LCWE, 2004.

Cheah, Pheng. *Inhuman Conditions: On Cosmopolitanism and Human Rights.* Cambridge, Mass.: Harvard University Press, 2006.

Clifford, James. *Person and Myth: Maurice Leenhardt in the Melanesian World.* Reprint ed. Durham, N.C.: Duke University Press, 1992. Original ed., 1982.

Clifton, James A., ed. *Applied Anthropology: Readings in the Uses of the Science of Man,* Boston: Houghton Mifflin Co., 1970.

Conn, Harvie M. *Eternal Word and Changing Worlds: Theology, Anthropology, and Mission in Trialogue.* Grand Rapids: Zondervan, 1984.

Davies, T. Witton. *Magic, Divination and Demonology among the Hebrews and Their Neighbors: Including an Examination of Biblical References and of the Biblical Terms.* New York: KTAV Publishing House, 1969. Reprint of the 1898 ed.

De Ridder, Richard R. *Discipling the Nations.* Grand Rapids: Baker Book House, 1975.

De Silva, K. M., ed. *Sri Lanka: A Survey.* Honolulu: University Press of Hawaii, 1977.

Dodd, Carley H. *Dynamics of Intercultural Communication.* 5th ed. Boston: McGraw-Hill, 1998.

Doubt, Keith. *Understanding Evil: Lessons from Bosnia.* New York: Fordham University Press, 2006.

Durkheim, Emile. *The Elementary Forms of Religious Life: A Study in Religious Sociology,* translated by Joseph Ward Swain. London: G. Allen & Unwin; New York: Macmillan, 1915.

Dyrness, William A. *Let the Earth Rejoice! A Biblical Theology of Holistic Mission.* Westchester, Ill.: Crossway Books, 1983.

Eder, James F. *On the Road to Tribal Extinction: Depopulation, Deculturation, and Adaptive Well-Being among the Batak of the Philippines.* Paperback ed. Berkeley, Calif.: University of California Press, 1992.

Ember, Melvin and Carol R. Ember, eds. *The Encyclopedia of Urban Cultures: Cities and Cultures around the World.* Danbury, Conn.: Grolier, Inc., 2002.

Engel, James F. *Contemporary Christian Communications: Its Theory and Practice.* Nashville: Thomas Nelson, 1979.

Engelsviken, Tormod. *Besettelse og åndsutdrivelse i Bibelen, historien og vår egen tid [Possession and Expulsion of Evil Spirits in the Bible, in History and in Our Own Time].* Oslo: Lunde Forlag, 1978.

———. *Spiritual Conflict in Today's Mission.* Lausanne Occasional Paper, No. 29, edited by A. Scott Moreau. Monrovia, Calif.: Lausanne Committee for World Evangelization, MARC Publications, 2001a.

———. *Spiritual Conflict in Today's Mission: A Report from the Consultation "Deliver Us from Evil."* August 2000. Nairobi: Association of Evangelicals of Africa/Lausanne Committee for World Evangelization, 2001b.

———. "Den misjonale kirke og utfordringen fra kirken i sør." In *Hva vil det si å være kirke? Kirkens vesen og oppdrag*, edited by Tormod Engelsviken and Kjell Olav Sandnes, 69-92. Oslo: Tapir Akademisk forlag, 2004.

Fanon, Frantz. *Black Skin, White Masks*, translated by Charles Lam Markmann. New York: Grove Press, 1967.

Fernando, Ajith. "Missionaries Still Needed—But of a Special Kind." *Evangelical Missions Quarterly* 24 (January 1988): 18-25.

Finnegan, Ruth. *Communicating: The Multiple Modes of Human Interconnection*. London: Routledge, 2002.

Fore, William F. *Television and Religion: The Shaping of Faith, Values, and Culture*. Minneapolis: Augsburg Publishing House, 1987.

Foster, Robert J. *Social Reproduction and History in Melanesia: Mortuary Ritual, Gift Exchange, and Custom in the Tanga Islands*. Cambridge Studies in Social and Cultural Anthropology. Cambridge: Cambridge University Press, 1995.

Frielander, Shems. *Ninety-Nine Names of Allah*. Lagos: Islamic Publications Bureau; Karachi: London Book House, n.d., 1978.

Frost, Michael and Alan Hirsch. *The Shaping of Things to Come: Innovation and Mission for the 21st-Century Church*. Peabody, Mass.: Hendrickson Publishers, 2003.

Geer, Curtis Manning, *The Hartford Seminary 1834-1934*. Hartford, Conn.: Case, Lockwood & Brainard Co., 1934.

Geertz, Clifford. *The Interpretation of Cultures: Selected Essays*. New York: Basic Books, Inc., 1973.

Gibbs, Eddie. *Church Next: Quantum Changes in How We Do Ministry*. Downers Grove, Ill.: InterVarsity Press, 2000.

Gibbs, Eddie and Ryan K. Bolger. *Emerging Churches: Creating Christian Community in Postmodern Cultures*. Grand Rapids: Baker Academic, 2005.

Gilliland, Dean. Interview with Paul E. Pierson, December 18, 2006. Unpublished e-mail, 2006.

Glover, Robert. *The Bible Basis of Mission*. Los Angeles: Bible House of Los Angeles, 1946.

Gluckman, Max. *Custom and Conflict in Africa*. Oxford: Basil Blackwell, 1955.

Goldschmidt, Walter. "Anthropology and the Coming Crisis: An Autoethnographic Appraisal." *American Anthropologist* 79, no. 2 (June 1977): 293-308.

Goodman, Nelson. *Problems and Projects*. Indianapolis and New York: The Bobbs-Merrill Co., Inc., 1972.

Goulet, Jean-Guy, and Bruce Granville Miller, eds. *Extraordinary Anthropology: Transformations in the Field*. Lincoln, Neb.: University of Nebraska Press, 2007.

Graham, Billy. *Just As I Am: The Autobiography of Billy Graham*. San Francisco: Harper San Francisco, 1997.

Gravem, Peder. "Kva er sanning? Til omgrepet sanning med tanke på religions- og livssynsteori." *Tidsskrift for teologi og kirke* no. 3 (2005): 181-211.

Greig, Herbert. "Letters to the Editor." *Practical Anthropology* 4, no. 5 (1957): 203-204.

Grimes, Barbara F., ed. *Ethnologue: Languages of the World*. 14th ed. Dallas: SIL International, 2000.

Gross, Edward. *Is Charles Kraft an Evangelical? A Critique of Christianity in Culture*. Christian Beacon Press, 1985.

Guder, Darrell L. "Foreword." In C. Van Engen. *You Are My Witnesses: Drawing from Your Spiritual Journey to Evangelize Your Neighbors*. New York: Reformed Church Press, 1992.

———. *Missional Church: A Vision for the Sending of the Church in North America*. Grand Rapids: W. B. Eerdmans Publishing Co., 1998.

———. *The Continuing Conversion of the Church*. Grand Rapids: W. B. Eerdmans Publishing Co. Rev. ed. of *Be My Witnesses*, 1985, 2000.

———. "Pointing toward the Reign of God." In *Treasure in Clay Jars: Patterns in Missional Faithfulness*, edited by Lois Y. Barrett et al., 126-138. The Gospel and Our Culture Series. Grand Rapids: W. B. Eerdmans Publishing Co., 2004.

Gudykunst, William B. *Bridging Differences: Effective Intergroup Communication.* 4th ed. Thousand Oaks, Calif.: Sage Publications, 2004.

Hardy, Spencer R. *The British Government and the Idolatry of Ceylon.* London: Krofts and Blenkarn, 1841.

Hauerwas, Stanley. *After Christendom? How the Church Is to Behave if Freedom, Justice, and a Christian Nation Are Bad Ideas.* Nashville: Abingdon Press, 1991.

Henry, Carl F. H. *The Uneasy Conscience of Modern Fundamentalism.* Grand Rapids: Eerdmans, 1947.

———. "The Cultural Relativizing of Revelation." *Trinity Journal* 1, no. 2 (Fall 1980): 153-164.

Henry, Jules. *Culture against Man.* New York: Vintage Books, 1963.

Hesselgrave, David J. *Communicating Christ Cross-Culturally.* Grand Rapids: Zondervan, 1978.

———. *Paradigms in Conflict: 10 Key Questions in Christian Missions Today.* Grand Rapids: Kregel Publications, 2005 .

Hiebert, Paul G. "Missions and Anthropology: A Love/Hate Relationship." *Missiology* 6 (April 1978): 165-180.

———. "The Flaw of the Excluded Middle." *Missiology* 10, no. 1 (January 1982): 35-47.

———. "Power Encounter and Folk Islam." In *Muslims and Christians on the Emmaus Road*, edited by J. Dudley Woodberry, 45-61. Monrovia, Calif.: MARC, 1989.

———. *Missiological Implications of Epistemological Shifts: Affirming Truth in a Modern/ Postmodern World.* Harrisburg, Penn.: Trinity Press International, 1999.

———. "The Missionary as Mediator of Global Theologizing." In *Globalizing Theology: Belief and Practice in an Era of World Christianity*, edited by Craig Ott and Harold A. Netland, 288-308. Grand Rapids: Baker Academic, 2006.

Hill, Harriet Swannie. "Communicating Context in Bible Translation among the Adioukrou of Côte d'Ivoire." Ph.D. dissertation, School of World Mission, Pasadena, Calif., Fuller Theological Seminary, 2003.

[Hisham, Ibn.] *The Life of Muhammad: A Translation of Ibn Ishaq's "Sirat Rasul Allah,"* translated by A. Guillaume. London: Oxford University Press, 1955.

Hobart, Mark and Robert H. Taylor, eds. *Context, Meaning, and Power in Southeast Asia.* Studies on Southeast Asia, No. 2. Ithaca, N.Y.: Cornell University Southeast Asia Program, 1986.

Hodges, Melvin L. *A Theology of the Church and Its Mission: A Pentecostal Perspective.* Springfield, Mo.: Gospel Publishing House, 1977.

Hoke, Stephen. "Nida, Eugene A." In *Evangelical Dictionary of World Missions*, edited by A. Scott Moreau, Harold Netland, and Charles Van Engen, Grand Rapids: Baker Books (2000), 689-690.

Holmberg, Alan R. "Adventures in Culture Change." In *Method and Perspective in Anthropology: Papers in Honor of Wilson D. Wallis,* edited by Robert F. Spencer, 103-113. Minneapolis: University of Minnesota Press, 1954.

———. "The Research and Development Approach to the Study of Change." *Human Organization* 17, no. 1 (1958): 12-16.

Hunsberger, George R. *Bearing the Witness of the Spirit: Lesslie Newbigin's Theology of Cultural Plurality.* Grand Rapids: W. B. Eerdmans Publishing Co., 1998.

Jenkins, Philip. *The Next Christendom: The Coming of Global Christianity.* New York: Oxford University Press, 2002.

———. *The New Faces of Christianity: Believing in the Bible in the Global South.* New York: Oxford University Press, 2006.

Jones, E. Stanley. *The Christ of the Indian Road.* New York: Abingdon Press, 1925.

Jongeneel, Jan A. B. *Missiologie.* Vol. 1, *Zendingswetenschap*; vol. 2, *Missionarie theologie.* The Hague: Boekencentrum, 1991.

Jørgensen, Knud. "The Role and Function of the Media in the Mission of the Church: With Particular Reference to Africa." Ph.D. dissertation, School of World Mission, Fuller Theological Seminary, Pasadena, Calif.: 1986.

Junod, Henri P. "Anthropology and Missionary Education." *International Review of Missions* 24, no. 94 (1935): 213-228.
———. *The Life of a South African Tribe*. 2 vols. New Hyde Park, N.Y.: University Books, Inc., 1962. Original ed., 1912.
Justin. *Dialogue with Trypho*. In *The Ante-Nicene Fathers: The Writings of the Fathers down to A.D. 325*, edited by Alexander Roberts and James Donaldson, vol. 1, *The Apostolic Fathers—Justin Martyr—Iraenæus*, 241-242. Grand Rapids: W. B. Eerdmans Publishing Co., 1981.
Kim, Caleb Chul-Soo. *Islam among the Swahili in East Africa*. Nairobi: Acton Publishers, 2004.
King, Roberta R. "Pathways in Christian Music Communication: The Case of the Senufo of Côte d'Ivoire." Ph.D. dissertation, Fuller Theological Seminary, School of World Mission, Pasadena, Calif., 1989.
Klutz, Todd E., ed. *Magic in the Biblical World: From the Rod of Aaron to the Ring of Solomon*. London: T&T Clark International, 2003.
Knauft, Bruce M. *Genealogies for the Present in Cultural Anthropology*. New York: Routledge, 1996.
Kraemer, Hendrik. *The Christian Message in a Non-Christian World*. London: Edinburgh House Press, 1947. Reprint, Kregel, Grand Rapids, 1961.
———. *The Communication of the Christian Faith*. Philadelphia: Westminster Press, 1956.
Kraft, Charles H. "Christian Conversion or Cultural Conversion." *Practical Anthropology* 10 (July-August 1963): 179-187.
———. "Dynamic Equivalent Churches." *Missiology* 1 (1973a): 39-57.
———. *Introductory Hausa*. Berkeley: University of California Press, 1973b.
———. "Toward a Christian Ethnotheology." In *God, Man and Church Growth: A Festschrift in Honor of Donald Anderson McGavran*, edited by Alan R.Tippett, 109-126, Grand Rapids: W. B. Eerdmans, 1973c.
———. *Christianity in Culture: A Study in Dynamic Biblical Theologizing in Cross-Cultural Perspective*. Maryknoll, N.Y.: Orbis Books, 1979a. Rev. ed. with Marguerite Kraft, 2005.
———. *Communicating the Gospel God's Way*. Ashland, Ohio: Ashland Theological Seminary, 1979. Reprint from the *Ashland Theological Bulletin* 12, no. 1 (Spring 1979b).
———. "The Place of the Receptor in Communications." *Theology, News and Notes* (October 1981): 13-15.
———. *Communicating the Gospel God's Way*. Pasadena, Calif.: William Carey Library, 1983a.
———. *Communication Theory for Christian Witness*. Nashville: Abingdon, 1983b .
———. *Christianity with Power: Your Worldview and Your Experience of the Supernatural*. Ann Arbor, Mich.: Servant Publications, 1989.
———. *Communication Theory for Christian Witness*. Rev. ed. Maryknoll, N.Y.: Orbis Books, 1991a.
———. "What Encounters Do We Need in Our Christian Witness." *Evangelical Missions Quarterly* 27, no. 3 (July 1991b): 258-265.
———. "Allegiance, Truth, and Power Encounters in Christian Witness." In *Pentecost, Mission and Ecumenism: Essays in Intercultural Theology*, edited by Jan A. B. Jongeneel, 215-230. Berlin and New York: Peter Lang, 1992a.
———. *Defeating Dark Angels: Breaking Demonic Oppression in the Believer's Life*. Ann Arbor, Mich.: Servant Publications, 1992b.
———. *Deep Wounds, Deep Healing: Discovering the Vital Link between Spiritual Warfare and Inner Healing*. Ann Arbor, Mich.: Servant Publications, 1993.
———. *Anthropology for Christian Witness*. Maryknoll, N.Y.: Orbis Books, 1996.
———. *I Give You Authority*. Grand Rapids: Chosen Books, 1997.
———. *The Rules of Engagement: Understanding the Principles That Govern the Spiritual Battles in Our Lives*. Colorado Springs: Wagner Publications, 2000.

———. "The New Wine of Independence." In *Culture, Communication and Christianity: A Selection of Writings*, Pasadena, Calif.: William Carey Library (2001): 172-176. Reprinted from *World Vision Magazine* 15 (February 1971): 7-9.

———. *Confronting Powerless Christianity: Evangelicals and the Missing Dimension.* Grand Rapids: Chosen Books, 2002a .

———. "Contextualization and Spiritual Power." In *Deliver Us from Evil: An Uneasy Frontier in Christian Mission*, edited by A. Scott Moreau, Tokunboh Adeyemo, David G. Burnett, Bryant L. Myers, and Hwa Yung (2002b): 276-289. Consultation on Deliver Us from Evil, Nairobi, 2000. Monrovia, Calif.: Lausanne Committee for World Evangelization, World Vision International.

Kraft, Charles H., ed. *SWM/SIS at Forty: A Participant Observer's View of Our History.* Pasadena, Calif.: William Carey Library, 2005a.

———. *Appropriate Christianity*. Pasadena, Calif.: William Carey Library, 2005b.

Kraft, Charles H., with Marguerite G. Kraft. *Christianity in Culture: A Study in Dynamic Biblical Theologizing in Cross-Cultural Perspective.* Rev. ed. Maryknoll, N.Y.: Orbis Books, 2005.

Kraft, Marguerite. "Spiritual Conflict and the Mission of the Church: Contextualisation." In *Deliver Us from Evil: An Uneasy Frontier in Christian Mission*, edited by A. Scott Moreau, Tokunboh Adeyemo, David G. Burnett, Bryant L. Myers, and Hwa Yung, 290-308. Consultation on Deliver Us from Evil, Nairobi, 2000. Monrovia, Calif.: Lausanne Committee for World Evangelization, World Vision International, 2002.

Kroeber, Alfred L. *Cultural and Natural Areas of Native North America.* Berkeley, Calif.: University of California Press, 1939.

———. "The Superorganic." *American Anthropologist* 19 (1917): 163-213.

Kuhn, Thomas S. *The Structure of Scientific Revolutions*. Chicago: University of Chicago Press, 1962.

———. *The Essential Tension: Selected Studies in Scientific Tradition and Change.* Chicago: University of Chicago Press, 1977.

Küng, Hans and David Tracy. *Paradigm Change in Theology*. New York: Crossroad, 1989.

Latourette, Kenneth Scott. *The Gospel, the Church and the World*. New York and London: Harper & Bros., 1946.

———. *A History of Christianity*. New York and London: Harper & Bros., 1953.

Lenning, Larry G. *Blessing in Mosque and Mission*. Pasadena, Calif.: William Carey Library, 1980.

Lewellen, Ted C. *The Anthropology of Globalization: Cultural Anthropology Enters the 21st Century*. Westport, Conn.: Bergin & Garvey, 2002.

Lewis, Oscar. "The Culture of Poverty." *Scientific American* 215, no. 4 (1966): 19-25.

Lindsell, Harold. *Christian Philosophy of Missions*. Wheaton, Ill.: Van Kampen, 1949.

———. *Missionary Principles and Practice*. Westwood, N.J.: Revell, 1955.

———. *The Battle for the Bible*. Grand Rapids: Zondervan Publishing House, 1976.

Lingenfelter, Sherwood G. *Agents of Transformation: A Guide for Effective Cross-Cultural Ministry.* Grand Rapids: Baker Books, 1996.

Lingenfelter, Sherwood G. and Marvin K. Mayers. *Ministering Cross-Culturally: An Incarnational Model for Personal Relationships.* Grand Rapids: Baker Academic, 1986. Second ed., 2003.

Luzbetak, Louis J. *The Church and Cultures: An Applied Anthropology for the Religious Worker.* Techny, Ill.: Divine Word Publications, 1963. Reprinted, 1970.

———. *The Church and Cultures: New Perspectives in Missiological Anthropology.* Maryknoll, N.Y.: Orbis Books, 1988.

———. "Prospects for a Better Understanding and Closer Cooperation between Anthropologists and Missionaries." In *Missionaries, Anthropologists, and Cultural Change.* Studies in Third World Societies, No. 25, guest edited by Darrell L. Whiteman, 1-53. Williamsburg, Va.: Department of Anthropology, College of William and Mary, 1985.

MacNutt, Francis. *Healing.* Notre Dame, Ind.: Ave Maria Press, 1974.

Madale, Nagasura T. "Kashawing: Rice Ritutal of the Maranaos." *Mindanao Journal* 1 (1974): 76-77.

Malinowski, Bronislaw. *Argonauts of the Western Pacific.* New York: E. P. Dutton and Co., 1922.

———. "Practical Anthropology." *Africa* 2, no. 1 (1929): 22-38. Reprinted in *Applied Anthropology: Readings in the Uses of the Science of Man,* edited by James A. Clifton, 12-25. Boston: Houghton Mifflin Co., 1970.

———. *Methods of Study of Culture Contact in Africa.* Memorandum 15, International Institute of African Languages and Cultures. London: Oxford University Press, 1938.

———. *A Scientific Theory of Culture and Other Essays.* Chapel Hill, N.C.: University of North Carolina Press, 1944.

Mandelbaum, David G., ed. *Selected Writings of Edward Sapir in Language, Culture, and Personality.* Berkeley, Calif.: University of California Press, 1951.

Mathew, C. V., ed. *Integral Mission: The Way Forward: Essays in Honor of Dr. Saphir P. Athyal.* Tiruvalla, Kerala, India: Christava Sahitya Samithi, 2006.

McCroskey, James C. *An Introduction to Rhetorical Communication: The Theory and Practice of Public Speaking.* Englewood Cliffs, N.J.: Prentice-Hall, Inc., 1968.

McGavran, Donald Anderson. *The Bridges of God: A Study in the Strategy of Missions.* Rev. and enlarged ed. New York: Friendship Press, 1981. Original edition, 1955.

———. *Understanding Church Growth,* revised and edited by C. Peter Wagner. 3rd ed. Grand Rapids: W. B. Eerdmans Publishing Co., 1990.

McGavran, Donald Anderson, ed. *Church Growth and Christian Mission,* New York: Harper & Row, 1965.

McLuhan, H. Marshall and Quentin Fiore. *The Medium Is the Message.* New York: Bantam Books, 1967.

McQuilkin, J. Robertson. "Limits of Cultural Interpretation." *Journal of the Evangelical Theological Society* 23, no. 2 (June 1980): 113-124.

Mead, Margaret. *Coming of Age in Samoa: A Psychological Study of Primitive Youth for Western Civilization.* New York: William Morrow and Co., 1928.

———. *Sex and Temperament in Three Primitive Societies.* New York: William Morrow and Co., 1935.

———. *New Lives for Old: Cultural Transformation—Manus, 1928-1953.* New York: William Morrow and Co., 1956.

Milbank, John. *Theology and Social Theory beyond Secular Reason.* Oxford: Blackwell Publishers, 1990.

Miller, Elmer S. "The Christian Missionary: Agent of Secularization." *Missiology* 1, no. 1 (1973): 99-107.

Mishkat al-Masabih, translated by James Robson. Lahore, Pakistan: Sh. Muhammad Ashraf, n.d.

Moltmann, Jürgen. *The Church in the Power of the Spirit: A Contribution to Messianic Ecclesiology.* New York: Harper & Row, 1977.

Moreau, A. Scott, Harold Netland and Charles Van Engen, eds. *Evangelical Dictionary of World Missions.* Grand Rapids: Baker Books, 2000.

Moreau, A. Scott, Tokunboh Adeyemo, David G. Burnett, Bryant L. Myers, and Hwa Yung, eds. *Deliver Us from Evil: An Uneasy Frontier in Christian Mission.* Consultation on Deliver Us from Evil, Nairobi, 2000. Monrovia, Calif.: Lausanne Committee for World Evangelization, World Vision International, 2002.

Mott, John R. *The Evangelization of the World in This Generation.* New York: Arno, 1900.

———. *The Present Day Summons to World Mission of Christianity.* Nashville: Cokesbury Press, 1930.

Murphy, Ed. *Handbook for Spiritual Warfare.* Nashville, Tenn.: Thomas Nelson Publisher, 1992.

Musk, Bill. *The Unseen Face of Islam: Sharing the Gospel with Ordinary Muslims.* London: MARC, 1989.

Nalunnakkal, George Mathew. *Re-Routing Mission: Towards a People's Concept of Mission (Indian Perspectives)*, edited by George Mathew. Tiruvalla, India: Christava Sahitya Samiti, 2004.

Neill, Stephen C. *The Unfinished Task*. London: Edinburgh House Press, 1957.

Nevius, John. *Planting and Development of Missionary Churches*. Nutley, N.J.: Presbyterian and Reformed, 1958.

Newbigin, Lesslie. *The Household of God: Lectures on the Nature of the Church*. London: SCM Press, 1952.

————. *Foolishness to the Greeks: The Gospel and Western Culture*. Grand Rapids: W. B. Eerdmans Publishing Co., 1986. Expanded version of the Warfield Lectures given at Princeton Theological Seminary, March 1984.

————. *The Gospel in a Pluralist Society*. Grand Rapids: W. B. Eerdmans Publishing Co., 1989.

Nida, Eugene A. *Morphology: The Descriptive Analysis of Words*. Ann Arbor, Mich.: University of Michigan Press, 1949.

————. *Learning a Foreign Language: A Handbook for Missionaries*. New York: Committee on Missionary Personnel of the Foreign Missions Conference of North America, 1950.

————. *God's Word in Man's Language*. New York: Harper & Row, 1952.

————. *Customs and Cultures: Anthropology for Christian Missions*. New York: Harper & Brothers, 1954.

————. *Message and Mission: The Communication of the Christian Faith*. New York: Harper & Row, 1960.

————. *Toward a Science of Translating: With Special Reference to Principles and Procedures Involved in Bible Translating*. Leiden: E. J. Brill, 1964.

————. "My Pilgrimage in Mission." *International Bulletin of Missionary Research* 12, no. 2 (April 1988): 62, 64-65.

————. "Culture, Communication, and Christianity." Missiology Lectures. School of World Mission, Fuller Theological Seminary, Pasadena, Calif., 2001.

Nida, Eugene A. and Charles R. Taber. *The Theory and Practice of Translation*. Leiden: E. J. Brill, 1969.

North, Eric M. "Eugene A. Nida: An Appreciation." In *On Language, Culture and Religion: In Honor of Eugene A. Nida*, edited by Matthew Black and William A. Smalley. The Hague: Mouton, 1974.

Ott, Craig and Harold A. Netland, eds. *Globalizing Theology: Belief and Practice in an Era of World Christianity*. Grand Rapids: Baker Academic, 2006.

Pachuau, Lalsangima. "Christian Mission from Below: Methodological Developments toward a Subaltern Affirmation." In *Re-Routing Mission: Towards a People's Concept of Mission (Indian Perspectives)*, edited by George Mathew Nalunnakkal, 19-38. Tiruvalla, India: Christava Sahitya Samiti, 2004.

Pantoja, Luis L., Jr., Sadiri Joy B. Tira, and Enoch Wan, eds. *Scattered: The Filipino Global Presence*. Manila: LifeChange Publishing, Inc., 2004.

Parsons, Talcott. *The Social System*. Glencoe, Ill.: The Free Press, 1951.

Parsons, Talcott and Edward A. Shils, eds. *Toward a General Theory of Action*. Cambridge, Mass.: Harvard University Press, 1951.

Peake, N. J. E. "Discussion." *Man* 21, no. 103 (1921): 174.

Philips, Abu Ameenah Bilal. *The Exorcist Tradition in Islaam* [sic]. Sharjah, United Arab Emerites: Dar Al Fatah, 1997.

Priest, Robert J. "Missionary Positions: Christian, Modernist, Postmodernist." *Current Anthropology* 42, no. 1 (2001): 29-70.

Pulei, Moses. "Communicating the Gospel to the Maasai: A Historical, Theological, and Practical Application for Evangelism." Unpublished manuscript, Fuller Theological Seminary, School of World Mission, Pasadena, Calif., 2000.

Radcliffe-Brown, A. R. *Method in Social Anthropology: Selected Essays,* edited by M. N. Srinivas. Chicago: University of Chicago Press, 1958.

———. *Structure and Function in Primitive Society: Essays and Addresses.* Paperback ed. New York: The Free Press, 1965. Original ed., 1952.

Reid, Gavin. *The Gagging of God: The Failure of the Church to Communicate in the Television Age.* London: Hodder & Stoughton, 1969.

Robeck, Cecil M., Jr., ed. "Signs, Wonders, Warfare, and Witness." *Pneuma* (Journal of the Society of Pentecostal Studies) 13, no.1 (Spring 1991): 1-5.

Rogers, Everett M. *Diffusion of Innovations.* 5th ed. New York: Free Press, 2003.

Rogers, Everett M. with F. Floyd Shoemaker. *Communication of Innovations: A Cross-Cultural Approach.* 2nd ed. New York: The Free Press, 1971.

Rogers, Everett M. and Thomas M. Steinfatt. *Intercultural Communication.* Prospect Heights, Ill.: Waveland Press, Inc., 1999.

Romarheim, Arild. "Åndenes makt. Folkelige forestillinger om hus hjemsøkt av ånder— og kirkens rolle" ("The Power of the Spirits: Popular Perceptions of Houses Haunted by Spirits—and the Role of the Church"). *Halvårsskrift for praktisk teologi* 21, no. 2 (2004): 61-69.

———. 2007 "Behöver vi en spökteologi?" ("Do We Need a Theology of Ghosts?"). *NOD—Forum for Tro, Kultur og Samhälle,* no. 1: 22-27.

Rommen, Edward, ed. *Spiritual Power and Missions: Raising the Issues.* Pasadena, Calif.: William Carey Library, 1995.

Rynkiewich, Michael A. "The World in My Parish: Rethinking the Standard Missiological Model." *Missiology* 30, no. 3 (July 2002): 301-321.

Said, Edward W. *Orientalism.* 1st ed. New York: Vintage Books, 1979.

Salamone, Frank A. "Missionaries and Anthropologists: An Inquiry into the Ambivalent Relationship." *Missiology* 14, no. 1 (January 1986): 55-70.

Salamone, Frank A., guest ed. *Missionaries and Anthropologists.* Part II. Papers presented at meetings of the 11th International Congress of Anthropological and Ethnological Sciences, Quebec, August 1983, and the African Studies Association, Boston, December 1983. Studies in Third World Societies, No. 26. Williamsburg, Va.: Department of Anthropology, College of William and Mary, 1985.

Samovar, Larry A. and Richard E. Porter. *Intercultural Communication: A Reader.* Belmont, Calif.: Wadsworth Publishing Co., 1972.

Sampson, Philip, Vinay Samuel, and Chris Sugden, eds. *Faith and Modernity: Essays in Modernity and Post-Modernity.* Oxford: Regnum Lynx Books, 1994.

Sanneh, Lamin. *Translating the Message: The Missionary Impact on Culture.* Maryknoll, N.Y.: Orbis Books, 1989.

Sapir, Edward. *Language, an Introduction to the Study of Speech.* New York: Harcourt, Brace and Co., 1921.

———. "Why Cultural Anthropology Needs the Psychiatrist." In *Selected Writings of Edward Sapir in Language, Culture, and Personality,* edited by David G. Mandelbaum, 569-570. Berkeley, Calif.: University of California Press, 1951.

Scharer, Matthias and Bernd Jochen Hilberath. *Kommunikative Theologie. Eine Grundlegung,* 2007.

Scherer, James A. and Stephen B. Bevans, eds. *New Directions in Mission & Evangelization 3: Faith and Culture,* Maryknoll, N.Y.: Orbis Books, 1999.

Schramm, Wilbur and Donald F. Roberts, eds. *The Process and Effects of Mass Communication.* Rev. ed. Urbana, Ill.: University of Illinois, 1971.

Schreiter, Robert J. "A New Modernity: Living and Believing in an Unstable World— Part Two." *New Theology Review* 20 (May 2007): 47-57.

———. *Reconciliation: Mission and Ministry in a Changing Social Order.* Maryknoll, N.Y.: Orbis Books, 1992.

Shannon, Claude E. and Warren Weaver. *The Mathematical Theory of Communication.* Urbana, Ill.: University of Illinois Press, 1949.

Sharp, Lauriston. "Steel Axes for Stone Age Australians." In *Human Problems in Technological Change,* edited by Edward H. Spicer, 69-72. New York: Russell Sage Foundation, 1952.

Shaw, R. Daniel. "The Legacy of Eugene A. Nida: A Contribution to Anthropological Theory and Missionary Practice." *Anthropos* 102 (2007): 2.

Shaw, R. Daniel and Charles E. Van Engen. *Communicating God's Word in a Complex World: God's Truth or Hocus Pocus?* Lanham, Md.: Rowman & Littlefield Publishers, 2003.

Shenk, Wilbert R. "The Role of Theory in Mission Studies." *Missiology* 24 (January 1996): 31-45.

Shenk, Wilbert R. and George R. Hunsberger. *The American Society of Missiology: The First Quarter Century.* Decatur, Ga.: The American Society of Missiology, 1998.

Sjödin, Ulf. *Mer mellan himmel och jord?* Stockholm: Verbum, 2001.

Skarsaune, Oskar and Tormod Engelsviken. "Possession and Exorcism in the History of the Church." In *Deliver Us from Evil: An Uneasy Frontier in Christian Mission*, edited by A. Scott Moreau, Tokunboh Adeyemo, David G. Burnett, Bryant L. Myers, and Hwa Yung, 65-87. Consultation on Deliver Us from Evil, Nairobi 2000. Monrovia, Calif.: Lausanne Committee for World Evangelization, World Vision International, 2002.

Slate, Carl Philip. *Communication Theory and Evangelization: Contributions to the Communication of Religious Innovations in the Euroamerican Culture Area.* D.Miss. dissertation, School of World Mission, Fuller Theological Seminary, Pasadena, Calif., 1976.

Small, W. J. T., ed. *A History of the Methodist Church in Ceylon 1814-1964.* Colombo, Sri Lanka: The Wesley Press, 1971.

Smalley, William A. "Cultural Implications of an Indigenous Church." In *Practical Anthropology* 5 (March-April 1958): 51-65.

Smalley, William A., ed. *Readings in Missionary Anthropology.* Tarrytown, N.Y.: Practical Anthropology, 1967.

———. *Readings in Missionary Anthropology II.* Enlarged ed. Pasadena, Calif.: William Carey Library, 1978.

Smedes, Lewis B., ed. *Ministry and the Miraculous: A Case Study at Fuller Theological Seminary.* Pasadena, Calif.: Fuller Theological Seminary, 1987.

Smith, Donald K. *Creating Understanding: A Handbook for Christian Communication across Cultural Landscapes.* Paperback ed. Grand Rapids: Zondervan Publishing House, 1992.

Smith, Edward M. *Beyond Tolerable Recovery: Moving Beyond Tolerable Existence into Genuine Restoration and Emotional Inner Healing.* Campbellsville, Ky.: Alathia, Inc., 1996.

Smith, Edwin W. *Handbook of the Ila Language.* London: Oxford University Press, 1907.

———. "Social Anthropology and Missionary Work." *International Review of Missions* 13, no. 52 (1924): 518-531.

———. "Anthropology and the Practical Man." Presidential address. *Journal of the Royal Anthropological Institute* 64 (January-June 1934): xiii-xxxvii.

Smith, Edwin W. and Andrew Murray Dale. *The Ila-Speaking Peoples of Northern Rhodesia.* 2 vol., 2nd ed. New Hyde Park, N.Y.: University Books, 1968. Original edition, 1920.

Smith, Gordon Hedderly. *The Missionary and Anthropology: An Introduction to the Study of Primitive Man for Missionaries.* Chicago: Moody Press, 1945.

Søgaard, Viggo B. *Everything You Need to Know for a Cassette Ministry: Cassettes in the Context of a Total Christian Communication Program.* Minneapolis: Bethany Fellowship, Inc., 1975.

———. *Media in Church and Mission: Communicating the Gospel.* Pasadena, Calif.: William Carey Library, 1993.

———. *Research in Church and Mission.* Pasadena, Calif.: William Carey Library, 1996.

Søgaard, Viggo B., ed. *Communicating Scriptures: The Bible in Audio and Video Formats.* Reading, U.K.: United Bible Societies, 2001.

Soper, Edmund Davison. *The Philosophy of the Christian World Mission.* Nashville: Abingdon Press, 1943.

Speer, Robert E. *Missions and Modern History*. London and Edinburgh: Fleming H. Revell, 1904.

Spencer, Robert F., ed. *Method and Perspective in Anthropology: Papers in Honor of Wilson D. Wallis*, 103-113. Minneapolis: University of Minnesota Press, 1954.

Stacey, Vivienne. "The Practice of Exorcism and Healing." In *Muslims and Christians on the Emmaus Road: Crucial Issues in Witness among Muslims*, edited by J. Dudley Woodberry, 291-303. Monrovia, Calif.: MARC, 1989.

Stanley, Brian. "Christian Missions and the Enlightenment: A Reevaluation." In *Christian Missions and the Enlightenment*, edited by Brian Stanley, 1-21. Grand Rapids: William B. Eerdmans Publishing Co., 2001.

Stanley, Brian, ed. *Missions, Nationalism, and the End of Empire*. Grand Rapids: W. B. Eerdmans Publishing Co., 2003.

Stine, Philip C. *Let the Words Be Written: The Lasting Influence of Eugene A. Nida*. Atlanta: Society of Biblical Literature, 2004.

Stipe, Claude E. "Anthropologists versus Missionaries: The Influence of Presuppositions." *Current Anthropology* 21, no. 2 (April 1980): 165-178.

Storkey, Elaine. "Modernity and Anthropology." In *Faith and Modernity: Essays in Modernity and Post-Modernity*, edited by Philip Sampson, Vinay Samuel, and Chris Sugden, 136-150. Oxford: Regnum Books, 1994.

Strathern, Marilyn. *The Gender of the Gift: Problems with Women and Problems with Society in Melanesia*. Berkeley, Calif.: University of California Press, 1988.

Sundermeier, Theo. "Spiritism: A Theological and Pastoral Challenge." In *LWF Studies*, edited by Ingo Wulfhorst, no. 2. Geneva: The Lutheran World Federation, 2004.

Sutlive, Vinson H., Jr. "Anthropologists and Missionaries: Eternal Enemies or Colleagues in Disguise?" In *Missionaries, Anthropologists, and Cultural Change*. Studies in Third World Societies, No. 25, guest edited by Darrell L. Whiteman, 55-90. Williamsburg, Va.: College of William and Mary, 1985.

Taber, Charles R. "Change and Continuity: Guest Editorial." *Missiology* 1, no. 1 (January 1973): 7-13.

———. *The World Is Too Much with Us: "Culture" in Modern Protestant Missions*. Macon, Ga.: Mercer University Press, 1991.

———. *To Understand the World, to Save the World: The Interface between Missiology and the Social Sciences*. Harrisburg, Pa.: Trinity Press International, 2000.

Tertullian. *Apologeticum*. In *The Ante-Nicene Fathers: The Writings of the Fathers down to A.D. 325*, edited by Alexander Roberts and James Donaldson. Vol. 3, *Latin Christianity: Its Founder, Tertullian*, 36-38. Grand Rapids: W. B. Eerdmans Publishing Co., 1980.

Thelle, Notto R. "Relation, Awareness, and Energy—Three Languages, Three Worlds." In *The Concept of God in Global Dialogue*, edited by Werner G. Jeanrond and Aasulv Lande, 48-62. Maryknoll, N.Y.: Orbis Books, 2005.

Thomas, Scott M. *The Global Resurgence of Religion and the Transformation of International Relations: The Struggle for the Soul of the Twenty-First Century*. New York: Palgrave Macmillan, 2005.

Tippett, Alan R. *Solomon Islands Christianity*. London: Lutterworth, 1967.

———. *People Movements in Southern Polynesia: Studies in the Dynamics of Church-Planting and Growth in Tahiti, New Zealand, Tonga, and Samoa*. Chicago: Moody Press, 1971.

———. "Missiology: 'For Such a Time as This!'—Editorial." *Missiology* 1, no. 1 (1973a): 15-22.

———. *Verdict Theology in Missionary Theory*. Pasadena, Calif.: William Carey Library, 1973b.

———. *Introduction to Missiology*. Pasadena, Calif.: William Carey Library, 1987.

Travis, Anna. *Undivided Heart Prayer Manual*. Unpublished, 2002.

Unger, Merrill Frederick. *Biblical Demonology: A Study of the Spiritual Forces behind the Present World Unrest*. Wheaton, Ill.: Scripture Press, 1963. Original ed., 1952.

United Nations (UN) Centre for Human Settlements. *Cities in a Globalizing World: Global Report on Human Settlements 2001*, edited by Willem Van Vliet. London: Earthscan Publications, 2001.

Van Der Geest, Sjaak. "Anthropologists and Missionaries: Brothers under the Skin." *Man* 25, no. 4 (December 1990): 588-601.

van der Toorn, Karl, Bob Becking, and Pieter W. van der Horst, eds. *Dictionary of Deities and Demons in the Bible*. Leiden: E.J. Brill, 1995.

Van Engen, Charles E. *The Growth of the True Church: An Analysis of the Ecclesiology of the Church Growth Movement*. Dissertation for the Free University of Amsterdam, Amsterdam: RODOPI, 1981.

———. *God's Missionary People: Rethinking the Purpose of the Local Church*. Grand Rapids, Mich.: Baker Book House, 1991.

———. *You Are My Witnesses: Drawing from Your Spiritual Journey to Evangelize Your Neighbors*. New York: Reformed Church Press, 1992.

———. *Mission on the Way: Issues in Mission Theology*. Grand Rapids: Baker Book House, 1996.

———. "Five Perspectives of Contextually Appropriate Mission Theology." In *Appropriate Christianity*, edited by Charles Kraft, 183-202. Pasadena, Calif.: WCL, 2005a.

———. "Toward a Contextually Appropriate Methodology in Mission Theology." In *Appropriate Christianity*, edited by Charles Kraft, 203-226. Pasadena, Calif.: WCL, 2005b.

———. "Toward a Missiology of Transformation." In *Transformation: Unifying Vision of the Church's Mission*, edited by Luis Bush, 93-117. Thailand: LCWE, 2005c. Reprinted in Mathew C. V., ed. *Integral Mission: The Way Forward: Essays in Honor of Dr. Saphir P. Athyal*, 71-96. Tiruvalla, Kerala, India: Christava Sahitya Samithi, 2006.

Van Engen, Charles E. and Jude Tiersma, eds. *God So Loves the City: Seeking a Theology for Urban Mission*. Monrovia, Calif.: MARC, 1994.

Van Vliet, Willem, ed. *Cities in a Globalizing World: Global Report on Human Settlements*. London: Earthscan Publications, 2001.

Wagner, C. Peter. *Spiritual Power and Church Growth*. Rev. printing. Altamonte Springs, Fla.: Strang Communications Co., 1986. Rev. ed. of *Look Out! The Pentecostals Are Coming*. Carol Stream, Ill.: Creation House, 1973.

———. *How to Have a Healing Ministry in Any Church: A Comprehensive Guide*. Ventura, Calif.: Regal Books, 1988a.

———. *The Third Wave of the Holy Spirit: Encountering the Power of Signs and Wonders Today*. Ann Arbor, Mich.: Servant Publications, 1988b.

———. *Warfare Prayer: How to Seek God's Power and Protection in the Battle to Build His Kingdom*. Ventura, Calif.: Regal Books, 1992.

———. *Confronting the Powers*. Ventura, Calif.: Regal Books, 1996.

Wagner, C. Peter, ed. *Signs and Wonders Today*. New exp. ed. Altamonte Springs, Fla.: Creation House, 1987.

Wagner, C. Peter and F. Douglas Pennoyer, eds. *Wrestling with Dark Angels: Toward a Deeper Understanding of the Supernatural Forces in Spiritual Warfare*. Papers presented at the Academic Symposium on Power Evangelism, December 13-15, 1988, Fuller Theological Seminary School of World Mission. Ventura, Calif.: Regal Books, 1990.

Walker, Robert, ed. "Signs and Wonders Today." *Christian Life* (October 1982): 18-76.

Wan, Enoch. "The Phenomenon of Diaspora: Missiological Implications for Christian Mission." In *Scattered: The Filipino Global Presence*, edited by Luis L. Pantoja, Jr., Sadiri Joy Tira, and Enoch Wan, 103-121. Manila: LifeChange Publishing, Inc., 2004.

Ward, Pete. *Liquid Church*. Carlisle, U.K.: Paternoster Press, 2002.

Warneck, Gustav. *Evangelische Missionslehre. Ein missions-theoretischer Versuch*. Vols. I-V. Gotha: F. A. Perthes, 1892-1905.

Warren, Max A.C. *The Calling of God.* London: Lutterworth Press, 1944.
————. *The Christian Mission.* London: Student Christian Movement Press, 1951.
————. *The Christian Imperative.* New York: Charles Scribner's Sons, 1955a.
————. *The Gospel of Victory.* London: Student Christian Movement Press, 1955b.
Webber, Robert E. *God Still Speaks: A Biblical View of Christian Communication.* Nashville: Thomas Nelson Publishers, 1980.
Whiteman, Darrell L. "Contextualization: The Theory, the Gap, the Challenge." *International Bulletin of Missionary Research* 21 (January): 2-7. Reprinted in *New Directions in Mission & Evangelization 3: Faith and Culture*, edited by James A. Scherer and Stephen B. Bevans, 42-53. Maryknoll, N.Y.: Orbis Books, 1999, 1997.
————. "Does Christianity Destroy Cultures: An Interview with Cultural Anthropologist Darrell Whiteman." *Heartbeat* 23 (Summer 2002): 1-8.
————. *Anthropology and Mission: The Incarnational Connection.* Third Annual Lewis J. Luzbetak, SBD Lecture on Mission and Culture. Chicago: Catholic Theological Union, 2003a.
————. "Anthropology and Mission: The Incarnational Connection." *Missiology* 31 (October 2003b): 397-415.
Whorf, Benjamin Lee. *Language, Thought, and Reality: Selected Writings of B. L. Whorf*, edited by John B. Carroll. Paperback ed. New York: John Wiley & Sons, Inc., 1965. Original ed., 1956.
Williams, F. E. *The Vailala Madness and the Destruction of Native Ceremonies in the Gulf Division.* Papuan Anthropology Reports 4. Port Moresby, New Guinea: Government Printer, 1923.
Wimber, John, with Kevin Springer. *Power Healing.* San Francisco: Harper & Row, 1987.
Wink, Walter. *Naming the Powers: The Language of Power in the New Testament.* Philadelphia: Fortress Press, 1984.
World Missionary Conference. *The Preparation of Missionaries.* Report of Commission V. Edinburgh: Oliphant, Anderson & Ferrier, 1910.
Woodberry, J. Dudley. "*How Jesus Would Encounter Power in Folk Islam.*" In *Wrestling with Dark Angels: Toward a Deeper Understanding of the Supernatural Forces in Spiritual Warfare.* Papers presented at the Academic Symposium on Power Evangelism, December 13-15, 1988, School of World Mission, Fuller Theological Seminary, edited by C. Peter Wagner and F. Douglas Pennoyer, 313-331. Ventura, Calif.: Regal Books, 1990
Woodberry, J. Dudley, ed. *Muslims and Christians on the Emmaus Road.* Monrovia, Calif.: MARC, 1989.
Young, David E. and Jean-Guy Goulet, eds. *Being Changed by Cross-Cultural Encounter: The Anthropology of Extraordinary Experience.* Peterborough, Ontario: Broadview, 1994.
Yung, Hwa. *Mangos or Bananas? The Quest for an Authentic Asian Christian Theology.* Oxford: Regnum International, 1997.
Zwemer, Samuel. *Thinking Missions with Christ: Some Basic Aspects of World-Evangelism: Our Message, Our Motive, and Our Goal.* Grand Rapids: Zondervan Publishing House, 1934.

Index

agency, role of, in anthropology, 38-39
agnostic pluralism, 81
Alphonse, Ephraim, 55-56
American Bible Society, 26-27
anthropologists, challenging positivism, 16, 17
anthropology: ambivalent relationship of, with mission, 3-4; American, joining British social anthropology and French structuralism, 35; applied, 4-6; central to missiology, for Americans, 28-31; Christians underrepresented in, 29; cognitive, 35; culturally determinist model of, 35; debated role of, in mission work, xiii; explaining cultural diversity, 4; growing importance of, to mission, 6-8; modernist, 33-34; positivism's influence on, 14; postmodern, 5, 18, 35, 39; post-postmodern, 18-19; relationship with missiology, historical overview, 23-28; shaped by cultures and worldviews, 13; symbolic, 35; uncovering role of, in mission, 1
Anthropology for Christian Witness (Kraft), 91
Anthropos, 23, 29
Aristotle, 57-58
arts, used to convey the gospel, 72-73
Asbury Theological Seminary, 27

baraka, 98-100
Barrett, David, 97
behavior, inner cause of, 35-36
Benedict, Ruth, 35
Bethel College (University), 8-9n2, 27
Bible: as casebook about mission, 78; including demons, magic, signs and wonders, 87; misunderstanding of, 53; as model for effective communication, 44
Bible translation: effect of, 12; receptor oriented, 17; work of, 47-48
biblical symbolism, 80
Biola University, 26
Boas, Franz, 34

Bodley, John, 39
Boniface, 88
breaking prayer, 108
Brewster, Betty Sue, xxvi
Brewster, Tom, xxvi
Bridges of God (McGavran), xxiii
Burgess, Paul, 49-50
Burridge, Kenelm, 4

cessationism, 88
Christian communicators, challenges facing, 65
Christianity, confused with Western civilization, 7
Christianity in Culture (Kraft), xiv, xix, xxxii, xxv, 29, 61, 69, 79, 91
Christian and Missionary Alliance, anthropologists from, 28
church, continuing conversion of, 77-78
Church Growth and Christian Mission (McGavran), 91
Church Next (Gibbs), 84
Cicero, 57-58
Clinton, J. Robert (Bobby), xxvi-xxvii
code models of communication, 69-70
cognitive environment, 70
collective cultural consciousness, 73
colonialism, 40-41
committed pluralism, 81
communication, xiv; arenas of intercultural negotiation, 71-75; audience-oriented, 62-63; code models of, 69-70; through community, 83-85; complexity of, 66-67; creating understanding as goal of, 70; cross-cultural, 79-80; cultural differences interfering with, 53; cyclical nature of, 67; employing all five senses, 71-72; at heart of God's mission, 43; incarnational method of, 60; inference model of, 70; integrated into missiology, 132-133; interaction model of, 69; intercultural, 44-45, 67-68; language and gestures used in, 50-52; message-oriented theories of, 60-61; methods of, 52-53; nonverbal, 72;

perfect, myth of, 18; principles of, for missiology, 62-65; receptor-oriented, xxxiv, 17, 44, 60, 62-63, 132; tailoring for receptors, xv; ten myths concerning, 61-62; as textbook on communication, 59-60; transaction model of, 69-70; types of, 57; understanding the process of, 57-58
communication theory: as central discipline on missiology, 43; in context of Christian witness, 81-82
Communication Theory for Christian Witness (Kraft), 57, 71, 79
community, communication through, 83-85
contextualization, xxv-xxvi, 72; effect of, on mission, 17; incarnational approach to, xxvii-xxviii; realizing importance of, 12
contextual theology: in Asia, 117; attempts to construct, xv
Corax, 57
Corpus Christianum, 77
critical realism, 19-22, 130
cross-cultural communication, 79-80
cross-cultural understandings, beginnings of, 20
cultural anthropology, xiv, 129; uncertain status of, 130-131
cultural re-entry, 54
cultural relativism, 3, 16-17
cultural tolerance, 54, 55-56
culture: anthropological developments in, informing missiology, 34-37; characteristics of, 36-37; differences in, interfering with communication, 53; using language to learn about, 50-52
cultures, increasing interactions between, 20
Customs and Cultures: Anthropology for Christian Missions (Nida), 1, 9, 26, 48

deep-level healing, xxviii, 106; basic model for, 107-111; case histories of, 111-113; lessons learned from, 113-115; need for, 106-107
deliverance prayer, 108, 110
"Deliver Us from Evil" (consultation on spiritual power, Nairobi 2000), 117-119, 123
demonic possession, 120-123, 135. *See also* exorcism
demons, belief in, 87-88
De Ridder, Richard, 102
De Silva, K. M., 15

devil, renunciation of, 88. *See also* evil; Satan
De Voogd, Albert, xiii
diaspora, role of, in anthropology and mission, 40
Dorsey, J. O., 36
dynamic equivalence, 44, 45, 83, 132

ecumenical mission conferences, 6
engaged pluralism, 81
Engel, James F., 58
Engelsviken, Tormod, 84, 89
ethnicity, role of, in anthropology, 38
ethnographic research, 28
ethnomusicology, 72-73
ethnotheology, xxii, xxv
evil, nature of, 134-136
exorcism, 87-88; Jesus practicing, 123; narratives of, in the New Testament, 121; need for missiologists to take seriously, 133-134

Feyerabend, Paul, 16
Fore, William, 58
Fuller Evangelistic Association, 94
Fuller School of Intercultural Studies, 58
Fuller Theological Seminary, signs and wonders at, 94-97. *See also* School of World Mission
functionalism, 5-6
functionalist integration, 35

Gagging of God, The (Reid), 60
Geertz, Clifford, 17
gestures, used in communications, 52
Gibbs, Eddie, 84
Gilliland, Dean, xxvi
Gilliland, Lois, xxvi
Gittins, Anthony, 25
Global South, shift of church's center of gravity to, 105
Gluckman, Max, 36
Goldschmidt, Walter, 3
gospel, as person-message, 75
Graham, Billy, 8
Greig, Herbert, 11
Grigolia, Alexander, 8, 25
Guder, Darrell L., 45, 77-78, 83

Hardy, Spencer, 15
healing, 87-88: as cultural phenomenon, 134-135; inner, xxviii. *See also* deep-level healing
healing prayer, 108-109
Henry, Carl F. H., xxv, 29-30

Herskovits, Melville, 35
Hesselgrave, David, 58
Hiebert, Paul, 1-2, 4
Hobart, Mark, 18
Hodges, Melvin, 91-92
Hoebel, E. Adamson, 35
Hubbard, David, 96

identity, role of, in anthropology, 37-38
incarnation, Kraft's fascination with,
    xxxvi
indigenization, xxv
inference model of communication, 70
information, methods of receiving, 52-53
information theory, growing importance
    of, 44
inner healing, Kraft's focus on, xxviii.
    See also deep-level healing
instrumentalism, 16-18
interaction model of communication, 69
intercultural communication, 44-45, 67-
    68
intercultural negotiation, 71-75
*International Bulletin of Missionary
    Research, The,* 29
Islam: elements of magic in, 99;
    phenomena in, associated with power
    and blessing, 100; popular approach
    to, 98-100

Jenkins, Philip, 97
Jesus: bringing about inner healing, 109-
    110; living in world of spirits, 100-
    102; personal communication of, 75;
    as prime example of receptor-oriented
    communication, 63, 75; spiritual
    power of, 92-93; teaching of, on evil
    spirits, 123-124
Jones, E. Stanley, 21-22
Jørgensen, Knud, 45, 58
Junod, Henri Philippe, 8
Justin Martyr, 122

Kegemni, 57
Kempers, John, xiii
Kennedy, Mrs. John Stewart, 10n
Kennedy School of Missions (Hartford
    Seminary), 9, 24
King, Roberta, xxvii, 44-45
Kirby, Jon, 25
Knauft, Bruce, 3n1, 33-34
Kraft, Charles (Chuck): bringing together
    anthropology, communication, and
    spiritual power, xxxi-xxxii; as catalyst
    for new programs at School of World

Mission, xxxii; on communication in
    context of Christian witness, 81-82;
    critical of traditional missionaries,
    xxv; developing expertise in areas of
    spiritual power, 96; on dynamic-
    equivalent church, 83-84; early years
    at Fuller, 91-92; education of, xxi-
    xxii; encouraging transition in
    approach to mission, xxxiii, xxxvii;
    fascination of, with the incarnation,
    xxxvi; on God and his communicative
    activity, 59-60; on importance of
    anthropology to theology, 33;
    impressions of, as teacher, xxxiv;
    influence of, xiii-xiv, xxxv, 2, 91, 130;
    intellectual background of, xxxiii-
    xxxiv; on interrelationship of power
    encounter, truth encounter, and
    allegiance encounter, 89, 100-101;
    love of experimentation, xix; at
    Michigan and UCLA, xxiii-xxiv; on
    miscommunication due to colonial
    practices, 60; missiological impact of,
    xxxii; mission work in Nigeria, xxii-
    xxiii; as participant observer of
    spiritual power, 92; on receptor as key
    participant in communication, 71; at
    School of World Mission, xxiv-xxvii,
    58, 60-61, 95-97; studying biblical
    perspectives on communication, 58;
    teaching courses on spiritual power,
    xxvii-xxviii; "Ten Myths Concerning
    Communication," 61-62; ten-point
    outline on receptors, 63
Kraft, Marguerite (Meg), xxi, xxiv
Kroeber, Alfred, 34
Kuhn, Thomas, 16

language: culture learning and, 50-52;
    functions of, 50; levels or registers of,
    51-52; vagaries of, 52
Lausanne movement, xxvi
Leenhardt, Maurice, 24
Lee University, 26
linguistics, growing importance of, 43
linguistic scholarship, 24
Linton, Ralph, 35
Liquid Church (Ward), 84
local people, attitudes toward, 55
Lowie, Robert, 35
Luzbetak, Louis, 4, 25

Malinowski, Bronislaw, 4-6, 35
Mangoes or Bananas (Yung), 77, 117
martyria, 82; mission as, 81-83

Mayans, missionary work with, xiii-xiv
McGavran, Donald, xxiv, 11, 27, 91
McQuilkin, Robertson, 29-30
Mead, Margaret, 35
meaning: greater significance of, 44; negotiating, 74
media, as extension of ministry, 82
Mennonites, anthropologists from, 28
Message and Mission: The Communication of the Christian Faith (Nida), 43-44
Methodists, anthropologists from, 28
migration, role of, in anthropology and mission, 39-40
Milbank, John, 29-30
Miller, William, 100
Ministering Cross-Culturally (Lingenfelter and Mayers), 73-74
Ministry and the Miraculous: A Case Study at Fuller Theological Seminary, 96
missiological anthropology, recommendations for strengthening, 31-32
missiological communication: characteristics of, 63-65; principles for, 62-65
missiology: American, 28-31; communication integrated into, 132-133; developments in, over past sixty years, xiv; linked to the pastoral, 77; paradigm shift in, xv-xvii; relationship with anthropology, 23-28, 131; research in, 30; uncertain status of, 131-132
Missiology, 11, 27, 29
missiology/intercultural studies, Ph.D. programs in, 27
mission: ambivalent relationship of, with anthropology, 3-4; incarnational approach to, xxxvi-xxxvii; lack of good communication in, 60-61; as *martyria*, 81-83; paradigm shift in, 1; post-colonial approach to, 1; tendency toward short-term, 30
missional church, 82-83
Mission and Anthropology, The: An Introduction to the Study of Primitive Man for Missionaries (Smith), 8
missionaries: challenging positivism, 16, 17; changing job description of, xxxv-xxxvii; double conversion of, 76; Nida's advice for success, 56; non-Western, 131-132; preserving indigenous cultures, 4; recognizing importance of anthropology to their work, 6-7; standing between two

worlds, 68; stereotyping of, by anthropologists, 4
Moberg, David, 8-9n2
modernist anthropology, 33-34
modernity: critique of, 18; influence of, on anthropology, 14-15
music, xxii, 15

narrative, power of, 133
neocolonialism, 40-41
Network of Christian Anthropologists, 27
Newbigin, Lesslie, 45, 79-80
Nida, Eugene, xxi-xxii, 1, 9, 24, 47-49, 58; influence of, on Kraft, xxxiii-xxxiv; and paradigm shift of communication theory's role in mission, 43-44; work for the American Bible Society, 26-27
Nigeria, Krafts' mission work in, xxii-xxiii
nonverbal communication, 72

occult, involvement in, 107
Olva, Saint, 88

Parsons, Talcott, 37
Paul, Apostle: guidelines from, on spiritual power, 102-104; spiritual power of, 93-94
person, role of, in culture, 37
Pierson, Paul, 95
Pike, Kenneth, 24
pluralism, types of, 81
polygamy, attitude toward, xxii-xxiii
Popper, Karl, 16
positivism, 13-14: challenged by anthropologists and missionaries, 16, 17; influence of, on anthropology, 14; influence of, on modern mission movement, 14-15, 22; influence of, on theology, 14, 22
postmodern anthropology, critiques of, 18
postmodernism, 16; bidding farewell to, 131; critique of, 18
post-postmodern anthropology, 18-19
power encounters, 87, 92, 135
Practical Anthropology, 10-11, 27, 29
Priest, Robert, on relationship between missiology and anthropology, 2
Puntel, L. B., 120n2

Quintillian, 57-58

Radcliff-Brown, A. R., 35
receptor-oriented communication, xxxiv, 17, 44, 60, 62-63, 132

receptors, negotiating the world of, 71
Reformed tradition, anthropologists from, 28
refugees, 39-40
Reid, Gavin, 60
relationships, negotiating, 74-75
relevance theory, 70
religions: dialogue among, 80-81; viewed through instrumentalist lens, 17-18
religious consciousness, 81
Reyburn, Bill, xxi-xxii
rhetoric, art of, 57
Robert, Dana, 28
Roman Catholic Church, anthropologists from, 27
Rules of Engagement, The (Kraft), 123n6
Rynkiewich, Michael, 2

Sapir, Edward, 34-35
Satan: reality of, generally rejected in Western theology, 119-120; varied work of, 118-119
Schmidt, Wilhelm, 23, 25
School of World Mission (Fuller Theological Seminary), xxiv-xxvii, 11, 27; expansion in curricula and ministry of, xxvi; spiritual power as part of curriculum, 95-96
Shaw, Dan, xxvi
Shaw, Karen, xxvi
Shenk, Wilbert, 34
Shils, Edward A., 37
signal systems, 72-73
signs and wonders, little early interest in, among Evangelicals, 88
Small, W. T. J., 15
Smalley, William (Bill), xxi-xxii, 84
Smith, Donald, 58
Smith, Edwin G., 6-7
Smith, Gordon Hedderly, 8
social science, Western, decentering of, 41
Society of the Divine Word (SVD), 25, 29
Søggard, Viggo, xxvii, 44
Southern Baptists, lacking anthropologists, 28
spirits: belief in, in Nordic European countries, 124; evil, 123-124; power over, xxvii
spirit-to-spirit healing, 110
spiritual conflict, as urgent task for church and pastoral leaders, 125
spiritual development, three stages of, 111n15
spiritual power, xiv, 133-136; biblical foundation for, 92-94; courses on, at

Fuller School of World Mission, xxvii; implications of, for present and future, 104-105; incidental to Hodges's writings, 91-92; inclusion of, in missiology, 94-97; issues of, in participating in God's mission, xv; paradigm shift related to, xxvii-xxviii, xxxi-xxxii; reasoning behind term, 87
spiritual realities, differing perceptions of, in West and Two-Thirds World, 118
spiritual struggle, eschatological character of, 119
Stipe, Claude, 9n
Summer Institute of Linguistics (SIL), 24-25
SWM. *See* School of World Mission
symbols, growing interest in, 43

Taber, Charles, 11, 14
Taylor, Robert B., 10, 26
Tertullian, 122
Thelle, Notto, 76, 80
theological positivism, 14
theology: basing on missionary experience, 78-79; contextual nature of, 21; critical realist approach to, 20-22; inherently missiological, 133
Theology of the Church and Its Mission, A: A Pentecostal Perspective (Hodges), 91-92
Tippett, Alan, xxiv-xxv, xxxiv, 11, 27, 84, 87, 88, 92
Townsend, Cameron, 24
transaction model of communication, 69-70
translation programs, xxxii
transnationals, role of, in anthropology and mission, 39-40
Travis, Anna, 89
Travis, John, 89
Trinity Evangelical Divinity School (TEDS), 27

understanding, negotiating, 74
Understanding Church Growth (McGavran), 91
Undivided Heart Prayer Manual (Travis), 108
United Bible Societies, 47

Vanguard University, 26
Victims of Progress (Bodley), 39

Wagner, Peter, 88
Walker, Bob, 95

Ward, Pete, 84
Weber, Robert, 58
Western theology: in Constantinian
    bondage, 76-77; rejecting spiritual
    warfare, 119-120; shaped by
    positivism, 14
Wheaton College, 8, 25-26
Wheaton Graduate School, 58
Whiteman, Darrell, 27
Whorf, Benjamin, 34-35
Wimber, John, xxvii, xxxiv, 88, 94-95

Winter, Ralph, xxiv
Woodberry, J. Dudley, 89
World Missionary Conference (Edinburgh
    1910), 6, 9-10n3
worldviews, negotiating, 73-74
Wrestling with Dark Angels (Wagner and
    Pennoyer), 97

Young Life, xxi
Yung, Hwa, 77, 117